THE CATHOLIC UNIVERSITY OF AMERICA
CANON LAW STUDIES
No. 143

IGNORANCE IN RELATION TO THE IMPUTABILITY OF DELICTS

AN HISTORICAL SYNOPSIS AND COMMENTARY

A DISSERTATION

Submitted to the Faculty of Canon Law of the Catholic University of America in Partial Fulfillment of the Requirements for the Degree of Doctor of Canon Law

BY

INNOCENT ROBERT SWOBODA, O.F.M., J.C.L.
Priest of the Franciscan Province of the Most Sacred Heart

THE CATHOLIC UNIVERSITY OF AMERICA PRESS
WASHINGTON, D. C.
1941

Imprimi Potest:

VINCENTIUS SCHREMPP, O.F.M.,
Minister Provincialis.
S. Ludovici, Mo., die XV Aprilis, 1941.

Nihil Obstat:

CLEMENS V. BASTNAGEL, J.U.D.,
Censor Deputatus.

Imprimatur:

✠ MICHAEL J. CURLEY, D.D.,
Archiepiscopus Baltimorensis et Washingtonensis.
Baltimorae, Md., die XVIII Aprilis, 1941.

Printed by
THE PAULIST PRESS
New York, N. Y.

 51

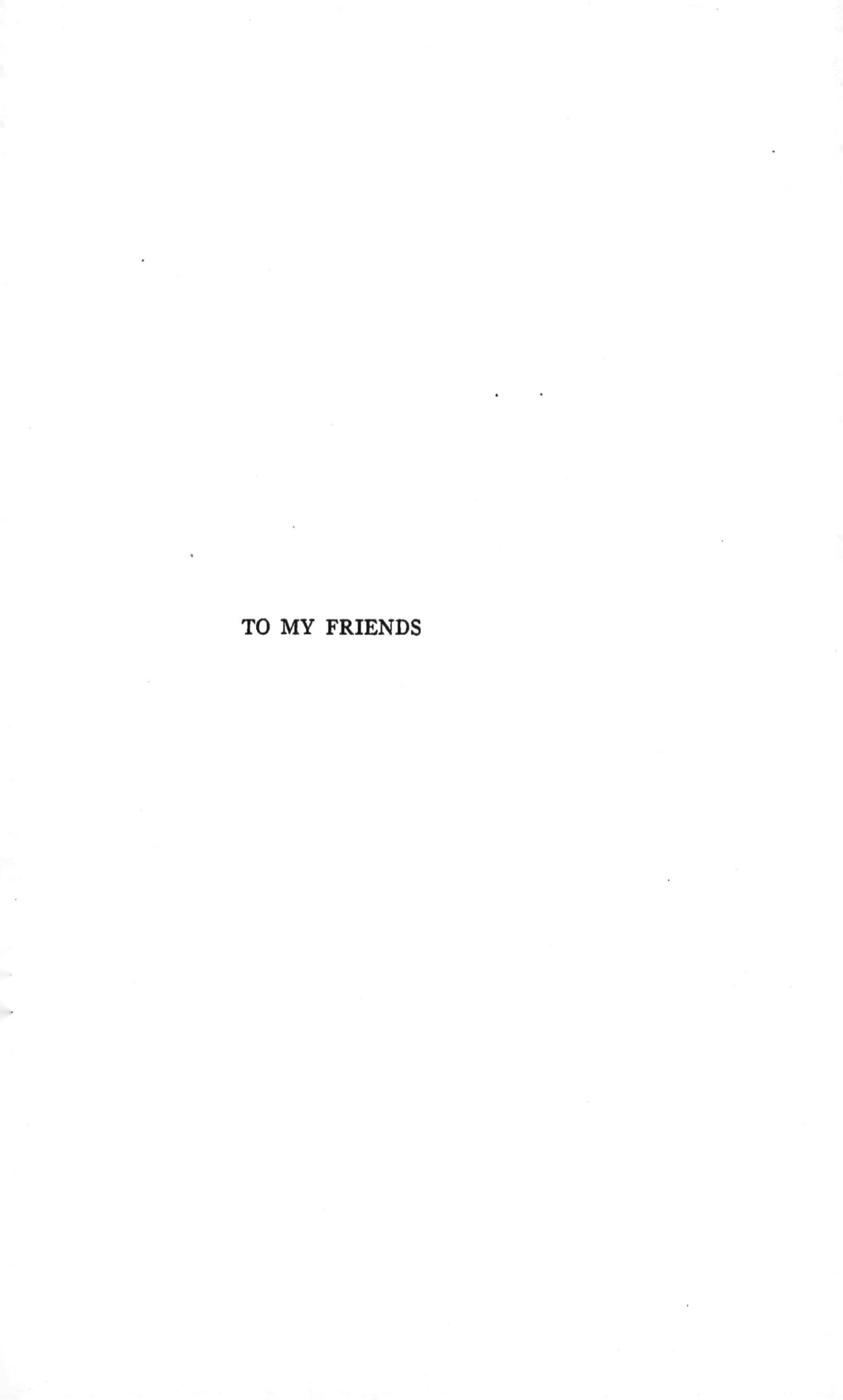

TO MY FRIENDS

TABLE OF CONTENTS

CHAPTER III

FROM THE TIME OF GRATIAN UNTIL THE TIME OF THE COUNCIL OF TRENT

CHAPTER IV

FROM THE TIME OF THE COUNCIL OF TRENT UNTIL THE CODE OF CANON LAW

PART II—CANONICAL COMMENTARY

CHAPTER V

THE IMPUTABILITY OF CRIME

PAGE

CHAPTER VI

THE NATURE AND THE DIVISIONS OF IGNORANCE

CHAPTER VII

EFFECTS OF IGNORANCE UPON PENAL IMPUTABILITY

CHAPTER VIII

EFFECTS OF IGNORANCE UPON RESPONSIBILITY FOR *LATAE SENTENTIAE* PENALTIES

INTRODUCTION

The problem of moral responsibility may be treated from the speculative viewpoint of the philosopher or from the practical standpoint of the jurist. The latter has special interest in the problem, because the more developed penal systems strive to measure a man's imputability and to proportion punishments not merely according to the gravity of the actual physical and moral damage inflicted upon society by the violation of its laws, but also according to the degree of imputability of the individual in his actual commission of a specific crime.

If the proper functioning of the mind is impeded through causes either within or beyond the individual's control, ignorance results. And no man can be held responsible for that which he has done blindly—through ignorance. Yet, if the delinquent is morally responsible for the ignorance itself, he must be considered liable for the results of his conduct even though he does not foresee them perfectly. It is the problem of the jurist to formulate and perfect rules which will aid in determining more precisely those results for which the delinquent, who has failed through ignorance, must be held accountable.

In an effort to contribute something toward the solution of this question the present study has been undertaken. This work, making no pretense of solving the ancient problem about the effects of ignorance upon penal imputability, merely takes inventory of past progress in this field of law and points out the possible directions of future developments.

The task had its difficulties, some of which may be considered peculiar to the nature of this topic. The greatest of these arose from the fact that the principles and rules for the imputability of delicts committed in ignorance had to be assembled from widely separated sources. Even when the law of the Church, after the time of Gratian, had developed into a legal system, the present question was treated under various aspects and in relation to numerous legal problems. Many of the principles which govern the imputability of crimes committed through ignorance developed out of the discussions of canonists in reference to specific delicts. Gradually the rules which had first been formulated in reference to some specific delict, were accepted as general principles applicable to all cases. Yet, to understand the rule perfectly it is necessary to study it in its source. Finally, the writings of the Scholastic Theologians and Moralists could not be overlooked, for the simple reason that canonical rules and moral principles developed both simultaneously and interdependently. Throughout, effort has been made to collect the more important fragments and to employ them in arriving at the true significance of present canonical rules and principles.

The plan of this work consists in presenting the historical background first of all. Then the basic notions of penal imputability and of ignorance are defined and delimited as to kind and species. Next follow those norms which are of general application to all cases of penal imputability and, finally, specific applications of these juridical principles are studied in regard to responsibility for *latae sententiae* penalties.

Finally, the writer wishes to take this occasion to express his sincere appreciation to all those who aided him in the preparation of this study. Gratitude is especially due to his Very Rev. Provincial, Vincent Schrempp, O.F.M., and to the former Provincial, the Very Rev. Optatus Loeffler, O.F.M., for the privilege of advanced study in Canon Law; to the faculty of the School of Canon Law of the Catholic University for their considerate, painstaking and generous assistance both in the immediate preparation of this work and in the lecture hall; and lastly to numerous friends for unfailing support and inspiring encouragement.

Part I
Historical Synopsis

CHAPTER I

IGNORANCE IN THE ROMAN PENAL LAW

The comparative study of the criminal law of the Romans and that of the Church reveals many striking similarities in the legal principles regarding ignorance and the infliction of penalties. More than that, the history of Canon Law offers many instances where a dependency is quite evident. Not only have a number of terms been taken over from the Roman Law, but also many of the legal concepts and norms regarding ignorance, at least as these existed at some time in the history of Canon Law, derive their origin from the same source. Consequently, this historical introduction would be defective without some consideration of Roman Law. Instead, however, of referring to Roman Law only upon occasion and breaking the continuity of the discussion by necessary but lengthy explanations of Roman Law, it was thought more practical to place the consideration of Roman Law in the beginning as an introductory chapter to the historical synopsis of the Canon Law principles. This method at once permits the presentation of the Roman Law materials in a more connected form and at the same time makes it possible to illustrate the connections and dependencies of Canon Law by a simple reference back to this chapter.

In this chapter ignorance will be considered in regard to both public and private delicts. While the distinction between these two kinds of delicts is important in other respects (especially in the matter of procedure) the rules of ignorance are very much the same in regard to both.[1] Particular differences will be noted upon occasion in the course of the discussion.

[1] Regarding the nature and the origin of public and private delicts, see Strachan-Davidson, *Problems of the Roman Criminal Law* (Oxford: Clarendon Press, 1912), I, 36-45; Mommsen-Duquesne, *Droit Pénal Romain* (Paris, 1907), I, 2-3.

Article I. The Subjective Element of Crime in Roman Law

To understand the rôle which ignorance plays in the imputability of crime it is necessary to approach the problem from a general consideration of the subjective element of crime according to the Roman Law system. As in other legal systems, it seems that the primitive law of Rome looked only to the material and objective violation of the law, irrespective of the state of mind of the individual delinquent.[2] However, the earliest historical records frequently mention that a crime to be punishable must be morally imputable, or in the legal language of the Romans, the crime must be done with *dolus*. Thus, in regard to one of the oldest of the public delicts, homicide, a distinction was made between homicide committed *dolo sciens* and *si quis imprudens occidisset hominem.* In the latter instance the law was satisfied with a sacrificial offering instead of the death penalty.[3] In the more primitive law the only distinction made was between a crime committed with *dolus* (intentional) and an unintentional violation of law. In the more developed system criminal responsibility can be either of two kinds: an intentional or deliberate violation of the law (*dolus*) or a culpable negligence resulting in a violation of the law (*culpa*).[4]

[2] Jolowicz, *Historical Introduction to the Study of Roman Law* (Cambridge: University Press, 1923), pp. 177-178; Mommsen-Duquesne, *Le Droit Pénal Romain,* I, 98. This is denied by Ferrini, at least so far as public crimes are concerned.—*Diritto Penale Romano* (Milano, 1899), pp. 77-78. For an interesting comparative study of the development of the concept of criminal imputability in the Roman, German and Common Law systems, cf. Bodenstein, "Phases in the Development of Criminal *Mens Rea*"—*South African Law Journal,* XXXVI (1919), 323-335.

[3] Thus, in two *leges,* attributed to Numa Pompilius, it is stated: "Si qui hominem liberum dolo sciens morti duit, paricidas esto . . . si quis imprudens occidisset hominem, pro capite occisi agnatis ejus in contione offerret arietem."—Girard, *Texts de Droit Romain* (5. ed., Paris: Rousseau, 1923), p. 8. (Hereafter this work will be cited as: Girard, *Texts.*)

[4] Cf. Mommsen-Duquesne, *Le Droit Pénal Romain,* I, 99; Falchi, *Diritto Penale Romano* (Treviso: Vianello, 1930), pp. 86-103; Ferrini, *Diritto Penale Romano,* pp. 73-124.

1. Dolus

In the Roman Law the deliberate violation of law is expressed by various terms. Among the most frequently used are: *dolo sciens,*[5] *sciens dolo malo,*[6] *dolo malo,*[7] and a number of more or less equivalent expressions.[8]

The term *dolus* and its equivalent expressions occur so frequently in numerous definitions of crimes, that one can scarcely doubt that a technical meaning was attached to them. The sources, however, do not contain a definition of *dolus.* True, there are two definitions of *dolus* in the *Digest,* but these evidently refer to *dolus* in purely civil matters and not to crimes.[9] The meaning of criminal *dolus*

[5] *Supra,* p. 2, note 3.

[6] *Lex Latina Tabulae Bantinae* (621-636 A. U. C.)—Bruns, *Fontes Iuris Romani Antiqui* (7. ed., Gradenwitz, Tubingae, 1909), I, 54. (Hereafter this work will be cited as: Bruns, *Fontes*) *Lex Acilia Repetundarum* (631-632 A. U. C.)—Bruns, *Fontes,* I, 60; D. (48, 15) 3, *pr.* (*Lex Fabia de Plagiariis*); D. (48, 10) 9, 3 (*Lex Cornelia de Falsis*).

[7] D. (48, 12), 2, 1 (*Lex Iulia de Annona*); D. (48, 10) 9, 2 (*Lex Cornelia de Falsis*); D. (47, 12) 3, *pr.* (*de Sepulchro Violato*).

[8] *Sciens*—D. (47, 2) 55, 4 (*de Furtis*); *sciens prudensque*—D. (47, 9) 9 (*de Incendio*); *voluntate*—C. (9, 16) 3 (*Lex Cornelia de Sicariis*); *consulto*—D. (48, 19) 5, 2 (in reference to *maiora delicta*); *data opera*—D. (47, 9) 12, 1 (*de Incendio*); or the *animus* or *voluntas* to commit a crime, v. gr. *animus furandi*—D. (47, 2) 52, 20; *animus occidendi*—D. (48, 8) 1, 3; *voluntas nocendi*—C. (9, 16) 1.

[9] " . . . dolus malus fit calliditate et fallacia: et ut ait Pedius, dolo malo pactum fit, quotiens circumscribendi alterius causa aliud agitur et aliud agi simulatur."—D. (2, 14) 7, 9. "Dolum malum Servius quidem ita definiit: machinationem quandam alterius decipiendi causa, cum aliud simulatur et aliud agitur. Labeo autem posse et sine simultatione id agi, ut quis circumveniatur; . . . itaque ipse sic definiit dolum malum esse omnem calliditatem fallaciam machinationem ad circumveniendum fallendum decipiendum alterum adhibitam."—D. (4, 3) 1, 2. According to Schulz (*Principles of Roman Law* [Oxford: Clarendon Press, 1936], pp. 45-46), the original meaning of civil *dolus* included only fraudulent misrepresentation, but was later extended to cover every kind of malicious act to the disadvantage of another person. Cf. Pauly-Wissowa, *Real-Encyclopaedie der Classischen Altertumswissenschaft* (Stuttgart, 1894-), V, P. I, 1292-1294, *s. v.* "dolus." In contrast to *dolus malus* there is also a *dolus bonus,* which consists in cunning or skill used to elude a thief or robber. Cf. D. (4, 3) 1, 3.

must be derived from a study of the term as used in the single definitions of various crimes. As a result a considerable amount of speculation and variety of opinion has arisen among Romanists concerning the exact meaning, the precise mental or psychological content of criminal *dolus.* It is admittedly important to know the exact meaning of *dolus,* because upon the solution of that problem depends to a great extent the answer to the question whether or not ignorance of law excuses.

Yet, this difficult problem must be left to the studies of Roman Law students.[10] It seems sufficiently clear that *dolus* does not contain the idea of secret and crafty malice,[11] nor does it imply the idea of premeditation and the deliberate despising of law and justice;[12] but, it can be defined as the simple deliberate or voluntary performance of the prohibited act. It does not, therefore, imply a clear knowledge and contempt of the particular penal law. This explanation of *dolus,* as the simple will to injure, accounts not only for the technical use of the word *dolus* in penal law, but also explains why the Roman jurists so frequently employed such expressions as *animus occidendi, data opera . . . incendium fecerit, voluntas nocendi*[13] instead of the term *dolus* itself.[14]

[10] Cf. Pernice, "Der verbrecherische Vorsatz im grieschish-römischen Rechte" —*Zeitschrift der Savigny-Stiftung für Rechtsgeschichte: Romanistische Abteilung,* XVII (1896), 205-251; Ferrini, *Diritto Penale Romano,* pp. 78-103; Falchi, *Diritto Penale Romano,* pp. 87-99.

[11] This theory was advanced by Binding (*Normen,* II, 278)—Ferrini, *op. cit.,* p. 79; Pernice, *ibid.*

[12] Ferrini (*op. cit.,* pp. 79-80) ascribes this theory to Leist, *Gräco-Italische Rechtsgeschichte,* p. 370.

[13] Cf. *supra,* p. 3, note 8.

[14] Thus, Mommsen-Duquesne (*Droit Pénal Romain,* I, 100) defines *dolus* as comprising "toute les illégalités conscientes"; Ferrini (*op. cit.,* p. 89) explains it as "l'intenzione cosciente di nuocere"; and Pernice ("Der verbrecherische Vorsatz"—*ibidem,* p. 205) understands *dolus* to mean "die bewuste Absicht bei der verbrecherischen That, welche die eigentliche Unsittlichkeit der rechtswidrigen Handlung ausmacht." It cannot, of course, be forgotten that *dolus* may have changed its meaning considerably during the various periods of Roman Law history. Cf. Falchi, *Diritto Penale Romano,* pp. 87-95.

2. Culpa

A penal law can be violated and a crime committed without the will's tending directly towards the action forbidden by law. Men living together in society must not only positively refrain from injury to one another, but they must also take reasonable precautions that their actions, however legitimate, do not result in harm to others. In a word, they must avoid negligence or *culpa*. Hence, a man may commit a crime and make himself liable for penal coercion, not only through *dolus*, but also through *culpa*.[15]

However, *culpa* or negligence is not recognized as a basis for penal action in all crimes.[16] Some delicts are not capable of being penalized in the *culposa* form, as, for example, theft and injury.[17] In several crimes the sources expressly state that *culpa lata* is sufficient for the imposing of penalties. As examples of such instances,

[15] "Refert et in maioribus delictis, consulto aliquid admittatur, an casu, et sane in omnibus criminibus distinctio haec poenam aut iustam elicere debet aut temperamentum admittere."—D. (48, 19) 5, 2. *Casus* is sometimes, as in this case, used to signify *culpa;* cf. D. (47, 9) 9: " . . . casu idest negligentia . . . " Cf. D. (47, 4) 2; D. (48, 19), 11, 2; D. (50, 16) 226.

[16] *Culpa* certainly sufficed for the commission of a private wrong or tort, whether arising out of contracts or otherwise. Cf. Schulz, *Principles of Roman Law,* pp. 250-251. Mommsen-Duquesne (*Le Droit Pénal Romain,* I, 103) admit *culpa* a sufficient only in private delicts but not in public delicts, Ferrini (*Diritto Penale Romano,* p. 109) holds that the only example of a *delictum ex culpa* is *homicidium culposum,* which after Hadrian (117-138) was punished *via extraordinaria.* But this innovation was not taken over into Justinian Law. Bodenstein ("Phases in the Development of Criminal *Mens Rea*"—*South African Law Journal,* XXXVI [1919], 327-335) maintains that Roman Law recognized *culpa* as a form of criminal imputability for the generality of crimes.

[17] Gaius (*Institutiones,* II, 50): " . . . furtum enim sine affectu furandi non committitur."—Seckel-Kuebler (6. ed., Lipsiae: Teubner, 1928), p. 64. *Inst.* (4, 2) 1: "Qui tamen ita competit haec actio [*vi bonorum raptorum*], si dolo malo quisque rapuerit: qui aliquo errore inductus suam rem esse et imprudens iuris eo animo rapuit, quasi domino liceat rem suam etiam per vim auferre possessoribus, absolvi debet." D. (48, 8) 7: "In lege Cornelia [sc. de sicariis] dolus pro facto accipitur. neque in hac lege culpa lata pro dolo accipitur."

homicide,[18] arson,[19] and allowing a prisoner to escape[20] may be mentioned.

Article II. Ignorance in General

Among the factors which destroy or diminish the necessary subjective element of a crime and consequently either exempt from penalty or give a basis for a mitigated sentence is ignorance or error. Ignorance may destroy *dolus* altogether or, if there is culpability in the ignorance itself, it may render a crime imputable *ex culpa.*

The most fundamental division of ignorance in Roman Law is that based on the unknown object. If the object is the law itself, the ignorance is called ignorance of law (*ignorantia iuris*); if it is something other than the law itself, yet pertaining to the crime as one of its objective or factual elements, the ignorance is called ignorance of fact (*ignorantia facti*). The distinction must be of great practical importance, since the jurists wrote special treatises on the distinction,[21] both the *Digest* as well as the Justinian Code contain separate titles on it[22] and the distinction between these two kinds of ignorance is constantly emphasized when the question of ignorance receives legal consideration. Despite its far-reaching importance the sources do not contain a definition of either of these classes of ignorance. The jurists themselves were content to teach and illustrate the division by examples rather than by definition. Ignorance of law can be described as a lack of knowledge concerning the law itself: its content, meaning and extension. Ignorance of fact is a failure to apprehend the factual circumstances which constitute the

[18] "Cum quidam per lasciviam causam mortis praebuisset, comprobatum est factum . . . quod eum in quinquenium relegasset."—D. (48, 8) 4, *pr.*

[19] "Qui aedes acervumve frumenti iuxta domum positum combusserit, vinctus verberatus igni necari iubetur, si modo sciens prudensque id commiserit. si vero casu, id est negligentia, aut noxiam sarcire iubetur aut, si minus idoneus sit levius castigatur."—D. (47, 9) 9. Cf. also D. (47, 9) 11.

[20] D. (48, 3) 12 and 14, 2.

[21] V. gr., Paulus, *Liber Singularis de iuris et facti ignorantia*—D. (22, 9) *pr.*

[22] D. (22, 6); C. (1, 18).

violation of the law.[23] The legal reason for making this distinction and predicating different effects upon ignorance of law than upon ignorance of fact is given by the jurists themselves.

> "In omni parte error in iure non eodem loco quo facti ignorantia haberi debebit, cum ius finitum et possit esse et debeat, facti interpretatio plerumque etiam prudentissimos fallat." [24]

These two forms of ignorance will, therefore, have to be considered separately.

Article III. Ignorance of Fact

In Roman penal law ignorance of fact is generally admitted as excluding criminal responsibility and, therefore, it exempts from penalty. This principle is frequently stated in the sources. For example, in reference to the *infamia* incurred by the man who marries a widow during the time required by law for the mourning of a deceased husband, it is expressly stated that that ignorance of fact excused.[25] One, who sells the slave of another, thinking that the slave is his own, does not incur the penalty imposed upon *plagium*.[26] By taking the property of another, erroneously believing that the owner consents, one does not become guilty of theft.[27] Whosoever violently recovered a thing which he wrongly supposed was his own, did not commit *rapina*; [28] nor did he incur the penalties inflicted upon *furtum* if he alienated the property of another in ignorance.[29]

[23] In the expression *ignorantia iuris* "ius" is taken in the sense of objective law and not of subjective right (*ius subjectivum*). Hence *ius ignorare* or *ignorantia iuris* is not the same as *ius suum* or *de iure suo ignorare*. The latter is not ignorance of law but ignorance of fact, *i. e.*, an error in regard to the facts of one's own juridical condition. Thus in D. (22, 6) 3, *pr.*: "Plurimum interest, utrum quis de alterius causa et facto non sciret an de iure suo ignorat," the distinction is not between *ignorantia iuris et facti*, but between *ignorantia facti proprii* and *ignorantia facti alieni*. Cf. Savigny, *System des heutigen Römischen Rechts* (Berlin, 1840-1849) III, 327.

[24] D. (22, 6) 2.

[25] "Notatur (*i. e.*, infamia) etiam 'qui eam duxit', sed si sciens: ignorantia enim excusatur non iuris, sed facti."—D. (3, 2) 11, 4.

[26] C. (9, 20) 14.

[27] D. (47, 2) 46, 7.

[28] Inst. (4, 2) 1.

[29] D. (41, 3) 36, 1.

However, not every error of fact, that can be alleged in connection with a criminal fact, excuses from penal liability. The error or ignorance must concern a substantial element of the delictual fact; that is, a circumstance which enters into the constitution of the crime.[80] While ignorance of an aggravating circumstance diminishes criminal responsibility, ignorance of an indifferent circumstance in the eyes of the law, does not excuse from penalty.[81] The simple mistake in regard to the person upon which the crime is inflicted does not excuse from penalty. Thus, if an injury intended for Titius is by mistake inflicted upon Seius, *praevalet quod principale est: iniuriam eum mihi facere velle.*[82] This is true, however, only in the case that the two (Titius and Seius of the example) are in the same juridical status, so that in either event the identical crime would result from the injury.[83] Again, it Titius injures a *filiusfamilias,* not knowing whose *filius* he is; or if he injures a married woman, not knowing whose wife she is, Titius is responsible in both instances.[84]

However, not every error of fact excludes penal responsibility; it must be a reasonable mistake, otherwise the delinquent may become liable in *culpa.* The sources do not afford detailed rules for discerning reasonable error from an error which is punishable because of *culpa.* Certain broad principles, however, can be deduced from the law which will serve at least to determine the extremes of excuse and non-excuse from penalty.

On the one hand, in order to excuse, the ignorance must be *iusta*[85] or *probabilis.*[86] Probable ignorance is that which cannot

[80] Thus a woman does not commit adultery when she marries a second time during the lifetime of her first husband, if only she can prove that she received false information concerning the death of her true husband.—D. (48, 5) 12, 12. Cf. also, D. (47, 2) 84, *pr.;* D. (9, 2) 45, 2.

[81] Ferrini, *Diritto Penale Romano,* pp. 140-144.

[82] D. (47, 10) 18, 3.

[83] V. gr., D. (47, 10) 3, 4: "Si quis hominem liberum ceciderit, dum putat servum suum, in ea causa est, ne iniuriarum teneatur."

[84] The reasoning of the jurisconsult is interesting: " . . . nam . . . cuicumque patri, cuicumque marito per filium, per uxorem vult facere iniuriam."—D. (47, 10) 18, 5.

[85] D. (48, 16) 1, 3; D. (31, 89), 7; D. (50, 17) 42.

[86] D. (41, 10) 5.

be dispelled by a diligent investigation; [37] and, since the understanding of facts often eludes even the most prudent,[38] it is not necessary that a man exercise the highest degree of diligence [39] or that he examine the facts with the curiosity of a spy.[40]

On the other hand, the law cannot tolerate the ignorance of the very negligent [41] or permit a man to enjoy the excessive security of being free from the effects of crass negligence.[42] Hence, the ignorance must not be *crassa* or *supina*,[43] *dissoluta* [44] or *captiosa;* [45] because in these cases the delinquent is guilty of *lata culpa* sufficient for delictual liability.[46]

Moreover, everyone is presumed to know his own condition and actions, and, hence, it is only ignorance of facts pertaining to third persons (*facta aliena*) that is tolerated by law.[47] In regard to *facta aliena* the law considered it *summa negligentia* to be ignorant of notorious facts, or those things which are known to everyone else in the locality.[48]

It must be admitted that the above rules regarding ignorance of fact are not always employed by the sources in regard to strictly penal matters. Yet, when one recalls what has been said of *culpa* in Roman penal law, it seems reasonable that these norms were used also in judging ignorance of fact in reference to delictual imputa-

[37] D. (50, 17) 42.

[38] D. (22, 6) 2.

[39] " . . . recte Labeo definit scientiam neque curiosissimi . . . hominis accipiendam . . . "—D. (22, 6) 9, 2.

[40] " . . . neque delatoria curiositas exigatur."—D. (22, 6) 6.

[41] " . . . recte Labeo definit scientiam . . . neque negligentissimi hominis accipiendam . . . "—D. (22, 6) 9, 2. Cf. also D. (18, 1) 13, 3.

[42] "Scientia enim hoc modo aestimanda est, ut neque negligentia crassa aut nimia securitas satis expedita sit . . . "—D. (22, 6) 6.

[43] D. (22, 6) 6.

[44] D. (21, 1) 55.

[45] D. (42, 8) 6, 10.

[46] D. (22, 6) 9, 2; D. (47, 9) 11; D. (50, 16) 226.

[47] " . . . quia in alieni facti ignorantia tolerabilis error est."—D. (41, 10) 5. Cf. *supra*, p. 7, note 23; C. (4, 44) 15.

[48] "Sed facti ignorantia ita demum cuique non nocet, si non ei summa neglegentia obiciatur: quid enim si omnes in civitate sciant, quod ille solus ignorat?"—D. (22, 6) 9, 2.

bility. The *Digest* itself indicates this[49] and interpreters of the *Digest* have so applied these rules.[50]

Article IV. Ignorance of Law

With regard to the effect of ignorance of the law upon criminal imputability there is considerable difficulty. Until quite recently it was generally held that ignorance of the law, except for a few determined exceptions, was not admitted in Roman penal law as an excuse from penalties. This opinion was contested by Binding, who considered *scientia iuris* to be an integral part of *dolus* and, consequently maintained that *ignorantia iuris* destroyed *dolus* and penal imputability.[51] Whatever may have been the true doctrine of the Classical Roman Law, it can scarcely be doubted that at Justinian's time ignorance of the law was not admitted as an excuse from penal liability. The ever recurring apposition of ignorance of law and ignorance of fact, with the frequent statement that the former does not excuse, leaves little doubt in the matter.[52] One thing is certain,

[49] D. (22, 6) 6. In this text, ascribed to Ulpian, *Ad Legem Iuliam et Papiam,* the rules for judging crass or supine ignorance are employed in penal matters.

[50] Cf. Savigny, *System des heutigen Römischen Rechts,* III, Beilage VIII, p. 395; Voet, *Commentaries* (trans. by Horwood, Cape Town and Johannesburg: Juta & Co., Ltd. [1929 ?]), bk. XXII, tit. VI, nn. 6-7; Falchi, *Diritto Penale Romano,* p. 105.

[51] In regard to this dispute, cf. Ferrini, *Diritto Penale Romano,* pp. 144-152. According to Ferrini, Binding defended this view in his *Normen und ihre Uebertretung* (Leipzig, 1872-1888), II, 311. Binding's views were contested by Heinemann (*Die Bindingsche Schuldlehre* [Berlin, 1889]) and Pernice (*Labeo,* II-2, 119 ff.).

[52] V. gr., "Regula est iuris quidem ignorantiam cuique nocere, facti vero ignorantiam non nocere."—D. (22, 6) 9, *pr.*; " . . . notatur etiam 'qui eam duxit,' sed si sciens: ignorantia enim excusatur non iuris, sed facti."—D. (3, 2) 11, 4; "Nonnumquam per ignorantiam delinquentibus iuris civilis uenia tribui solet, si modo rem facti quis, non iuris ignoret . . . "—*Mosaicarum et Romanarum Legum Collatio* (ed. Hyamson, Oxford: The University Press, 1913), I, 12, 1; "Constitutiones Principum nec ignorare quemquam nec dissimulare permittimus."—C. (1, 18) 12. Ferrini (*Diritto Penale Romano,* pp. 145-147) finds in none of these cases an expression of general principle in regard to penal imputability. He maintains that the single delicts must be considered individually.

during the Middle Ages when the influence of Roman Law began to be felt in Canon Law, the common opinion was that ignorance of law does not excuse; and to support this view the Roman Law was expressly appealed to. Consequently, the dispute as to the true doctrine of classical Roman Law is irrelevant so far as Canon Law is concerned.[53]

However, Roman Law did not punish the mere objective violation of the law without any regard to the subjective or moral guilt of the delinquent. Because it is practically impossible for the judge in a criminal case to ascertain the subjective state of the criminal before him, Roman Law did not admit ignorance of law as an excuse in the generality of cases.

In the first place, ignorance of the natural law and of the *ius gentium* did not excuse. It was the general presumption of the law that anyone who was capable of *dolus* had also the knowledge of these laws. Thus, even women, who were generally presumed ignorant of law,[54] were not excused because of ignorance of the natural law or of the *ius gentium.* They were, for example, subject to the same penalty for incest prohibited by the *ius gentium* as were men. In other words, there was no excuse at all. This was not the case with incest prohibited *iure nostro.*[55] This explains why in most cases there is no excuse for ignorance of law; for, generally speaking, penal laws place a sanction upon those laws which have at least a foundation in natural law.[56]

[53] Cf. *glossa* of Accursius, *ad* C. (1, 18) 12; Kantorowicz, *Studies in the Glossators of the Roman Law* (Cambridge: University Press, 1938), p. 79.

[54] Cf. *infra,* p. 13.

[55] " . . . quia multum interest, errore matrimonium illicite contrahatur an contumacia . . . Quare mulier tunc demum eam poenam, quam mares, sustinebit, cum incestum iure gentium prohibitum admiserit: nam si sola iuris nostri observatio interveniet, mulier ab incesti crimine erit excusata."—D. (48, 5) 39, 1-2. Cf. *glossa* of Accursius ad D. (22, 6) 9, *v.* "regula." Kantorowicz (*op. cit.,* p. 79) holds that Roman Law did not make a distinction between natural or quasi-natural law and civil law so far as ignorance was concerned. This text seems to indicate the contrary. However, at least from the time of Bulgarus (d. 1166), as Kantorowicz admits, the distinction was made by the glossators and commentators of Roman Law.

[56] Cf. Falchi, *Diritto Penale Romano,* pp. 109-110; Mommsen-Duquesne, *Droit Pénal Romain,* I, 108.

At the extreme opposite of the natural law and quasi-natural law (*ius gentium*) are municipal laws; those laws, namely, which originate from local authority and are peculiar to a certain locality. Ignorance of municipal law is sustained as an excuse from penalty. "Municipali lege ita cautum erat: si quis extra curiam iudicabit, curia movetor et praeterea multam mille denarium dato. Quaesitum est, an poenam sustinere debeat, qui ignorans adversus secretum fecit. Respondit, et huiusmodi poenas adversus scientes paratas esse." [57]

Between the extremes of the natural law and the municipal law is the broad field of positive civil legislation which comes from the highest lawgiver in the State and is universally binding upon all. There is an express obligation to know this law [58] and, hence, ignorance of these laws is generally not permitted. There are, however, expressly admitted exceptions to this universal rule in regard to certain classes of people. There are four classes of people (the unlearned or illiterate, minors [*i. e.*, those not yet twenty-five years old], women and soldiers) who are presumed to be ignorant of the law. Consequently, they are more readily excused from penalty if they actually violate the law because of ignorance of law. Several concrete examples of this are to be found in the sources themselves:

1. Thus, the young soldier is exempted from the penalties inflicted upon the *emansor* [59] if he is ignorant of military discipline.[60]

2. The illiterate or rustics were considered not to have *dolus malus* and, therefore, not held to the penalty if they violated the law in ignorance.[61]

[57] D. (50, 9) 6.

[58] "Constitutiones principum nec ignorare quemquam nec dissimulare permittimus."—C. (1, 18) 12; "Leges sacratissimae, quae constringunt omnium vitas, intelligi ab omnibus debent . . . " C. (1, 14) 9. Cf. the *glossa* of Accursius to these texts.

[59] "Emansor est, qui diu vagatus ad castra regreditur."—D. (49, 16) 3, 2.

[60] " . . . et datur venia valetudini, affectioni parentium . . . sed et ignoranti adhuc disciplinam tironi ignoscitur."—D. (49, 16) 4, 15.

[61] "Doli mali autem ideo in verbis edicti fit mentio, quod, si per imperitiam vel rusticitatem vel ab ipso praetore iussus vel casu aliquis fecerit, non tenetur." —D. (2, 1) 7, 4. For application of this principle, cf. D. (29, 5) 3, 22.

3. Women were generally excused when they violated such penal laws as were not based upon the natural law,[62] as is expressly stated in the *Digest*.[63] A practical application of this is found in the *Mosaicarum et Romanarum Legum Collatio*. "Si qui (affinem) uel cognatam contra interdictum duxerit, remisso mulieri iuris errore ipse poenam adulterii lege Iulia patitur, non etiam ducta." [64]

4. Minors, *i. e.*, those below the age of twenty-five years, were generally excused on account of ignorance of law.[65] Thus, a minor can be excused from the crime of incest because of ignorance of law.[66]

Conclusion

These legal rules of Roman Law have been dwelt upon at some length because they are of the greatest importance in the development of the Canon Law doctrine of penal imputability and its relation to ignorance. Yet, the influence of Roman Law was not exerted upon the law of the Church until the revival of Roman Law studies in the twelfth century. One recognizes in these principles not only many of the phases in the historical development of the Canon Law, but also many canonical rules of law that are still in force. During the first eleven centuries of Canon Law history, however, its development is almost completely independent of the Roman Law.

[62] Cf. *supra*, p. 11, note 55.

[63] " . . . ius ignorare permissum est. quod et in feminis in quibusdam causis propter sexus infirmitatem dicitur: et ideo sicubi non est delictum, sed iuris ignorantia, non laeduntur."—D. (22, 6) 9. *pr.* The text is corrupted but the meaning is sufficiently clear. Cf. Mommsen-Duquesne, *Droit Pénal Romain,* I, 108, note 1.

[64] *Coll.* VI, 3, 3—ed. Hyamson, p. 84. The "affinem" is supplied from the edition of Huschke. Cf. also D. (48, 10) 15, *pr.*

[65] " . . . minoribus viginti quinque annis ius ignorare permissum est."—D. (22, 6) 9, *pr.* Cf. (1, 18) 11; *Codex Theodosianus* (3, 5) 3.

[66] "Incestum autem, . . . excusari solet sexu vel aetate . . . "—D. (48, 5) 39, 7.

CHAPTER II

IGNORANCE IN THE ANCIENT PENITENTIAL SYSTEM UNTIL THE TIME OF GRATIAN

THE Church, in accord with the teaching of her Divine Founder,[1] has always taught that knowledge and the will to transgress the law form the necessary internal or moral elements of all sin. Against the legalistic views of the Jews and Gnostics the early Fathers[2] and ecclesiastical writers[3] expressly taught that the mere objective violation of law did not constitute moral guilt without the deliberate consent of free will.[4]

ARTICLE I. THE DOCTRINE OF ST. AUGUSTINE

Among the Fathers of the Church St. Augustine stands out prominently for his clear statement of the moral principles of imputability and the relation of ignorance to personal guilt for sin. He is not only a valuable witness of the past but also from a doctrinal point of view has had a lasting influence upon the foundations of the doctrine, or the body of principles, concerning the influence of ignorance upon criminal responsibility. Gratian introduces texts on ignorance into the *Decretum* from the writings of St. Augustine[5] and the commentators of Gratian built up their doctrine in no small manner around these texts.[6] Moreover, St. Augustine had consider-

[1] "For from the heart come forth wicked purposes—murders, adulteries, fornications, thefts, false witness, blasphemies."—Matt. XV, 19. Cf. also Matt. XXIII, 27; Matt. V, 28; Matt. XII, 34.

[2] "Usque adeo peccatum voluntarium est malum, ut nullo modo sit peccatum, si non sit voluntarium."—St. Augustine, *De Vera Religione,* XIV, 27—Migne, *Patrologiae Cursus Completus, Series Latina* (221 vols., Paris, 1844-1864), XXXIV, 133. (Hereafter this work will be cited as *MPL.*)

[3] Tertullian, *De Poenitentia,* cap. III—*MPL,* I, 1232.

[4] Michiels, *De Delictis et Poenis* (Lublin: Universitas Catholica, 1934), I, 87-88.

[5] Cf. *infra,* p. 31.

[6] Cf. Kuttner, *Kanonistische Schuldlehre von Gratian bis auf die Dekretalen Gregors IX,* Studi e Testi, n. 64 (Città del Vaticano: Biblioteca Apostolica Vaticana, 1935), pp. 133-151. (Hereafter this work will be cited as: Kuttner, *Schuldlehre.*)

able indirect influence upon canonical doctrine through the writings of the Scholastic Theologians. The latter relied, at least to some extent, upon St. Augustine's teachings in attempting the solution of the moral problem of ignorance in relation to sin.[7] St. Augustine, therefore, contributed also through this channel to the doctrinal development of the canonists. Hence, his doctrine is not without interest to the historians of Canon Law.

In St. Augustine's doctrine of sin the intellect plays an indispensable part. Sin is a voluntary evil;[8] but to be voluntary it must first be known and thus freely embraced.[9]

St. Augustine made several distinctions of ignorance which were later to become part of the Canon Law doctrine. First of all, ignorance is not the same as error; for, ignorance is *existimare scire quod nescit,* while error is *approbare falsum.*[10] On the basis of the object which is not known, he distinguishes between those things which should be known and those things about which knowledge is either harmful or indifferent.[11] St. Augustine seems not to have made any further distinction on the basis of the unknown object. He does not expressly distinguish between ignorance of law and ignorance of fact. That distinction was to be introduced into Canon Law much later and that from the Roman Law. However, from the practical solutions which Augustine makes in various places it appears that he implicitly recognized a difference between these two kinds of ignorance.

In the first place ignorance of the divine law does not free from

[7] Müller, *Ethik und Recht in der Lehre von der Verantwortlichkeit* (Regensburg: Habbel, 1932), p. 27. (Hereafter this work will be cited as: Müller, *Ethik und Recht.*)

[8] *Retractationes,* I, c. 14, n. 4: " . . . peccatum sine voluntate esse non posse verissimum est."—*Corpus Scriptorum Ecclesiasticorum Latinorum* (Vindobonae, 1866-), XXXVI, 75. (This work will be cited *CSEL.*)

[9] "Nam et qui nesciens peccauit, non incongruenter nolens peccasse dici potest . . . ," *ibid.*—*CSEL,* XXXVI, 74. And in one of his letters (*Epistola XCIII,* IV, 15) he writes: "Certe nullius crimen maculat nescientem."—*CSEL,* XXXIV, 2, 459.

[10] *Enchiridion,* c. 17—*MPL,* XL, 239—c. 11, D. XXXVIII.

[11] *Loc. cit.*

moral guilt. Yet, the degree of moral imputability is not always the same; for there are some who simply do not know and there are others who positively will to remain ignorant. The first are somewhat less guilty on account of ignorance, while the latter are not excused at all.[12] A practical application of this principle is made by St. Augustine relative to the divine law prohibiting adultery. In this case it is not true to say: *Ergo si nescit non peccat.* Because the ignorance itself cannot but be sinful, guilt is only diminished by the lack of knowledge. *Sunt etiam peccata ignorantium, quamvis minora quam scientium.*[13]

On the other hand there is an ignorance which excuses entirely. In several particular cases St. Augustine admitted complete excuse according to the principle: *certe nullius crimen maculat nescientem.* Thus, in one of his letters he defends the faithful against the unjust accusations of the Donatists. The faithful are not to be blamed on account of their association with Cecilianus, because they were unable to know of a crime which even the accusers of Cecilianus were unable to prove in court. He continues: "Certe nullius crimen maculat nescientem . . . quis locus innocentiae reservatur, si crimen est proprium nescire crimen alienum?" [14] Similarly, a man is not guilty of a lie who in ignorance of the facts tells an untruth; for, "ream linguam non facit nisi rea mens." [15]

[12] *De Gratia et Libero Arbitrio,* cap. III, n. 5: "Nec tamen ideo confugiendum est ad ignorantiae tenebras, ut in eis quisque requirat excusationem. Aliud est enim nescisse, aliud scire noluisse. Voluntas quippe in eo arguitur, de quo dicitur 'Noluit intelligere ut bene ageret' (Ps. XXXV, 4). Sed et illa ignorantia quae non est eorum qui scire nolunt, sed eorum qui tanquam simpliciter nesciunt, neminem sic excusat, ut sempiterno igne non ardeat . . . sed fortasse ut mitius ardeat."—*MPL,* XLIV, 884-885. Out of this distinction the *ignorantia invita-simplex-affectata* division was developed by the Decretists.

[13] *De Adulterinis Coniugiis,* lib. I, c. 9—*CSEL,* XLI, 356.

[14] *Epistola,* XCIII, IV, 15—*CSEL,* XXXIV, 2, 459-460—cc. 1-2, C. I, q. 4.

[15] *Sermo CLXXX,* c. 2—*MPL,* XXXVIII, 973. It is interesting to note the similarity of this sentence of St. Augustine with the Common Law doctrine of *mens rea* (guilty mind), which is summarized in the axiom: *Reum non facit nisi mens rea.* Some trace this expression back to St. Augustine's comment upon an inadvertent lie. Cf. Lévitt, "The Origin of the Doctrine of *Mens Rea*"—*Illinois Review* (1922-1923), XVII, 117-137.

Article II. The Theory and Practice of the Ancient Discipline

It is frequently asserted that the Church always attended to the moral imputability of the delinquent in her juridico-penal system and, consequently, always admitted ignorance as an excuse from penalty.[16] When, however, the actual practice of the early Church is studied as it is revealed to us in the ancient penitential discipline and later on in the penitential books, a number of instances are to be found which seem to indicate the contrary. It does seem that in the early ages, practically until the ninth century, the external anti-juridical fact constituted the basis of penal imputability with little regard for the subjective state of mind of the individual author of the deed.[17]

1. Early Doctrine and Legislation

On the one hand, ignorance is sometimes expressly admitted as an excuse from penalty. In the records of the ancient penitential system several instances can be pointed out in regard to which it was explicitly stated that those committing the crime were not to be considered guilty, if they did so in ignorance. One of the earliest instances has been preserved in the *Pastor Hermae* (ca. 140-155). According to the penitential discipline of the time a husband who continued to live with an unfaithful wife made himself guilty of her sin. However, according to the author of the *Pastor,* a husband who did not separate from an adulterous wife because he was ignorant of the fact of her crime, was not considered liable for his wife's adultery.[18]

The tendency to punish only morally imputable crimes is evi-

[16] Roberti, *De Delictis et Poenis* (Romae: Libraria Pontificii Instituti Utriusque Iuris, 1938), I, 107; Chelodi, *Ius Poenale* (4. ed., Tridenti: Ardesi, 1935), p. 9, note 6.

[17] Cf. Michiels, *De Delictis et Poenis,* I, 89.

[18] "Et dixi illi: Domine, si quis habuerit uxorem fidelem in Domino, et hanc invenerit in adulterio, numquid peccat vir, si convivat cum illa? Et dixit mihi: Quamdiu nescit peccatum ejus, sine crimine est vir vivens cum illa."—Lib. II, mand. IV, cap. 1—Migne, *Patrologiae Cursus Completus, Series Graeca,* II, 919-920. (Hereafter this work work will be abbreviated *MPG.*)

denced by a decree of an African council, held at the end of the fourth century. This council ordered that children baptized by heretics and later admitted into the Church were not to be prohibited from receiving sacred orders. The children were not to be held responsible for the errors of their parents.[19]

St. Ambrose (d. 397) besides giving his own view on the subject, has left a valuable testimony in regard to the generally admitted judicial practice of his time. In refuting the Manichaeans and proving that men themselves are to be blamed for the real evils that befall them, he used an *a priori* argument to illustrate the point. Therefore, he must have been stating something admitted by his opponents when he argued:

> Ideo etiam in judiciis istius mundi voluntarios reos, non ex necessitate compulsos, culpa constringit, poena condemnat. Neque enim si per furorem aliquis innocentem peremerit, obnoxius morti est. Quin etiam ipsius divinae legis oraculo (Exod. XXI, 13), si quis per imprudentiam intulerit necem, accipit impunitatis spem . . . Mala enim non sunt nisi quae crimine mentem implicant et conscientiam ligant.[20]

Even the Penitential Books, with their minute specifications of penalty according to rigid rules for each individual case, contain general admonitions to the effect that penance is to be moderated according to the penitent's guilt. Thus, the *Ordo Romanus,* under the title, *Ordo Feriae IIII in capite jejunii,* instructs the priest receiving the penitents in the following words:

> Non omnibus vero una eademque discretio sit; unicuique eorum hoc est inter divitem et pauperem, . . . infantem et puerum . . . *scientem et ignarum* . . . utrum voluntarie vel casu . . . discernat.[21]

To some extent these principles are exemplified in the early legislation of the Church. Thus, the Council of Ancyra (314) pro-

[19] III Council of Carthage (397), c. 48—Mansi, *Sacrorum Conciliorum Nova et Amplissima Collectio* (Parisiis, 1901-1927), III, 891. (Hereafter this work will be cited as: Mansi.)

[20] *Hexaemeron,* lib. I, cap. VIII, 31—*MPL,* XIV, 140-141.

[21] The text is from the *Codex Manuscript. Valicellanum* D. 5 (tenth century)—Schmitz, *Die Bussbücher und die Bussdisciplin der Kirche* (Mainz, 1883), p. 88.

vided that voluntary homicide be punished with lifelong penance, while involuntary (*non sponte*) homicide be penalized with a seven-year (according to an older definition) or a five-year (according to a more recent regulation) penance. It seems that the Council left the imposition of either of these latter two penances to free choice.[22]

According to an old decree, of uncertain date and origin,[23] a distinction is to be made in regard to the penalty to be inflicted upon those who give Holy Communion to a heretic in ignorance of the prohibition of the Church and those who do so knowing the law. The former are to perform penance for one year after becoming aware of the fact. The latter, who knowingly violate the law, must undergo a penance of ten years or, according to a milder practice, a penance for a period of from five to seven years. The same penance is to be imposed upon those who receive Holy Communion from the hands of a heretic. This example of a mitigated penalty for the violation of a law in ignorance is noteworthy because it is one of the earliest instances in which ignorance of law was expressly admitted as a mitigating circumstance.[24]

2. The Penitential Practice of the East

The actual penitential practice of the ancient Church was not, however, uninfluenced by the primitive penal systems of the times and the popular conceptions of criminal imputability. The penitential system served a double purpose. It served to secure the amendment of the sinner and his reconciliation with God; and, secondly,

[22] Cc. 21-22—Harduin, *Acta Conciliorum et Epistolae Decretales ac Constitutiones Summorum Pontificum* (Parisiis, 1714-1725), I, 279-280. (Hereafter this work will be cited as: Harduin.)

[23] Incorporated in the *Decretum Gratiani,* c. 41, C. XXIV, q. 1. According to Richter-Friedberg, two codices ascribe the decree to Pope Julianus (?), while five others attribute it to Pope Lucianus (253-254).—*Corpus Iuris Canonici* (2 ed., Lipsiae: Tauchnitz, 1928), I, 983, note 646. The edition of the *Correctores Romani* (Romae, 1582) ascribe it to Pope Julius (337-352). The *Decretum Burchardi* (ca. 1012) attributes the same decree to Pope Eutychianus (283-296).—*MPL,* CXL, 1004-1005.

[24] Hinschius, *Das Kirchenrecht der Katholiken und Protestanten in Deutschland* (Berlin, 1869-1879), V, 922, note 2. (Hereafter this work will be cited as: Hinschius, *Kirchenrecht.*)

to safeguard the external social order. In the latter function it assumed the rôle of criminal law, which, especially in the more primitive legal systems, does not consider so much the moral guilt of the individual delinquent but rather the objective fact of the crime.

The penal character of the penitential discipline assumed new prominence in Asia Minor during the fourth century as a reaction to the decline of the Graeco-Roman and Christian culture brought about by the inroads of the barbarians. To counteract the moral evils of these times the penitential discipline took on a new severity. Moreover, the lower moral and ethical consciousness of the peoples left its stamp upon the penitential practice. Like the primitive juridical systems, it considers not so much the moral guilt of the delinquent but rather the objective fact that he violated the law. Hence, even the purely material violation of law through ignorance is considered a sufficient basis for the imposition of penalties.[25]

Evidence of this is to be found in the three famous letters which St. Basil wrote to Amphilochius, Bishop of Iconium, between the years 374 and 375. For example, in his first canonical letter to Amphilochius, St. Basil enumerates a series of crimes which were to be severely punished. In regard to serious crimes against chastity (*immunditia*) he makes the express provision that a thirty-year penance is to be imposed upon those who commit these crimes in ignorance.[26]

A similar tendency is evident from St. Basil's application of a ruling made by the council of Neocaesarea (314). According to canon 8 of this council, a layman is not to be admitted to the clerical rank if his wife has violated conjugal fidelity and this becomes

[25] Cf. Müller, *Ethik und Recht*, pp. 36-42.

[26] C. 7—*MPG*, XXXII, 674-675. The editors (col. 674, note 58) consider the number 30 incorrect, despite the fact that all the readings consulted by them had that number. They argue especially from the fact that St. Basil imposed much milder penances upon like crimes. Thus, he prescribed a penance of fifteen years for deliberate adultery (c. 58) and a penance of twenty years for incest with one's sister (c. 67). Müller (*Ethik und Recht*, pp. 38-39), however, considers the number correct. He argues that St. Basil in canon 7 is giving expression to a rule already in existence; while Basil himself is inclined to a more lenient penance.

publically known. If the infidelity of the wife occurred after the ordination of the cleric, the latter must either leave her or abstain from all sacred functions. The motive of this legislation is evident. Man and wife are united so intimately, that the public infidelity of one dishonors the other. Hence, it would be unbecoming to admit the dishonored husband to orders or the exercise of sacred functions.[27] According to St. Basil a priest, who *insciens illicitis nuptiis implicatus est* is not permitted to exercise any sacred functions. While no special penance was imposed and the priest could retain his rank among the clergy, yet, he is not considered entirely free from guilt; because St. Basil admonishes him to beseech the Lord to pardon the sin committed in ignorance.[28]

The tendency to regard merely the objective transgression is also shown in the advice which St. Basil gives to a woman who unknowingly married a man already joined in valid wedlock. Because the *fornicatio* is *imprudens,* she is not forbidden to enter a valid marriage, yet it would be better for her to remain unmarried.[29]

3. The Penal Discipline of the Penitential Books

The new form of penitential discipline, which arose in the British Isles and later spread to the continent, is fundamentally different from the ancient penitential system of the Church. It is not necessary to discuss the changes that came about during these centuries. There is a gradual decline of the ancient severity of the penitential canons. Despite this fact, the penitential books continue to prescribe penalties for purely objective or material transgressions of law. In this the penitential books show a dependency upon the primitive Germanic Law, which demanded expiation for the material criminal fact, even though the individual criminal could not be considered morally responsible.[30]

[27] Hefele-Leclercq, *Histoire des Conciles* (Paris, 1907-1938), I, 331.

[28] *Epistola Canonica* II, c. 27—*MPG,* XXXII, 723.

[29] "Quae viro ad tempus ab uxore derelicto insciens nupsit, ac deinde demissa est, quod prior ad ipsum reversa sit, fornicatio quidem est, sed imprudens. A matrimonio ergo non arcebitur, sed melius est si sic permaneat."—*Epistola Canonica* II, c. 46—*MPG,* XXXII, 730.

[30] Müller, *Ethik und Recht,* p. 44.

As far as the imposition of penalties is concerned, the Penitential Books precisely fix the exact punishment that is to be meted out according to an inflexible rule covering the various forms of each delict. Hence, instead of allowing a mitigation of a prescribed penalty according to the concrete circumstances of the individual case, the Penitential Books determine beforehand what is to be done in each case.

Ignorance is not admitted as an excuse from penalties nor can the priest imposing the penance vary or mitigate the same in order to fit the subjective guilt of the penitent before him. In the Penitential Books exact regulations are found, which determine minutely what penance is to be imposed upon the deliberate violation of law and upon the transgression of the same law through ignorance.

A few examples will illustrate this point. The *Poenitentiale Cummeani* (ca. 650) has these regulations in regard to the crime of perjury:

> Si quis perjurium fecerit, laici III annos peniteant, clerici V, subdiaconi VI, diaconi VII, presbyteri X, episcopi XII.
> Qui ducit alium in perjurio ignorantem, VII annos peniteat.
> Qui ductus est in perjurio ignorans et postea recognoscit annum peniteat.
> Qui vero suspicatur, quod in perjurio ducitur, tamen jurat per consensum, II annos peniteat.[31]

The penances for lying are apportioned in the same minute manner:

[31] *Excarpus,* C. V, cc. 1, 6, 7, 8—Schmitz, *Bussbücher,* pp. 628-629. The *Codex Paris 3182* contains a fragment which attributes these penitential canons to a Synod of Victoria in Wales (ca. 520). Cf. Schmitz, *op. cit.,* pp. 491, 494; Hefele-Leclercq, *Histoire des Conciles,* II, 1045. Haddan-Stubbs (*Councils and Ecclesiastical Documents Relating to Great Britain and Ireland* [Oxford, 1869-1871], I, 116-118) seem to consider these decrees as really originating in a council held by Bishop St. David (d. 601) at Luci Victoria (sometimes used without Luci). These canons are repeated in many other Penitential Books; v. gr., *Poenitentiale Cummeani, Capitula Iudiciorum,* C. XV, 1, 3, 4—Schmitz, *op. cit.,* pp. 664-665; *Poenitentiale Valicellanum I, Leges Canonicae* (VIII cent.), cc. 48, 49, 51—Schmitz, *op. cit.,* pp. 290-291; *Poenitentiale Casinense* (700-750), cc. 32-34—Schmitz, *op. cit.,* pp. 408-409.

> Mendax vero per ignorantiu[a]m et non nocuit, confiteatur ei, cui mentitus est, et sacerdoti et hora tacendi damnetur vel XII psalmos canat.
> Si vero de industria, III dies tacendi vel XXX, si preest.[32]

Some penitential canons impose a different penalty for a sin committed in ignorance, negligence and contempt. For instance, the *Poenitentiale Cummeani* has the following rule for drunkenness of a priest:

> Sacerdos si inebrietur per ignorantiam, VII dies peniteat in pane et aqua, si per negligentiam, XV dies peniteat, si per contemptum, XL dies penit.[33]

The same plan is followed in the *Poenitentiale Arundel* (end of the IX Cent.) in apportioning the penances to be imposed upon a mother who kills her own child:

> 17. Mulieres, qui partus suos sponte necaverint, . . . X annis poeniteant, et omnibus diebus vitae suae fletibus insistant.
> 19. Mulier quae filium suum non baptizatum ignoranter oppresserit, VII annos poeniteat; qui baptizatum IV.
> 21. Si infans baptizatus quidem infra VII annos parentum negligentia perierit, III annis peniteant, nec tamen communionem aut ecclesiam amittant.[34]

Similar prescriptions in regard to other crimes could be adduced. The underlying principle in all these regulations is the same: a delict committed in ignorance has its own special penalty. Ignorance is, therefore, not considered as an excuse from penalty, but, as a reason for mitigating the ordinary penance. The mitigation of the penalty is not in the hands of the judge or the priest administering the law, but is determined very minutely by the legislator in the law itself.[35]

[32] *Poenitentiale Cummeani, Excarpus,* C. V, cc. 12-13—Schmitz, *op. cit.*, p. 629; *Valicellanum I,* c. 76—Schmitz, *op. cit.*, p. 301.

[33] *Excarpus,* C. I, c. 6—Schmitz, *op. cit.*, pp. 615-616; cf. also *Poenitentiale Casinense,* cc. 42-43—Schmitz, *op. cit.*, p. 410.

[34] Schmitz, *op. cit.*, pp. 443-444; cf. *Poenitentiale Valicellanum* I, cc. 7, 9, 10—Schmitz, *op. cit.*, pp. 259-262.

[35] Cf. Müller, *Ethik und Recht,* 42-68.

Article III. The Discipline after the Ninth Century

After the beginning of the ninth century a notable change is to be noted in ecclesiastical penal law. The change is marked by a revival of ancient law and a reaction against Germanic Law tendencies. There is a notable return to patristic Moral Theology which leads to a more profound consideration of the subjective element of crime.[86] Instead of the mere objective violation of the law being considered as the basis for the application of a rigid penalty found in the Penitential Books, penalties are adjusted more according to subjective guilt. In accord with the principle announced several centuries before and frequently to be cited later on, *rem quae culpa caret, in damnum vocari non convenit,*[87] the necessary subjective element of crime received more attention; first in regard to specific crimes, such as homicide,[88] and then gradually applied by analogy also to other crimes.

The doctrine and practice regarding ignorance consequently developed along the same line. It is not surprising to find that ignorance received more consideration in reference to various delicts and also that it was more and more admitted as an excuse from penalty. Moreover, penalties were greatly increased in number during these centuries. The use of general censures and the gradual introduction of *ponae latae sententiae* greatly encouraged the development of principles applicable to those who violated statutes and sentences in ignorance. Principles are evolved in discussing specific laws, deci-

[86] Müller, *Ethik und Recht,* pp. 68-69; Michiels, *De Delictis et Poenis,* I, 90-91.

[87] *Ex Registro Gregorii* I (IX, 104) *Fortunato Episcopo Neapolis* (599)—Jaffé, *Regesta Pontificum Romanorum* (2. ed. Lipsiae, 1885-1888), n. 1629 (ed. P. Ewald)—Comp. I, c. 2, *de constitutionibus,* I, 1; c. 2, X, *de constitutionibus,* I, 2. While the Pope in this letter speaks of the *"ignorantes"* as not incurring penalty, it would be wrong to deduce too much from this passage. Pope Gregory is speaking of the effect of law after its proper promulgation, namely that it affects the future and not the past. He says nothing of the ignorance which follows the effective promulgation of law. ". . . ne detrimentum ante prohibitionem possint ignorantes incurrere, quod eos postmodum dignum est vetitos sustinere."

[88] C. 49, D. L. (Pope Nicolas I); c. 50, D. L. (Council of Worms [868], c. 29—Mansi, XV, 874); c. 51, D. L. (Council of Friburg [895], c. 36).

sions and responses of the Roman Pontiffs. These become the germ of a more systematic doctrine begun at the time of Gratian and perfected in its essential elements by the sixteenth century.

A consideration of some of the specific laws and decisions will afford some idea of the way in which ignorance came to be admitted as a complete excuse from the penalties of the law.

1. Papal Decrees

A noteworthy instance in which ignorance is admitted as an excuse is contained in a rescript of Pope Nicolas I to Hincmar of Rheims (864-867). This is a response of the Pope to Emperor Charles concerning the abettors of and those who communicated with the excommunicated and unfaithful wife of Count Boso, Engeltrude.[39] The Pope, insisting that he is not teaching something entirely new, explained that a distinction is to be made with regard to a crime committed out of necessity or ignorance and one committed with deliberate design. Those who failed out of ignorance are not to be punished hastily, but rather their ignorance is to be examined to find out whether it be true (*vera*) or simulated, *i. e.*, wilful. Those who offended wilfully or out of wilful ignorance can be absolved only by the Pope himself; while those who failed through *ignorantia non simulata* are to be freed from the excommunication immediately by Hincmar on the authority of the Pope.[40]

The principle that knowledge is a requisite for incurring the excommunication imposed upon communication with excommunicated persons is more clearly stated in a letter of Pope Urban II to

[39] Mansi, xv, 389. The response is incorporated in a number of collections of canons; v. gr., *Decretum Ivonis,* XIV, 46; *Panormia,* V, 106; *Collectio Trium Partium,* I, 62, 34; c. 102, C. XI, q. 3.

[40] From the strict wording of the text it would seem that the Holy Father refers to absolution from a censure already incurred. He says: " . . . auctoritate nostra per te absolvantur." However, this can be understood in the sense of a release from a sentence which had been unjustly pronounced and hence without juridical effect. Note also the similarity between the distinctions of ignorance used by the Pope with those formulated by St. Augustine. With regard to wilful ignorance the Pope cites the same Psalm XXXV, 4, as St. Augustine had done. Cf. *supra,* p. 16, note 12.

the bishop of Constance (1089). The Pope enumerates the various causes which excuse from the excommunication in these words:

> Sanctis quippe canonibus cautum constat, ut quicumque excommunicatis communicauerit excommunicetur. Ipsius tamen penitenciae atque absolutionis modos eo moderamine decernimus, ut quicumque seu ignorantia, seu timore, seu necessitate negocii . . . contaminauerint, cum minoris penitenciae medicina societatis nostrae participium sortiantur. Eos vero, qui aut spontanee, aut negligenter inciderint, sub ea uolumus disciplinae cohercione suscipi, . . .[41]

Ignorance is clearly admitted as an excuse from the excommunication. However, the text seems to imply also that the ignorance must be inculpable; because it states that those who *negligenter* communicate with excommunicates fall under the penalty.

The censures and penalties which were inflicted by the Popes during the investiture and simony struggles occasioned a decision by Pope Gregory VII. It is of considerable importance because it is frequently appealed to by canonists in treating of ignorance. At a Roman Council, held under Gregory VII (1078), the sentence of excommunication and other penalties were inflicted on and threatened to a number of refractory children of the Church. However, the Council saw fit to mitigate its severe sentence. As the Council expressly says, it realized that many were perishing spiritually through ignorance, simplicity or fear on account of the numerous penalties, and, therefore, felt it necessary to temper the penalties. The Council then proceeds to exempt whole classes of people; women (*uxores*), children, slaves, servants, "rustici et omnes alios qui non adeo curiales sunt, ut eorum consilio scelera perpetrentur, et illos qui ignoranter excommunicatis communicant, seu illos qui communicant cum eis qui communicant excommunicatis." It is evident that the ignorance here referred to was ignorance of fact. Yet, it does not necessarily imply that ignorance of law is completely excluded. That distinction was not yet formally introduced into Canon Law and the words of the text *nimia simplicitate* and

[41] Harduin, VI, P. II, 1651—c. 110, C. XI, q. 3.

non adeo curiales are very well applicable to those who are ignorant of the law itself.[42]

2. The Decisions of Particular Councils

The decisions of several particular councils manifest a similar tendency. Of great importance for the subsequent development of the doctrine of penal imputability in general, as well as of imputability for ignorance, is the decree of the Council of Worms (868) in regard to homicide. In determining the responsibility of the woodchopper who killed a man while cutting down a tree, the Council distinguishes two kinds of penal imputability: *Voluntas* or *votum* and *negligentia* or *incuria.* It is determined that either *voluntas* or *negligentia* suffices for penal liability. In this the Council approaches the modern classification of delicts, on the basis of subjective responsibility, into *delicta ex dolo* and *delicta ex culpa.*[43] Ignorance, however, is dealt with as a separate source of criminal liability, as can be seen from the words of the Council in speaking of those who are not held for homicide. "Quod si non voto, non incuria illius, non denique scientia contigit, sed dum ille operi necessario fortassis incumberet, iste insperatus occurrens, sub arborem improviscus devenit, et sub ipsa, nemine valente penitus adjuvare, suppressus est, incisor arboris homicidae procul dubio non est comparandus."[44] According to this ruling ignorance of fact is

[42] Mansi, XX, 505-506—c. 103, C. XI, q. 3. The decree was evidently intended to be something provisional. Cf. Hinschius, *Kirchenrecht,* V, 925, note 9. However, it was given universal and permanent character by its incorporation in the *Corpus Iuris* and several other collections, v. gr., *Decretum Ivonis* (XIV, 43), *Panormia* (V, 125). Cf. Kober, *Kirchenbann nach den Grundsätzen des canonischen Rechts* (2. ed., Tübingin, 1863), pp. 406-407); Lega, *Praelectiones in Textum Iuris Canonici, De Delictis et Poenis* (2. ed., Romae, 1910), p. 66, note 1. (Hereafter this work will be cited as: Lega, *De Delictis et Poenis.*)

[43] Cf. Kuttner, *Schuldlehre,* p. 68.

[44] C. 29—Mansi, XV, 874. The decree is incorporated in the *Decretum Gratiani* with some modifications. The text of the Correctores Romani and of the critical edition (Richter-Friedberg) do not agree. According to the Correctores Romani c. 50, D. L reads: "Quod si non voto, non incuria illius non debet omnino submitti. . . ." According to the Richter-Friedberg edition the text is as follows: "Quod si non uoto, sed incuria illius, non hoc eum sen-

admitted as a complete excuse from penal liability, if it is invincible or, in the words of the council, if the presence of the man is *insperatus* (unlooked for) and *improvisus* (unknown).

At the close of the century the Council of Tribur (895) made similar provisions for adultery relative to the penalty of privation of marital rights. In this case, also, ignorance of fact is admitted as an excuse from the privation.[45]

These decrees became general law through their acceptance in the *Decretum Gratiani* and were applied by analogy to similar cases. They were cited later on to prove that ignorance of fact excuses from penalty and became important materials out of which the Decretists developed a systematic doctrine.[46]

Conclusion

From these historical considerations several conclusions can be drawn. The Christian principles of moral imputability are to be found already in the writings of the early writers and Fathers of the Church, notably St. Augustine. Yet, it cannot be denied that in the early penitential system the external, objective violation of the law, with but little regard for individual subjective guilt, was considered the basis for penal responsibility. Under the influence of the popular conceptions of penal liability and the primitive legal systems the Christian idea of moral guilt was lost sight of until the beginning of the ninth century. In the Penitential Books the influ-

tencia contingit." The first reading leaves out *scientia,* while the second, besides omitting *scientia,* distinguishes *incuria* from *negligentia,* declaring that the former does not suffice for penal imputability.

[45] C. 43: "Si quis cum qualibet fornicatus fuerit, et eo nesciente, filius ejus vel frater ejusdem rei inscius, cum eadem se polluerit . . . et hoc se nescire cum juramento confirmaverint . . . post peractam congruam poenitentiam, legitimo utatur matrimonio. . . ." C. 45: ". . . definimus . . . qui cum duabus sororibus fuerit pollutus, ut usque in exitum vitae poenitens et continens permaneat. Soror autem, quae . . . scienter se cum eodem commaculaverit, usque in finem vitae poenitens et continens perduret. Si autem improvise contingit, condigna stringatur castigatione: et si velit, legitima utatur viri conjunctione." —Mansi, XVIIIa, 153-154—c. 6, C. XXXIV, q. 1-2.

[46] Cf. Kuttner, *Schuldlehre,* pp. 67-71; Müller, *Ethik und Recht,* pp. 69-71; Michiels, *De Delictis et Poenis,* I, 90-91.

ence of Germanic Law is quite evident. According to the practice of the Penitential Books, every violation of law must receive its penalty. Accordingly, there are minute determinations of penances to be imposed according to the different degrees of delictual culpability. In measuring individual guilt the objective gravity of the crime was considered more important than the knowledge and will of the delinquent. In the Penitential Books, therefore, ignorance is not admitted as a complete excuse from penalty. It is admitted as a mitigating circumstance and the law itself provides a milder penance for delicts committed in ignorance.

After the ninth century a number of pontifical decrees and decisions of councils show a marked change in regard to ignorance. The legal system of the Church is gradually breaking away from the primitive legal ideas of the previous centuries and returns to the truly Christian principles of Patristic Theology.

Ignorance of fact, and in a few exceptional and extraordinary cases also ignorance of law, is recognized as an excuse from penalties, or, at least as a cause for mitigating the penalties imposed by law. That is about all that can be affirmed as a matter of general principle. No distinctions seem to have been made in regard to the kinds and degrees of culpability in the ignorance itself. Hence, the doctrine regarding imputability of crimes committed in ignorance is still rather primitive and its principles are too rigid to meet the demands of a legal system which attempts, at least, to apportion penalties in accord with individual guilt.

CHAPTER III

FROM THE TIME OF GRATIAN UNTIL THE TIME OF THE COUNCIL OF TRENT

THIS period extends roughly from the middle of the twelfth century until about the middle of the sixteenth century. The starting point is obviously the *Decretum Gratiani,* which occasioned important doctrinal developments in the whole of the ecclesiastical law of penalties. The close of this period is not arbitrarily chosen. The reason for extending this period until the middle of the sixteenth century is twofold: First, because by this time the nature of censures and their differentiation from other canonical penalties was clearly recognized and fully appreciated; and secondly, the moral doctrine of imputability reached new heights of perfection at about the same time.

A separate consideration of these four centuries is of particular value, because during this time the fundamental doctrine of ignorance in regard to penal, as well as moral, imputability was gradually worked out. In a word, the canonists and moralists of this period developed not only a system of divisions and definitions for the various kinds of ignorance, but also proposed the basic principles upon which the law in force today is based.

This doctrine developed through the discussions of numerous canonists and moralists in reference to concrete cases or particular canons and decrees. The immediate result was, as can be expected, considerable variety, not only in the definitions and divisions of ignorance, but also in the results arrived at, namely, the principles or rules of law in regard to penal imputability for crimes committed in ignorance.

ARTICLE I. GRATIAN AND THE DECRETISTS—ORIGIN OF A SYSTEMATIC DOCTRINE [1]

Several important factors contribute to the clarification of the nature of penal responsibility for ignorance. The first, most obvious

[1] Only the more general trends of the devolopment during this period can be considered. Those points of law will be discussed which have had a more

and also most important, is the amount of consideration given to the problems of ignorance in the *Decretum Gratiani* itself. Gratian himself considered the question in several places [2] and introduced several important texts from St. Augustine,[3] as well as a number of canons from various councils [4] and pontifical decrees.[5]

Moreover, the revival of Roman Law in the schools and the evident borrowing of Roman Law principles together with the development of the doctrine of ignorance in the theological schools greatly contribute towards the foundation of a highly developed canonical doctrine. The importance of this period for the legal principles of Canon Law cannot be overestimated. What Kantorowicz says of the Roman Law Glossators can be applied literally to their Canon Law contemporaries: "There is scarcely any type of legal literature, any legal method, any legal doctrine or concept, that was not created or foreshadowed in the successive medieval law schools." [6]

The dependence of the canonists either upon the doctrine of the Scholastic Theologians or upon the Roman Jurists gave rise to a twofold development which must be considered separately.

1. Principles of Theological Origin

Abelard had attempted the solution of a theological and scriptural problem, namely, the guilt of the Jews crucifying Christ in ignorance and Christ's prayer for their pardon,[7] by means of a dis-

lasting influence. For a complete treatment of this period, see Kuttner, *Schuldlehre,* III, "Unwissenheit und Irrtum," pp. 133-184. This article relies almost entirely upon Dr. Kuttner's profound research in the doctrine of this period. See also Lottin, "Le problème de l' *ignorantia iuris* de Gratien à St. Thomas d'Aquin"—*Recherches de Théologie ancienne et médiévale,* V (1933), 345-368.

[2] *Grat. init.* D. XXXVIII; *Grat. Dict. p.* c. 12, C. I, q. 4; *Grat. Dict. p.* c. 2, C. XV, q. 1.

[3] V. gr., c. 4, C. XXII, q. 2; c. 37, C. XXIII, q. 4; c. 1, C. XV, q. 1.

[4] V. gr., Council of Worms (868)—c. 50, D. L; Council of Tribur (895) —c. 6, C. XXIV, q. 1-2.

[5] Nicolas I (ca. 864-867)—c. 102, C. XI, q. 3; c. 49, D. L.; Gregory VII (1078)—c. 103, C. XI, q. 3; Urban II (1089)—c. 110, C. XI, q. 3.

[6] *Studies in the Glossators of the Roman Law,* p. 1.

[7] Cf. Luke, XXIII, 34.

tinction between *ignorantia invincibilis* and *negligentia*. Even the latter, he taught, excluded sin in the strict sense and was only *quod nos facere minime convenit*.[8] In this manner a fundamental distinction had been established between ignorance which excuses and that which does not excuse. Abelard was completed by the Scholastic Theologians who substituted *ignorantia vincibilis* (the opposite of *invincibilis*) for the *negligentia* of Abelard's distinction.[9]

By distinguishing between actions which proceed from infirmity and actions which proceed from the will Gratian had found a basic norm for determining, whether acts performed in ignorance were to be imputed to the agent or not.[10] By the application of this principle of distinction he was able to solve the discordance between the text of St. Paul, *si quis ignorat ignorabitur*,[11] and the proposition he had set up according to his dialectic method, namely, *non sunt peccata nolentium, nisi nescientium*.[12] The difficulty was, therefore, solved by showing that there is an ignorance which excuses (namely, that which proceeds from infirmity) and an ignorance which does not obviate guilt (namely, that which proceeds from the will). Gratian did not develop this distinction any further, nor did he give any norm according to which these two forms of ignorance are to be distinguished. The Decretists, however, completed

[8] *Ethica*, c. 14—*MPL*, CLXXVIII, 657. This opinion, in so far as it was applied to the guilt of the Jews crucifying Christ, was condemned by the Council of Sens (1140) at the instigation of St. Bernard. Cf. Denzinger-Bannwart-Umberg, *Enchiridion* (21-23. ed., Friburgi-Brisgoviae: Herder, 1937), n. 377.

[9] "Est enim ignorantia, quae excusat peccatum; et est ignorantia talis, quae non excusat; est autem ignorantia invincibilis, et ignorantia vincibilis."—Peter Lombard, *Libri Quatuor Sententiarum* (2. ed., PP. Collegii S. Bonaventurae, Ad Claras Aquas: Typographia Collegii S. Bonaventurae, 1916), lib. II, dist. XXII, cap. 5.

[10] "Peccata namque alia penes voluntatem animi, alia circa naturae infirmitatem videntur consistere."—*Dict. Grat. pr.* C. XV, q. 1.

[11] I Cor. XIV, 38.

[12] C. 1, C. XV, q. 1. The text is taken from St. Augustine, *Quaestionum in Heptateuchum Libri VII*, lib. IV, q. 24 *ad Num.*, XV, 24-29— *CSEL*, XXVIII (2), 333.

Gratian's distinction by introducing the *vincibilis-invincibilis* divison of the Scholastic Theologians.[13]

Yet this fundamental distinction based solely upon the objective possibility of gaining knowledge is not sufficient for an accurate determination of subjective responsibility. Further development occurs along two more or less distinct lines.

A. *Ignorantia invita-simplex-affectata*

The first adopted a tripartite division of ignorance into *ignorantia invincibilis (invita), simplex (media)* and *affectata.*[14] Invincible ignorance, or that which can by no means be overcome,[15] excuses entirely. *Ignorantia simplex,* or that which one neither desires nor avoids,[16] somewhat diminishes but does not destroy imputability.[17]

[13] "Sed anime infirmitas bipartito dividitur; alia est enim pena tantum, ut invincibilis ignorantia."—Rufinus, *Summa Decretorum, ad Grat. Dict.,* c. 1, C. XV, q. 1, *vv.* "Quod autem ea, qua mente alienata fiunt" (ed. Singer [Paderborn, 1902], p. 345). "Et sciendum, quod duplex est ignorantia, vincibilis et invincibilis, invincibilis est pena peccati tantum et non peccatum, vincibilis autem . . . est peccatum."—*Summa Bambergensis, ad pr.* C. XV, q. 1—Kuttner, *Schuldlehre,* p. 139, note 4.

[14] Stephanus Tornacensis, *Summa, ad pr.* D. XXXVIII: " . . . ignorantia alia est invincibilis, alia vincibilis . . . Vincibilis alia affectata, alia simplex."—ed. Schulte (Giessen, 1891), p. 57. Sicardus, *ad* C. I, q. 4: " . . . ignorantia . . . alia necessaria, alia perniciosa; . . . perniciosa . . . quoque duplex: nam alia simplex, alia affectata."—Kuttner, *Schuldlehre,* p. 141, note 1. The distinction comes from Peter Lombard, *Libri Quattuor Sententiarum,* lib. II, dist. XXII, cap. 5.

[15] Stephanus, *ad pr.* D. XXXVIII: " . . . ut quando quis laborat, ut sciat, sed . . . proficere non potest . . . "—ed. Schulte, p. 57; Rolandus, *ad* C. XXII, q. 5: " . . . ea quae excludi nullatenus potest."—Kuttner, *Schuldlehre,* p. 141.

[16] Stephanus, *loc. cit.*: " . . . ut quando nec appetit nec fugit discere." —ed. Schulte, p. 57.

[17] Sicardus *ad* C. I, q. 4: " . . . hec excusat a maiori pena, set non ab omni, quia non excusat ut omnino non ardeat, set ut mitius ardeat."—Kuttner, *Schuldlehre,* p. 142, note 2.

Ignorantia affectata is the result either of neglect or of contempt;[18] such ignorance never excuses from penalties.[19]

B. *Ignorantia Culpa and Ignorantia Poena*

The Decretists, moreover, employed several other distinctions which were independent of Peter Lombard's *invincibilis-vincibilis* (or *invincibilis-simplex-affectata*) division. The idea of *ignorantia affectata,* nevertheless, remained as the criterion for ignorance which does not excuse. These Decretists distinguished between *ignorantia poena* and *ignorantia culpa. Ignorantia culpa* results from neglect, contempt or even a positive desire to remain ignorant. This ignorance never excuses. *Ignorantia poena* is a passion or defect of mind which hinders one from acquiring knowledge; consequently, it excuses.[20]

The idea of negligence in the various forms of non-excusing ignorance (especially *affectata*) led to the employment of further distinctions according to the degrees of subjective culpability. The distinction was borrowed from the Roman Law [21] and was first introduced into the theological schema by Rolandus Bandinelli (d. 1181);[22] and it differentiated between vincible ignorance which is

[18] Stephanus *ad pr.* D. XXXVIII: "Affectata ut quando quis potest discere, sed neglegit et contemnit . . . "—ed. Schulte, p. 57; Sicardus *ad* C. I, q. 4: " . . . affectata, cum neglegit immo et discere contemnit."—Kuttner, *Schuldlehre,* p. 142, note 4.

[19] Stephanus *ad pr.* C. XV, q. 1: " . . . hec a nulla pena excusat."; *Summa Coloniensis ad pr.* D. XXXVIII: " . . . affectata gravat."; Sicardus *ad* C. I, q. 4: " . . . hec incusat . . . "—Kuttner, *loc. cit.*

[20] Thus, v. gr., Huguccio *ad pr.* D. XXXVIII: " . . . ignorantia quedam est culpa, quedam est pena. ignorantia culpa est negligentia, vel contemptus, qua vel quo quis neglegit vel contempnit scire ea que debet scire vel facere, vel voluntas qua querit ignorare ea . . . hec neminem excusat a peccato vel pena . . . ignorantia pena est animi passio vel defectus, quo animus impeditur ad comprehendum vel intelligendum ea que sunt necessaria . . . "—Kuttner, *Schuldlehre,* p. 144, note 1. Cf. Lottin, "Le problème de l'*ignorantia iuris*"—*—op. cit.,* pp. 349-350.

[21] Cf. *supra,* p. 9.

[22] Kuttner, *Schuldlehre,* p. 145.

crassa vel supina and that *quae caderet in discretissimum virum.*[23] Crass ignorance did not excuse. In regard to the ignorance *quae caderet in discretissimum virum,* Rolandus and many other Decretists distinguished between that which resulted *ex culpa praecedente* and that which did not.[24] If the ignorance resulted from *culpa praecedens* it excused from penalties in the eyes of the Church, but did not exempt from sin before God.[25]

To sum up what has been said, in the words of Dr. Kuttner: "With the introduction of *culpa praecedens* the ways and means of distinguishing excusing and non-excusing ignorance, on the principle of the theologico-canonical distinction of *invincibilis-vincibilis,* are exhausted. To sum up and coordinate what has been said. Two sets of distinctions arising from this principle can be distinguished: the one following Lombard divides *ignorantia vincibilis* into *affectata* and *simplex*; the other, introduced by Roland, distinguished according to the Roman concepts of *crassa vel supina* and *quae caderet in discretissimum virum.* The latter again borrows from the canonical concepts and introduces the subdivision of *ex culpa praecedenti* and *sine culpa praecedenti.* Completely excusing are: *Ignorantia invincibilis* and that *ignorantia vincibilis* which would befall even the most discreet man without any previous fault of his own. Partially excusing are: *Ignorantia simplex,* the merited *(ex culpa praecedenti) ignorantia vincibilis,* which would befall even the most prudent man. (This form of ignorance excuses from guilt before the Church but not before God.) Imputable are the *ignoran-*

23 " . . . item vincibilis . . . quandoque est resupina et crassa; quandoque est talis quae caderet in discretissimum virum."—*Sententiae,* p. 125—Kuttner, *Schuldlehre,* p. 145, note 2.

24 The *culpa praecedens* in this division is not so much moral guilt or responsibility; but rather, the result of just divine punishment. For example, the theory was used to explain the ignorance or blindness of Lamech. It was explained that his ignorance was a punishment for the crime of bigamy. In the same way the ignorance of Eve was explained. Cf. Müller, *Ethik und Recht,* pp. 152-153.

25 Cf. Stephanus, *ad dict. p.* c. 12, C. I, q. 4—ed. Schulte, p. 152; Kuttner, *Schuldlehre,* p. 148, note 1.

tia vincibilis affectata, i. e., scire posse sed nolle (vel negligere et contemnere) or the *ignorantia vincibilis crassa et supina.*" [26]

2. Principles of Roman Law Origin

A second and independent system of distinctions was borrowed from the Roman Law. Gratian himself formally introduced this distinction into the Canon Law for the first time in connection with the question whether a son might retain a benefice, which, unknown to him, had been procured for him by his father through simony.[27] This distinction, of the greatest importance to the subsequent developments in canonical doctrine, divided ignorance on the basis of the unknown object into ignorance of law and ignorance of fact.[28] The further development of this distinction by the Decretists forms an important phase in the history of canonical doctrine. Ignorance of law and ignorance of fact must be considered separately, since during this period they remain essentially independent.

A. *Ignorance of Fact*

Gratian distinguishes ignorance of fact into *factum quod oportet scire* (which does not excuse) and *factum quod non oportet scire* (which excuses). This distinction, unknown to Roman Law, is based solely upon the objective obligation of knowing the fact.[29] It is of minor importance and disappears entirely in the later Decretalists.

The Decretists introduce into this purely Roman Law division another distinction which had been developed by canonists and theologians in dependence upon Roman Law. They divide *ignorantia facti quod oportet scire* into *crassa vel supina* and its opposite, *quae*

[26] *Schuldlehre,* pp. 148-149. Cf. also Müller, *Ethik und Recht,* III, § 1 "Die Lehre der Frühscholastik," pp. 118-169.

[27] *Dict. Grat. ad* c. 1, C. I, q. 4.

[28] Kantorowicz (*Studies in the Glossators of the Roman Law,* p. 80) calls attention to the striking similarity between the *Dictum Gratiani,* part. IV, § 2, *ad* C. I, q. 4 and Bulgarus (d. 1166), *de iuris et facti ignorantia Summula,* §§ 3, 4, 6. This similarity led Kantorowicz to the conclusion that Gratian derived this text from Bulgarus, the famous glossator of Roman Law.

[29] *Dict. Grat.* pars IV, § 1 *ad* C. I, q. 4.

caderet in discretissimum. Crass or supine ignorance [30] consists essentially in negligence; for example, it would be crass ignorance not to know that which everyone in the city knew [31] or that which proceeds from *lata culpa.*[32]

In opposition to crass ignorance is that which would befall even the most prudent man. The criterion *vir prudentissimus* or *constantissimus* [33] is gradually replaced by *vir diligens* [34] and *discretus* or *peritus.*[35] This type of ignorance is most frequently called *probabilis* and more rarely *iusta* or *verisimilis.*[36] Probable ignorance of fact is more easily admitted in regard to facts pertaining to others than concerning those pertaining to oneself, though both excuse if they are truly probable.[37]

B. *Ignorance of Law*

Ignorance of law receives a fundamentally different treatment. It is especially in regard to ignorance of law that the Decretists show dependence upon Roman Law, or more precisely, upon the Roman Law Glossators.[38]

[30] Also called *dissoluta.*—Kuttner, *Schuldlehre,* p. 157. Cf. *supra,* p. 9.

[31] This Roman Law criterion (cf. *supra,* p. 9, note 48) is frequently employed; v. gr., *Glossa Ordinaria ad pr.* D. XXXVIII, *v.* "cum itaque"; *ad* D. XVI, c. 14: " . . . nulli licet ignorare quae publice facta sunt."

[32] *Summa Bambergensis ad* D. XXXVIII: " . . . unde presbiter, qui ignorat, que in synodo facta sunt, dicitur esse in lata culpa."—Kuttner, *Schuldlehre,* p. 158, note 2.

[33] Stephanus, *Summa ad Grat. Dict. p.* c. 12, C. I, q. 4—ed. Schulte, p. 152.

[34] Simon, *ad* c. 6, C. XXXIV, q. 1-2—Kuttner, *ibidem,* p. 155, note 1.

[35] V. gr., Huguccio *ad* C. 1, q. 4—Kuttner, *loc. cit.*

[36] Cf. Kuttner, *ibidem,* p. 155.

[37] "Ignorantia facti semper excusat, sive ignorat de alieno facto, sive de propriis, dumtamen probabilis sit . . . magis tamen excusat error in alieno facto . . . " (citing D. [41, 10] 5—*supra,* p. 9, note 47)—*Glossa Ordinaria ad Grat. Dict. p.* 12, C. I, q. 4, *v.* "omnis ignorantia."

[38] Compare Gratian (*Dict.* pars IV, § 2 *ad* C. I, q. 4): "Item ignorantia iuris alia naturalis, alia civilis. Naturalis omnibus adultis dampnabilis est; ius vero civile aliis permittitur ignorare, aliis non" with Bulgarus (*de iuris et facti ignorantia summula,* § 6): "In iuris errore distinguitur naturale et civile ius, quia plus est culpa, naturale ius ignorare quam civile."—Kantorowicz, *Studies in the Glossators of the Roman Law,* p. 245.

Gratian distinguishes between ignorance of the natural law, which is never permissible to adults, and ignorance of the civil law, which can be permitted to some. The term "adultus" is explained by the Decretists to mean *discretus*[39] or simply *doli capax*.[40] Hence, ignorance of the natural law is permitted only to the mentally weak or, by some, to children; otherwise it is declared to be universally inexcusable.[41]

In regard to ignorance of civil law, Gratian simply states that it is permitted to some. The Decretists complete Gratian by declaring that ignorance of civil law (the latter term is interpreted to include also canon law)[42] is permitted to minors,[43] women, soldiers and *rustici*.[44] On the other hand, clerics are frequently expressly excluded from any excuse on account of ignorance of law.[45] However, these exceptions in regard to ignorance of law for certain classes of people do not seem to have meant a great deal so far as penal law is concerned. Many Decretists expressly limit the excuse

[39] " . . . si est adultus vel discretus . . . "—*Glossa Ordinaria ad pr.* D. XXXVIII.

[40] *Summa Bambergensis ad Grat. Dict. p.* c. 12, C. I, q. 4—Kuttner, *Schuldlehre*, p. 165.

[41] Cf. *Summa Paucapaleae* (ed. Schulte [Giessen, 1890], p. 55) and *Glossa Ordinaria ad* c. 12, C. I, q. 4; Kuttner, *Schuldlehre*, pp. 164-165; Lottin, "Le problème de l'*ignorantia iuris* de Gratien à St. Thomas d'Aquin"—*Recherches de Théol. ancienne et médiévale*, V (1933), 345-368.

[42] *Glossa Ordinaria, ad Dict. Grat. cit.* c. 12, C. I, q. 4; cf. Kuttner, *Schuldlehre*, p. 164, note 4.

[43] Gratian himself (*Dict. Pars* IV, § 2, *p.* c. 12, C. I, q. 4) admitted excuse for minors, as can be seen from the example he gives: " . . . ut, si minor pecuniam dederit filiofamilias, repetit [ignorantia ei non obest]; in maiore uero quasi delictum est." A minor is explained according to the Roman Law as one below the age of twenty-five years.—Paucapalea, *Summa, loc. cit.*

[44] "Ignorantia iuris civilis vel canonici . . . aliquos . . . excusat, ut milites, mulieres, rusticos, minores."—*Glossa Ordinaria* (Joannes Teutonicus) *ad pr.* D. XXXVIII. The reasons are given by Stephanus Tornacensis (*Summa, ad Dict. Grat. p.* c. 12, C. I, q. 4, *v.* "aliis permittitur"—ed. Schulte, p. 153): "Ut pupillo ob beneficium aetatis, et militibus, qui propter rempublicam occupantur in castris . . . et rusticis propter commodum agriculturae, et quandoque mulieribus propter sexum." For dependence upon the Roman Law, cf. *supra*, pp. 12-13.

[45] Cf. Kuttner, *Schuldlehre*, p. 168, note 2.

for ignorance of civil law to purely "civil" matters in contradistinction to exemption from penalties.[46]

Besides the Roman Law distinction on the basis of status in society, some Decretists introduce some purely canonical distinctions in relation to ignorance of law and, in so doing, open the way for the later relaxation of the old rigorous view in regard to ignorance of law. Thus, Joannes Teutonicus considers the distinction on the basis of status secondary and divides ignorance of canon law into affected and invincible ignorance. Invincible ignorance excuses, unless the knowledge were necessary on account of one's office.[47] Others distinguish solely on the basis of negligence and judge ignorance of law in the same way as ignorance of fact. According to these, ignorance of law excuses if the delinquent cannot discover the law by the use of due care.[48]

Yet in penal matters the excuse admitted even by these canonists for ignorance not resulting from negligence, is extremely limited. Ignorance of natural law and *quasi iuris naturalis*[49] never excuses from penalties. Since most of the Church's penal laws are but positive sanctions to natural laws, the excuse admitted for ignorance

[46] Stephanus Tornacensis, *Summa, ad Dict. Grat. p.* c. 12, C. I, q. 4, *v.* "si negotium": "quoniam facilius succurritur in negotio, quam in delicto."—ed. Schulte, p. 153. For others cf. Kuttner, *ibidem*, note 1. This is also the doctrine of the Roman Law Glossators. For example, Bulgarus (*de iuris et facti ignorantia summula*) says: "Similiter distinguitur, quid iuris civilis error contingat, delictum an negotium. Nam in negotio facilius succurritur."—Kantorowicz, *Studies in the Glossators of the Roman Law*, p. 245.

[47] *Glossa Palatina ad Dict. Grat. p.* c. 12, C. I, q. 4—Kuttner, *Schuldlehre*, p. 169, note 2.

[48] "Ignorantia iuris canonici sive civilis neminem excusat . . . et hoc intellige, cum ius tale est, quod aliquis de facili per seipsum scire potuit, vel etiam per alios, dum tamen habuerit copiam peritorum . . . "—*Glossa Ordinaria, ad* c. 12, C. I, q. 4, *v.* "omnis ignorantia." The *Summa Bambergensis* (*ad pr.* D. XXXVIII) applies the term *crassa et supina* even to ignorance of law. This is an isolated instance of the use of this division of *ignorantia facti* in connection with *ignorantia iuris*. Cf. Kuttner, *Schuldlehre*, p. 169 and note 3.

[49] Damasus (*Add. ad Glos. Ord.* Tancredi ad c. 3, Comp. I, *de apostatis et reiterantibus baptisma*, V, 9): " . . . immo iura canonica loquencia de receptione baptismi quasi naturalia sunt, quia modificant ius naturale . . . unde nec etas nec rusticitas per ignorantiam excusatur in eo."—Kuttner, *Schuldlehre*, p. 170, note 3.

of law becomes almost negligible. About the most that can be said is that in certain specific instances ignorance of canon law is admitted, if not as a total excuse, at least as a reason for mitigating the penalty of the law.[50]

Article II. From the Decretals of Gregory IX to the Council of Trent

1. General Characteristics

The promulgation of the Decretals of Gregory IX (1234) along with the Commentaries upon the Decretals written before the *Liber Sextus* (1298) brought practically no change in the general principles regarding ignorance. While no general principles regarding ignorance were introduced into the Decretals of Gregory IX, the canonists could, nevertheless, point to several instances in which the doctrine of the Decretists had been officially adopted in the law in regard to individual laws.[51] The general doctrine, as in the preceding period, developed in the scattered commentaries of canonists upon numerous specific crimes, especially in regard to homicide,[52] the use of false decretals [53] and crimes which require a peculiar personal character, for example, the striking of a cleric [54] and adultery.[55]

[50] For example, in regard to receiving Communion from a heretic. Cf. *supra*, p. 19. Cf. Hinschius, *Kirchenrecht*, V, 922-924.

[51] V. gr., c. 1, X, *de ordinatis ab episcopo, qui renunciavit episcopatui*, I, 13: (In speaking of one ordained by a bishop who had renounced both his see and his dignity) "Ubi autem non scienter, poterit, nisi crassa et supina fuerit ignorantia, discretus pontifex dispensare." The text is from a rescript of Alexander III to the Archbishop of Toledo (1158-1181)—Jaffé (ed. Loewenfeld), n. 14114; c. 9, X, *de clerico excommunicato, deposito vel interdicto ministrante*, V. 27: (In regard to the celebration of Mass while under suspension) "Verum, quia tempore suspensionis ignari celebrastis divina, vos reddit ignorantia probabilis excusatos. Ceterum, si forte ignorantia crassa et supina aut erronea fuerit, propter quod dispensationis gratia egeatis . . . " A rescript of Gregory IX to the Canons of Prague (1227)—Potthast, n. 7882.

[52] Cc. 6, 19, 22, 23, X, *de homicidio voluntario vel casuali*, V, 12; c. 7, X, *de poenitentiis et remissionibus*, V, 38.

[53] C. 7, X, *de crimine falsi*, V, 20.

[54] C. 32, X, *de sententia excommunicationis*, V, 39.

[55] C. 3, X, *de adulteriis et stupro*, V, 16.

As stated above, the doctrine of the Decretalists until the later commentators of the *Liber Sextus* remained essentially the same as that of the Decretists. The Decretalists merely repeat what is already to be found in the commentators of Gratian. The doctrine of this period, however, shows a greater degree of uniformity, principally because the earlier commentators of the Decretals adopt almost exclusively those distinctions which were developed in close dependence upon Roman Law. A number of the distinctions invented by the commentators of Gratian in connection with the comparatively numerous and dissimilar texts of the *Decretum* disappear entirely from Canon Law literature. Even the canonico-theological *vincibilis-invincibilis* distinction is rarely to be found in the writings of canonists until the next period.

Finally, the ethical or moral aspects of ignorance in reference to the imputability of sin received considerable attention in the works of the great Scholastic Theologians of this period. St. Thomas considered the problem on several occasions [56] and the solutions he offered exerted a great influence upon canonists and moralists alike, especially during the classical period of Moral Theology.[57]

In order to illustrate the continuity of the development and to show what part of the doctrine of the preceding period was accepted by the Decretists a few of the more outstanding questions discussed by the commentators of the Decretals of Gregory IX will be considered.

2. Doctrine of the Decretalists concerning Ignorance of Fact

Ignorance of fact is uniformly considered. The one question to be asked is: Is the ignorance probable or crass? Probable igno-

[56] Cf. especially *Summa,* I-II, q. 6, arts. 3, 8; I-II, q. 76; II-II, q. 150, art. 4; *De Malo* (*Opera Omnia* [Parisiis: apud L. Vivès, 1871-1880], XIII, 320-618), q. 3, art. 8. Cf. Lottin, "La problème de l'*ignorantia iuris* de Gratien à St. Thomas d'Aquin"—*Recherches de Théologie ancienne et médiévale,* V (1933), 365-368.

[57] In regard to developments in Moral Theology, cf. Müller, *Ethik und Recht,* pp. 170-191; Michiels, *De Delictis et Poenis,* I, 186-188.

rance is always to be admitted as an excuse from all penalties.[58] On the other hand, crass or supine ignorance never excuses from penalties.[59] It may also be noted here that the term *ignorantia affectata* was used for the first time in a legislative text by the Second Council of Lyons (1274). The way in which the term was employed naturally led to the conclusion that affected ignorance is equivalent to knowledge. In canon 15 the Council declared: "Eos qui clericos parochiae alienae absque superioris ordinandorum licentia, scienter, seu affectata ignorantia, vel quocumque alio figmento quaesito, praesumpserint ordinare. . . ." [60] The text was incorporated into the *Liber Sextus* [61] and immediately led to the interpretation that affected ignorance must be considered the same as knowledge.[62] Furthermore, the clause immediately following (*vel quocumque alio figmento quaesito*) caused some to define affected ignorance as simulated ignorance.[63] Finally, to anticipate somewhat, this text was often appealed to by those authors who held that affected ignorance did not excuse even when the law intended to punish only such crimes as were committed with perfect *dolus*. The fact that

[58] The Decretalists could point to the official approbation of this principle in c. 9, X, *de clerico excommunicato, deposito vel interdicto ministrante,* V, 27: " . . . quia tempore suspensionis ignari celebrastis divina, vos reddit ignorantia probabilis excusatos." Cf. *Glossa Ordinaria hoc loco, v.* "probabilis." Panormitanus (*Commentaria in Quinque Libros Decretalium* [Venetiis, 1588], *loc. cit.*) observes: "Nota primo . . . quod non quaelibet ignorantia excusat, sed probabilis tantum." Hostiensis (*Commentaria in quinque Decretalium Libros* [Venetiis, 1581], *loc. cit. v.* "probabilis") explains that it is possible to have probable ignorance even if the sentence is *publici lata*: " . . . quia . . . et ipsi latebant, nec denuntiati erant, et ideo excusati sunt."

[59] "Ceterum, si forte ignorantia crassa et supina aut erronea fuerit, propter quod dispensationis gratia egeatis . . .—c. 9, *ibid.*

[60] Schroeder, *Disciplinary Decrees of the General Councils* (St. Louis: Herder, 1937), p. 600.

[61] C. 2, *de temporibus ordinationum et qualitate ordinandorum,* I, 9 in VI°.

[62] *Glossa ad hunc loc., v.* "affectata": "Aequipollent ergo scientia et affectata ignorantia."

[63] *Glossa, loc. cit.* " . . . et dicitur affectata, ex quo scire potuit, sed noluit: immo dissimulavit."

this decree said *scienter, seu affectata ignorantia* certainly supported that contention.[64]

If probable ignorance is pleaded as an excuse it must be proved, because the law generally presumes that the delinquent knows what he is doing.[65] Due to the difficulty of proving ignorance, which is an internal state of mind, the oath became the special means of proof. The admission of an oath by the delinquent to prove ignorance had already been prescribed by the Council of Tribur, held at the close of the ninth century.[66] This becomes the traditional doctrine and is frequently spoken of by canonists. The oath must be taken to prove probable ignorance and a refusal to take it would be considered as an admission of crass ignorance.[67] If the oath is taken it suffices to overcome the simple *praesumptio iuris* that a man had the knowledge.[68]

There are several interesting cases which prove how thoroughly this doctrine regarding ignorance of fact had become a part of universally admitted principles. One case is that in which Pope Alexander III had permitted the bishop to dispense in a case where a candidate in probable ignorance had received orders from a bishop who had resigned.[69] Commentators, however, sought to find a reason why the penalty should have been incurred at all, since the ignorance was probable. Many thought that the ordinand was at fault in knowingly permitting himself to be ordained by any other than his own proper bishop. The Gloss and Hostiensis, however, considered this theory contrary to the facts of the case and explained that this was not a penalty in the strict sense. The dispensation was

[64] Cf. v. gr., Kober, *Kirchenbann*, p. 208; Hinschius, *Kirchenrecht*, V, 923, note 7.

[65] Cf. c. 20, X, *de electione*, I, 6: " . . . parcentes non modicum . . . quod eis nec poenam infligimus . . . nec probare cogimus ignorantiam quam allegant." *Glossa ad hunc loc.*: " . . . unde probare debebant isti ignorantiam quam allegabant . . . "

[66] C. 43—Mansi, XVIIIa, 153.

[67] Cf. *Glossa ad loc. cit.*; c. 4, X, *de sententia excommunicationis*, V, 39.

[68] *Glossa ad* c. 6, X, *qui matrimonium accusare possunt, vel contra illud testificare*, IV, 19, *v.* "iuramento": " . . . nota hic, quod plus valet iuramentum unius quam praesumptio iuris . . . "

[69] C. 1, X, *de ordinatis ab episcopo, qui renunciavit episcopatui*, I, 13.

necessary because the candidate had not received the "execution" of the orders thus conferred; this the bishop could not give because he did not have it.[70]

Another frequently discussed difficulty is found in the interpretation of a rescript of Pope Innocent III. In 1198 this Pontiff had decreed that all who used a papal rescript must first carefully examine it to ascertain its authenticity. The penalties inflicted upon those who used false papal briefs were not to be escaped by those who pleaded ignorance.[71] The obvious conclusion might have been that the lawgiver had in this instance, for reasons of public welfare, intended to include also those acting in ignorance, in order to make the use of papal briefs more secure. However, the commentators pointed out that Roman Law required *dolus* for this type of crime,[72] and, therefore, the Holy Father could have intended to punish only those who acted in crass or affected ignorance, otherwise the penalty would be unjust.[73] Crass or affected ignorance were sufficient because according to the Roman Law they were equivalent to *dolus*.[74]

3. The Beginnings of a Change in Attitude towards Ignorance of Law

During the thirteenth century there is little evidence indicating

[70] "Respondeo: hic necessaria est dispensatio: quia saltem scienter fecit, se a non suo episcopo ordinari secundum omnes. Hoc non placet: quia quod praemissum est, contradicit, sed haec est sola ratio, quia alius transferre non potuit executionem, quam non habebat . . . "—Hostiensis, *Commentaria, hoc loco,* n. 8.

[71] " . . . si falsis litteris se usos dixerint ignoranter eorum sera poenitentia evitare nequibit poenas . . . ita tamen, ut . . . malitia gravius quam negligentia puniatur . . . "—c. 7, X, *de crimine falsi,* V, 20.

[72] " . . . si . . . per errorem huiusmodi instrumenta proferantur, ignoscatur eis . . ."—D. (48, 10) 31; " . . . non nisi dolo falsum committentes crimini subiugentur. . . ."—C. (9, 22) 20.

[73] Thus Joannes Teutonicus (*ad* c. 4, Comp. III, *de crimine falsi,* V, 11) writes: " . . . alias videretur iniustum, si vellet dicere iustum errorem, et non esset admittendus . . . set dic, quod ideo non excusat hic ignorantia, quia non est probabilis ignorantia in suo facto. . . . "—Kuttner, *Schuldlehre,* p. 162, note 2.

[74] Cf. *Glossa Ordinaria, ad* c. 7, *h. t.,* V, 20, *vv.* "examinent" and "dixerint."

any change in the ancient rigor towards ignorance of law. While the Decretals of Gregory IX put the stamp of approval upon the doctrine concerning ignorance of fact as an excuse from penalties, at least in several important particular instances; these same Decretals, with possibly one exception, contain no text which would justify the admission of ignorance of law as an excuse from penalty.[75] The early Decretalists repeat the doctrine of the Decretists. For example, Hostiensis (d. 1271) holds that ignorance of law is never an excuse for a cleric.[76] While, in general, ignorance of law is tolerable in certain classes of people, the rule fails when there is question of the natural law.[77]

During the fourteenth century, however, a relaxation of the frequently cited Roman Law maxim, *ignorantia facti, non iuris*

[75] The apparent exception is found in c. 32, X, *de sententia excommunicationis,* V, 39. This is part of a rescript of Pope Innocent III (1201).—Potthast, n. 1326. In it the Pope allows abbots to dispense their subjects in certain cases of ignorance of fact, as well as ignorance of law (". . . vel factum quidem scientes, iuris ignari nesciunt exinde se teneri.") from the suspension incurred for receiving orders while under excommunication on account of a violation of the *privilegium canonis.* The rescript makes it plain that the penalty is incurred, but permits abbots to absolve their subjects in cases of ignorance of fact or of law. The faculty, moreover, was clearly meant to be a privilege: "Praecipimus autem abbatibus, ut formam istam diligenter observent, ne privilegium mereatur amittere . . ." The *Glossa Ordinaria* (*v.* "iuris peritiam," *hoc loco*) remarks that ignorance of positive law, but not of natural law, allows a mitigation of penalty.

[76] ". . . nam et si dicat quod in iure erravit non relevabitur cum iuris ignorantia clericum et maxime praelatum non excusat."—*Commentaria, ad* c. 45, X, *de appellationibus, recusationibus et relationibus,* II, 28, par. 6. This became the doctrine of the Scholastic Theologians in general; cf. Lottin, "Le problème de l'*ignorantia iuris*"—*Recherches de Théologie ancienne et médiévale,* V (1933), 351-368.

[77] ". . . licet enim feminis liceat allegare . . . ignorantiam iuris . . . non tamen . . . ignorantia evangelicae veritatis . . . nec ignorantia iuris naturalis probabilis est."—Hostiensis, *Commentaria,* c. 4, X, *de eo qui duxit in matrimonium quam polluit,* IV, 8, n. 2. The same is true in regard to minors: ". . . illud tamen non habet locum in articulis fidei, vel sacramentis, vel iure naturali."—Henricus Boich (d. *ca.* 1350), *In Quinque Decretalium Libros Commentaria* (Venetiis, 1576), c. 1, X, *de delictis puerorum,* V, 23.

excusat [78] is plainly evident. This change in the ancient and traditional rigor toward ignorance of law is due in a large measure to the increase of *latae sententiae* penalties. Leaving aside the question of the origin of this form of penalties,[79] it seems fairly clear that before the eighth century the Church employed *ferendae sententiae* penalties almost exclusively. The *Decretum Gratiani* contained only a few instances of *latae sententiae* penalties. Until the publication of the *Liber Sextus,* the number of *latae senteniae* penalties was estimated at about thirty. From this time, however, the number steadily increased. There were about thirty-two in the *Liber Sextus* and fifty in the *Clementinae* (1317). The *Bulla in Coena Domini* and later papal constitutions brought the number well over two hundred by the beginning of the eighteenth century.[80]

The gradually mounting number of *latae sententiae* penalties, especially excommunications, accounts in a large measure for the change, from an almost complete denial of any excuse for ignorance of law to the admission of even crass and affected ignorance of law in some instances; a reversal of opinion, which is for the most part commonly accepted doctrine by the seventeenth century. This development became almost a necessity by the very nature of the case. For, *latae sententiae* penalties operate automatically in the conscience of the guilty subject without the action of a court. In the conscience of the individual legal presumptions have no value; hence, the presumption of knowledge of law gives away to actual hence, the presumption of knowledge of laws gives sway to actual began to examine the case on the basis of fact. The question was: Did the individual know the law? and if he did not, was he morally

[78] D. (22, 6) 9, *pr.;* Reg. 13, R. J., in VI°.

[79] Kober (*Kirchenbann,* pp. 55-59) traces their origin back to the very beginning of the Church; Van Espen (*Ius Ecclesiasticum* [Lovanii, 1753], P. III, tit. XI, c. VII, n. 19) considers *latae sententiae* penalties unknown during the first ten centuries.

[80] Cf. Benedict XIV, *De Synodo Diocesana* (Romae, 1806), lib. X, cap. I, n. 6; cap. II, n. 1; Navarrus, *Enchiridion sive Manuale* (*Opera Omnia,* vol. I [Venetiis, 1618]), cap. XXVII, nn. 49-50. Pichler (*Candidatus Iurisprudentiae Sacrae* [3, 4. ed., August., 1723-1733], lib. V, tit. 39) enumerates 233; Ferraris (*Bibliotheca Canonica Iuridica Moralis Theologica* [Romae, 1885-1899], *v.* "excommunicatio," art. II-IV) recounts about 179 excommunications alone.

at fault in not knowing the law? If he was not at fault, then in the secrets of his own conscience he was not guilty of a crime and could not be liable to severe canonical penalties.

Finally, both canonists and moralists saw the necessity of a more lenient attitude towards ignorance of law for another reason. The very spiritual welfare of the delinquent (the highest consideration of ecclesiastical legislation) is in danger if the delinquent can without his own knowledge fall under severe canonical penalties, especially excommunication.[81] These considerations, rather than the legal arguments advanced by the more liberal opinion (which must very often be considered weak) are more important for the proper understanding of the development which will be described in the following pages.

4. The Milder Interpretation Occasioned by the *c. Ut Animarum*[82]

Since a great deal of the development in doctrine concerning ignorance of law occurred in connection with the commentaries on the *c. Ut Animarum* of the *Liber Sextus*, a good idea of the changing views of canonists can be gained by a consideration of this text and its numerous interpretations.

A. *The c. Ut Animarum in its original meaning*

The wording of the text is as follows:

> Ut animarum periculis obvietur, sententiis per statuta quorumcumque ordinariorum prolatis ligari nolumus ignorantes: dum tamen eorum ignorantia crassa non fuerit aut supina. Statuto episcopi, quo in omnes, qui furtum commiserint, excommunicationis sententia promulgatur, subditi eius, furtum extra ipsius diocesim committentes, minime ligari noscuntur, quum extra territorium ius dicendi non pareatur impune.[83]

[81] Cf. *infra*, pp. 67-69; Hinschius, *Kirchenrecht*, V, 924.

[82] *Ut Animarum* is the opening phrase of the important constitution under consideration. For the sake of brevity this constitution will henceforth be referred to as *c. Ut Animarum*.

[83] C. 2, *de constitutionibus*, 1, 2 in VI°. The first sentence is of primary interest in the present study. The second part contains the famous disposition regarding the territoriality of penal laws. Cf. Van Hove, *Commentarium Lovaniense*, vol. I, tom. II, *De Legibus Ecclesiasticis* (Mechlinae: Dessain, 1930), pp. 124-127. (Hereafter to be cited as: Van Hove, *De Legibus Ecclesiasticis*.)

This constitution of Boniface VIII is a parallel to the decree of Gregory I, contained in c. 2, X, *de constitutionibus,* I, 2, which declares that a law containing something new refers only to the future and not the past. It completed the latter constitution of the Gregorian Decretals by giving a particular application of the principle stated therein: *Rem quae culpa caret, in damnum vocari non convenit.*[84]

From the clear wording of the text itself it is evident that this decretal was originally intended to include only ignorance of particular statutes of local ordinaries. The phrase, *per statuta quorumcumque ordinariorum,* in its literal sense can be understood only of particular laws and not of general laws passed by the supreme legislator.[85] The context, moreover, leads to the same conclusion. For, the second part of the same decree speaks only of particular laws which have binding force only within the territorial jurisdiction of the legislating bishop. And, finally, the early commentators of this constitution understood it in this sense.[86]

B. *Extensive Interpretations of the c. Ut Animarum*

Successively wider interpretations of this text led eventually, though not without opposition, to a general admission of probable ignorance of all law as an excuse from penalties.

The first dispute arose over the question, whether ignorance of a particular law excuses if the statute prohibited something already previously forbidden either by general positive law or by the natural law. Joannes Andreae seems to have been one of the first to advance the opinion that ignorance of a particular statute excuses even in those cases where it merely places penal sanctions upon an

[84] With regard to the decree of Gregory I, cf. p. 24, note 37.

[85] Cf. Hinschius, *Kirchenrecht,* V, 922.

[86] Thus the *Glossa Ordinaria, hoc loco, v.* "statuta": "De generalibus ergo statutis canonum non loquitur, quae ab omnibus scire et custodire debent." The *inscriptio* by Joannes Andeae says the same. Cf. also, *In Sex Decretalium Libros Novella Commentaria* (Venetiis, 1581), *loc. cit., v.* "per statuta." There was precedent for this in Roman Law in regard to ignorance of municipal law.

already existing divine or canon (general) law.[87] Despite the fact that canonists had to admit that the juridical foundations of Joannes Andreae's opinion were weak, it soon became the accepted view.[88]

The *c. Ut Animarum* was extended to include also ignorance of the general law, the *statuta Romani Pontificis*. Joannes Andreae did not admit this extension;[89] and the earlier commentators still considered the *c. Ut Animarum* an exception from the general rule not to be extended beyond its express limits to the prescriptions of common law.[90]

The argument in favor of the extension was that the Pope was also an Ordinary in the sense of the canon, namely an ordinary for the whole world. Furthermore, the reason which Pope Boniface assigned in the *c. Ut Animarum* for excusing the ignorant from the penalties of local statutes was equally valid in the case of general laws. For, the danger to souls (*ut animarum periculis obvietur*) was equally grave if ignorance were not an excuse from general laws.[91] These reasons were generally accepted and the opinion fa-

[87] *Novella Commentaria, loc. cit., v.* "ignorans": "Intelligo hoc etiam cum statutum punit illud prohibitum lege divina vel canonica, et secundum hoc terminetur hic id, quod scripsit Joannes de Deo (*ad* c. 1, C. II, q. 3) et Papa (Innocentius IV) ibi, quaerit an sint excommunicati impubes, qui falsificavit instrumentum, et monachus qui tulit falsum testimonium ignorantes constitutionem episcopi, qui tales excommunicat, quicquid ibi dicat satis uterque potuit probabiliter ignorasse, quod si ita est, locus est hinc decretum. Et licet pena iuris in eis locum possit habere, cessabit tamen pena statuti, quod probabiliter ignoratur."

[88] Panormitanus (*Commentaria*, c. 21, X, *de sententia excommunicationis*, V, 39, n. 9), admitting that the contrary view of the *Glossa Ordinaria* was in accord with the *rigor iuris*, says that the view of Joannes Andreae is *aequior*. Sylvester (Mozolinus Sabaudus, d. 1523) writes: "Mihi videtur dicendum quod ignorantia etiam in facto damnato excusat a poena statuti humani: nisi forte esset statutum Papae . . ." He concedes that Bartholus a Saxoferrato, the great Romanist of the fourteenth century, and Antonius de Butrio (d. 1408) are against this view. In his favor he mentions, besides Joannes Andreae, the *Summa Pisana* (before 1338) and Panormitanus.—*Summa Summarum* (Venetiis, 1601), *v.* "excommunicatio."

[89] Cf. *supra*, p. 48, note 86.

[90] Henry Boich, *Commentaria*, c. 2, X, *de constitutionibus*, I, 2.

[91] Sylvester, *Summa*, *v.* "ignorantia," n. 17.

voring the extension of the *c. Ut Animarum* to canon laws or the general laws of the Church was the commonly accepted doctrine already early in the following period.[92]

Here the previous question returned. Did ignorance of a general law excuse if the latter prohibited something already forbidden by natural or positive divine law? Sylvester hesitated in this instance to admit an excuse from penalties.[93] An argument for excuse even in this case was derived from the context of the decree itself. For, in the very next sentence it referred to an excommunication placed upon theft, which is a crime forbidden by the natural law. Hence, it was argued, the natural law must be understood also in the first part which dealt with ignorance. Furthermore, the danger for souls, which the Pope sought to avoid, was equally great in both instances.[94] Whatever may be said for the argument as such, the opinion in support of which it was advanced gained adherents especially in regard to the penalty of excommunication. In this way a result was reached which approaches very nearly to the later principle that *ignorantia solius legis* and *solius poenae* excuses at least from censures. The latter, however, developed on other grounds than any arguments derived from the *c. Ut Animarum* as will be seen in the discussion of *ignorantia solius poenae.*[95]

4. Ignorance of Law Judged on the Basis of Negligence

Toward the close of this period another opinion in regard to ignorance of law was advanced which cannot be passed over in silence. It shows a certain amount of independence from the *c. Ut Animarum* and approaches the question from an entirely different angle. According to this view ignorance of law is to be measured by the same standard which is now commonly used in judging igno-

[92] Cf. Passerinus, *Commentaria in Sextum Librum* (Venetiis, 1698), lib. I, tit. II, cap. II, n. 47; Sanchez, *De Sancto Matrimonii Sacramento* (Antverpiae, 1607), lib. IX, disp. XXXII, n. 11; Suarez, *De Censuris* (*Opera Omnia*, 1856-1866), disp. IV, sect. IX, nn. 8, 11-13; Sayrus, *Casuum Conscientiae Thesaurus*, tom. I, *De Censuris Ecclesiasticis* (Venetiis, 1609), lib. I, cap. XVIII, nn. 21-23.

[93] *Summa Summarum, v.* "excommunicatio," n. 16.

[94] Cf. Sayrus, *De Censuris Ecclesiasticis*, lib. I, cap. XVIII, nn. 27-38.

[95] *Infra*, pp. 62-70. Cf. Suarez, *De Censuris*, disp. IV, sect. IX, n. 14.

rance of fact. In treating of ignorance of fact the observation was made that the Decretalists abandoned many of the distinctions and criteria devised by the Decretists for ignorance of fact and retained only the *crassa-probabilis division,* which is based upon the presence or absence of negligence on the part of the delinquent.

Already the Decretists had begun to apply the negligence norm to ignorance of law [96] but it seems that no new important developments occurred in this direction until the later part of the period under consideration. Several of the Decretists had distinguished between ignorance of law that occurred after the passage of a law (*conditio*) but before its promulgation and ignorance which was had after the promulgation. Before proper publication ignorance of the law is to be considered ignorance of fact, while after that time ignorance becomes ignorance of law. The very promulgation of the law changed the ignorance of fact into ignorance of law.[97] Damasus, in accordance with *Novella* 66, c. 1, extended the time during which the ignorance could be considered *ignorantia facti* until two months after the promulgation of the law.[98] After this time the ignorance must be considered *ignorantia iuris* and cannot be pleaded as an excuse from the law.

This opinion is adopted and developed by the commentators of the Gregorian Decretals. Two months after proper promulgation,[99] unless the law expressly provides otherwise, the law is presumed to be known by all.[100] This presumption of knowledge can be overcome only by such evidence as would prove that it was *impossible* for the delinquent to have known the law.[101] He must be able to

[96] *Supra,* p. 39.

[97] Cf. Kuttner, *Schuldlehre,* pp. 173-175. This is the opinion of the *Summa Monacensis,* Huguccio and Joannes Teutonicus.—*Op. cit.*, p. 174, note 1.

[98] *Brocarda ad* c. 2, D. LXXXII—Kuttner, *loc. cit.*

[99] According to Henry Boich (*Commentaria,* c. 2, X, *de constitutionibus,* I, 2) if the law is merely declarative of a previously existing law the time must be reckoned from the moment of promulgation and not two months later.

[100] Cf. *Glossa Ordinaria,* Hostiensis (*Commentaria*), Henry Boich (*Commentaria*) *ad* c. 2, X, *de constitutionibus,* I, 2.

[101] Hostiensis (*loc. cit.*) merely says: " . . . nisi forte dilucide probaret suam ignorantiam." However from the context it seems quite clear that anything

prove through documents or witnesses that he was insane at the time, or a *pupillus non doli capax,* or imprisoned or on some uninhabited island away from the society of men.[102] Finally, if the law is a particular statute it might be of avail to show that one was not present in the territory at the time of the promulgation of the law.[103]

Outside of these cases it would be impossible for the delinquent to escape penalty by attempting to prove ignorance of law.[104]

This seems to have been the common doctrine until about the close of this period. Panormitanus apparently was the first to introduce an important change in these principles by applying the Roman Law doctrine of *culpa* also to ignorance of law. In other words, *ignorantia iuris* is to be judged, according to Panormitanus, by the same norm hitherto applicable only to ignorance of fact, namely, the diligence or negligence of the delinquent in attempting to find out.[105]

Panormitanus begins with the general principle that no law affects the truly ignorant. While knowledge of law is presumed two months after promulgation, yet this presumption is not *iuris et de iure,* but admits of contrary proof. If the ignorance can be shown to be without any guilt or *culpa* there can be no penalty. If there is *lata culpa* (the equivalent of crass ignorance) the penalty is incurred. But if the law or statute expressly or tacitly require *dolus,* the penalty of the law is not to be inflicted for *lata culpa,* but he can be punished by other penalties.[106] The same is true of those

short of proving the impossibility to know would be of little avail, because the ignorance would not be considered probable.

[102] Cf. Henry Boich, *Commentaria, loc. cit.*

[103] *Glossa Ordinaria, ibidem, v.* "ante prohibitionem."

[104] ". . . nec credo quod maior compos sui et inter homines conversans ad probandam ignorantiam huiusmodi per iuramentum admitti deberet . . . nam supposito, quod probaret etiam per testes . . . se ignorasse post duos menses constitutionem taliter publicatam, non prodesset sibi talis iuris ignorantia sed noceret et oporteret probare tale quod ex quo necessario sequeretur ipsum ignorasse, ut furorem, vel infantiam . . . "—Henry Boich, *loc. cit.*

[105] For the exception to this statement, cf. *supra,* p. 39.

[106] As an example he cites c. 29, C. XVII, q. 4 (*Si quis suadente diabolo*)—

cases in which *lata culpa* is not equivalent to *dolus* because the law tacitly requires *dolus*.[107] In these cases the penalty of the law or statute is avoided but other penalties can be applied according to the degree of guilt; in other cases *culpa lata* and *dolus* are to be punished in the same manner.

If there is only *levis* or *levissima culpa,* Panormitanus finds the opinion of the Roman Law jurists, from whom he is borrowing, divided among themselves. On the one hand, Cynus Pistoriensis (d. 1336 or 1337)[108] admitted that civil redress but no strict penalty could be imposed for *levis* or *levissima culpa*.[109] Others, as for example the Gloss of Accursius and Bartolus a Sassoferrato (d. 1357)[110] admit that criminal punishment can be inflicted but *pro modo culpae.* Panormitanus attempts to harmonize these views by admitting only civil redress where the law provided this remedy. If civil redress could not be had, then the penalty has to be applied, but *pro modo culpae,* lest crime should go unpunished.[111]

What is perhaps remarkable about this opinion is that it applies the complete Roman Law doctrine of *culpa* also to ignorance of law. The development is now complete. It is true that the distinction between ignorance of law and ignorance of fact remains, but from now on both will be judged on the basis of negligence by the delinquent.

II Lateran Council, c. 15; c. 4, X, *de sententia excommunicationis,* V, 39. Both instances deal with violations of the *privilegium canonis.*

107 As examples, Panormitanus cites D. (12, 3) 5, 3: "Sed in his omnibus ob dolum solum in litem iuratur, non etiam ob culpam . . ."; and the *Gloss* of Bartolus to D. (16, 3) 32.

108 Cynus had received his legal training in the School of Orleans.

109 In his *Gloss ad* C. (1, 3) 5.

110 *Ad.* D. (48, 19) 11, 2.

111 *Commentaria,* c. 2, X, *de constitutionibus,* I, 2. The same is repeated in practically the same words by Felinus Sandaeus (d. 1503), *Commentaria in Quinque Libros Decretalium* (Venetiis, 1570), *hoc loco.* Cf. also Sylvester, *Summa, v.* "ignorantia," n. 15.

CHAPTER IV

FROM THE TIME OF THE COUNCIL OF TRENT UNTIL THE CODE OF CANON LAW

ARTICLE I. THE INFLUENCES OF MORAL THEOLOGY

THE development of this period is wholly independent of any new positive legislation on the part of the Church. The last important legal document before the promulgation of the Code is the *c. Ut Animarum* of the *Liber Sextus*. Furthermore, after the Protestant Revolt of the sixteenth century criminal court proceedings are limited almost exclusively to clerical cases and most of these are handled in an administrative way, with the result that there is practically no important court jurisprudence in the matter of ignorance. The entire development occurs within the doctrine of canonists and moralists. The juridical norms are based upon moral or legal reasonings and their binding force must be sought in the general acceptance of the Church through custom.[1]

The influence of moral theologians in the production of the principles which were to become the commonly accepted doctrine, is plainly evident. In the preceding period the development occurred in the commentaries of canonists upon individual laws, which sometimes announced a general principle and, more frequently, contained some rule of law in regard to a specific crime. Beginning with the more recent *Summae pro Confessoribus* the method of treating ignorance changed.[2] Ignorance is not treated merely as occasion presents itself but the doctrine is brought together and discussed according to the scholastic method of definition, division and statement of principles.[3]

[1] Cf. Hinschius, *Kirchenrecht,* V, 923-924.

[2] V. gr., *Summa Pisana,* Bartholomaeus a Sancto Concordio (1338); *Summa Rosella,* Trovamala (ca. 1483); *Summa Summarum,* Sylvester Prierias (ca. 1460) all have separate articles on ignorance. Cf. Müller, *Ethik und Recht,* pp. 109-117.

[3] V. gr., Covarrubias y Leyva (d. 1577), *In Bonifacii VIII Constitutionem, quae incipit, Alma Mater, Commentarii* (*Opera Omnia,* vol. I, Coloniae Allo-

With regard to the definition and divisions of ignorance there is little that is new to be recorded in this period.[4] The distinction between ignorance of law and ignorance of fact remains, but its importance is gone. Both forms of ignorance are judged by the same standard of diligence in acquiring the necessary knowledge. Suarez reviewed the various criteria employed to determine whether ignorance of law excuses and arrived at the conclusion that the *primum documentum* must always be whether or not the ignorance is the result of negligence. The duty of one's state in life or office, as well as the fact that everybody knew the law or fact is not the primary consideration; for even the diligent man sometimes remains ignorant in things pertaining to his office or he can forget what he had once known.[5] This is now the accepted doctrine.[6]

The influence of the moralists is plainly evident in regard to the divisions of ignorance in use during this period. The old *probabilis-crassa,* developed by canonists in dependence upon Roman Law, practically disappears. The term *"probabilis"* [7] is replaced by the more or less synonymous theological terms: *invincibilis, involun-*

brogum, 1679), Pars I, X. (Hereafter this work will be cited as: Covarrubias, *Alma Mater*); Sanchez, *De Matrimonio,* lib. IX, disp. XXXII; Alterius, *De Censuris Ecclesiasticis* (Romae, 1616), lib. III, disp. II, cap. III; Passerinus, *Commentaria in Sextum Librum,* lib. I, tit. II, cap. II, q. 1; Pirhing, *Ius Canonicum Nova Methodo Explicatum* (Dilingae, 1674-1678), lib. V, tit. XXXIX, sect. II, nn. 42-46; Suarez, *De Censuris,* disp. IV, sect. VIII-XI.

[4] More will be said on this subject in the commentary on the Code.

[5] Suarez, *De Censuris,* disp. IV, sect. VIII, n. 12-19.

[6] Cf. v. gr., Sanchez, *De Matrimonio,* lib. IX, disp. XXXII, n. 33; Passerinus, *Commentaria in Sextum Librum,* lib. I, tit. II, cap. II, q. I, art. 5; Wernz, *Ius Decretalium* (Romae et Prati, 1906-1913), VI, 30-32; Alterius, *De Censuris Ecclesiasticis,* lib. III, disp. II, cap. III.

[7] It is somewhat difficult to fit the old legal term *"probabilis"* into the theological scheme of distinctions. Perhaps the nearest equivalent would be *ignorantia moraliter invincibilis.* It might be described simply as that kind of ignorance which the law "approves" (*probare*) or accepts as an excuse from penalty. Its opposite is *crassa* or *supina* or as it is sometimes called *ignorantia improbabilis.* Cf. Navarrus, *Consiliorum sive Responsorum Libri Quinque* (Romae, 1602), P. I, lib. I, *de constitutionibus,* cons. I, n. 2.

taria or *inculpabilis*. The direct opposite of this form of ignorance is, not *crassa*, but *vincibilis, voluntaria* or *culpabilis*.[8]

A few words concerning the *involuntaria-voluntaria* division may be in place. The first to employ this division, as it is understood during this period[9] and at the present time, seems to have been Alexander of Hales (d. 1245). He distinguished two kinds of voluntary ignorance, the *affectata simpliciter* of the *volentes nescire* and the *affectata secundum quid* of the *nolentes scire*. Neither of these excuse from guilt. *Ignorantia involuntaria* which springs from an involuntary principle excuses entirely.[10] The distinction is found in the *Summa Theologica* of St. Thomas[11] who divides voluntary ignorance into *ignorantia directa et per se voluntaria* and *indirecta et per accidens voluntaria*.[12]

The ignorance which is *directe et per set volita* is called *ignorantia affectata*. The exact meaning of this term as used by the Decretists is not always clear. It seems that they consider it a form of negligent ignorance which is practically identical with crass or supine ignorance.[13] From now on affected ignorance signifies ignorance which is directly procured for the express purpose of avoiding the obligation of the law. Crass ignorance also takes on a slightly altered meaning. It is ignorance which is indirectly willed because it results from negligence and that of a peculiarly high degree.

Another distinction of completely theological origin is the tripartite division of ignorance into *antecedens, concomitans* and *sub-*

[8] The precise meaning of these terms will be considered in the Commentary on the Code, *infra*, chapter VI, art. II.

[9] Already Gratian speaks of voluntary ignorance. "Cum itaque voluntaria ignorantia omnibus sit noxia sacerdotibus est periculosa."—*Dict. Grat.* Pars I, *pr.* D. XXXVIII.

[10] *Summa Theologiae* (ed. PP. Collegii S. Bonaventurae, Ad Claras Aquas: Typographia Collegii S. Bonaventurae, 1924-1930), lib. II, P. II, inq. III, tract. II, sect. I, qu. II, tit. I, cap. 8.

[11] I-II, q. 76, art. 4.

[12] This distinction is also taken over into Canon Law literature. Cf., v. gr., Gonzalez Tellez, *Commentaria Perpetua* (Lugduni, 1715), lib. V, tit. XXVII, c. 9, n. 1; Passerinus, *Commentaria in Sextum Librum*, lib. I, tit. II, cap. II, q. I, arts. 5-6.

[13] Cf. *supra*, p. 34.

sequens. Apparently this division resulted from an amplification of the *culpa praecedens* theory found already in the writings of the Decretists.[14] Thus Praepositinus of Cremona (d. 1217) distinguishes between ignorance which proceeds from *culpa* and that which does not. To these he added a third member, namely, ignorance which accompanies guilt. The first of these is called *ignorantia praecedens,* the second *ignorantia subsequens* and the third *ignorantia coherens.*[15]

The Scholastics converted this primarily temporal relationship between the ignorance and the guilt of the ignorant party into a purely causal relationship between the will of the ignorant person and the action which results from the ignorance, as well as the ignorance itself. Accordingly, ignorance is consequent to the act of the will, in so far as the ignorance itself is voluntary (either directly or indirectly). Ignorance is concomitant, when there is ignorance of what is done but, so that even if it were known, it would be done. For example, a man does not know whether the object before him is a man or beast. He strikes the fatal blow. Actually he does not know at the moment whether or not he is killing a man, but he is so minded that he would kill even if he knew. Ignorance is antecedent to the act of the will, when it is not voluntary; in other words when it precedes any deliberate action on the part of the ignorant person. For example, a man is invincibly ignorant that today is Friday, because he does not even advert to the fact. His ignorance antecedes any voluntary act on his part.[16]

[14] Cf. *supra,* p. 35.

[15] ". . . triplex est ignorantia scl. precedens, coherens et subsequens. . . . Et nota, quod ille proprie dicitur peccare ex ignorantia, qui peccat ex prima ignorantia, quia ex ea tamquam precedente est peccatum. Ille vero, qui peccat ex secunda ignorantia, dicitur minus proprie ex ignorantia peccare, sed tamen dicitur ex ignorantia peccare, non quia ex ea precedat peccatum, sed quia sine ea non est. In tertia vero de scito peccato venit in ignorantiam."—*Summa,* lib. II, q. "Quis plus peccaverit Adam vel Eva."—Müller, *Ethik und Recht,* pp. 150-151, note 100.

[16] This division is used in this way by Odo Rigaldi, *Summa in IV Libros Sententiarum,* sent. II, dist. XXII, q. 1—Müller, *Ethik und Recht,* p. 151, note 101; St. Thomas, *Summa Theologica,* I-II, q. 6, art. 8; and by many canonists and moralists after them. V. gr., Suarez, *De Censuris,* disp. IV, sect.

The introduction of this division into penal law brought a new difficulty which was much discussed during the early part of this period. The problem arose concerning concomitant ignorance and the question asked was: Is the delinquent who acts with concomitant ignorance (even invincible) excused from penal liability? Suppose a man cannot discover whether the object before him is a human being or not. He intends to kill in any event, even if he could or did discover that it actually is a man. Does such ignorance exempt him from the penalties imposed upon homicide? Concomitant ignorance evidently does not exclude the will to transgress the law, and, therefore, some authors held that it did not excuse from penalty.[17]

Those who insisted that concomitant ignorance excused from penalties separated the internal affection for sin from the guilt in respect to the external violation of the law. The individual is *de facto* not guilty of the external violation of the law because of the ignorance; and, consequently, he incurs no penalty in the eyes of the Church, because only external violations of the law are punished.[18] Suarez apparently goes even further and denies that any moral effects are imputable in this case. His conclusion was that there is neither guilt nor penalty and, therefore, thought that this distinction should not be applied at all in penal matters.[19] As this

VIII, n. 5; Sylvester, *Summa Summarum, v.* "ignorantia," n. 2; Sanchez, *De Matrimonio*, lib. IX, disp. XXII, n. 26; Navarrus, *Consilia*, Pars I, lib. I, *De constitutionibus*, cons. I, n. 3; Fagnanus, *Commentaria in Quinque Libros Decretalium* (Romae, 1661), lib. III, tit. XXXI, c. XI, nn. 22-26.

[17] According to Sanchez (*De matrimonio*, lib. IX, disp. XXXII, n. 26) this was the view of Ugolinus ([1610] *De Censuris Ecclesiasticis*, tab. I, c. IX, par. 8) and Jacobus de Graffis (P. I, *Decisionum*, lib. IV, cap. IX, n. 42); Covarrubias, *Alma Mater*, X, 15. Cf. also Montes, "La ignorancia en el derecho penal"—*Ciudad de Dios*, CL (1927), 42-47.

[18] Sanchez, *De Matrimonio*, lib. IX, disp. XXXII, n. 26.

[19] ". . . quod autem sit concomitans (ignorantia), semper est impertinens ad . . . effectus morales . . . Ignorantia ergo concomitans omittenda prorsus est in praesenti materia, quia nihil omnino refert ad excusandam vel incurrendam culpam aut censuram, quia per se, nec voluntariam, nec involuntariam reddit actionem."—*De Censuris*, disp. IV, sect. VIII, n. 8-10.

solution of the problem is generally accepted [20] the importance of the *antecedens-concomitans-consequens* division is gone. Concomitant ignorance is of no interest or concern to penal law at all, and the other two members of the division are frequently identified with inculpable (antecedent) and culpable (consequent) ignorance.[21]

The present article would be incomplete without mention of another achievement of this period, due largely to the clarification of the concept of an *indirectum voluntarium.* It is difficult to define the exact limits of criminal liability for negligent conduct. Some writers on penal law thought that one who unknowingly was the cause of injury while engaged in illicit conduct should be held responsible. Consequently a distinction was made between the ignorance of one *dans operam rei licitae* and *dans operam rei illicitae.* The latter must suffer the consequences of his action even if he did not foresee them. Thus, the cleric who kills a man while engaging in forbidden chase should be held liable for homicide.

This conclusion is but an application of a much broader principle, the doctrine of *versari in re illicita.* Historically this doctrine was devised by the Decretists to overcome legal difficulties in the interpretation of the *Decretum.* The Decretists taught as a matter of principle, that no penalty could be imposed if the delinquent was not at fault morally; *pro solo peccato pena est infligenda.*[22] Yet, the commentators of the *Decretum* found a number of ancient penitential canons incorporated which demanded penalty even if there were no subjective guilt.[23] To solve these difficulties the Decretists invented several explanations, one of which developed into the doctrine of *versari in re illicita.* The proponents of this explanation went upon the historically unsound basis that wherever the laws found in the *Decretum* prescribed a penalty personal moral guilt

[20] Cf. Montes, "La ignorancia en el derecho penal"—*loc. cit.;* Pirhing, *Ius Canonicum,* lib. V, tit. XXXIX, sect. II, n. 43.

[21] Cf. Passerinus, *Commentaria in Sextum Librum,* lib. I, tit. II, cap. II, q. I, arts. 7 and 15; Ferraris, *Bibliotheca Canonica Iuridica Moralis Theologica,* *v.* "ignorantia."

[22] Huguccio *ad* c. 2, D. V, *v.* "poenam vertimus ei in culpam"—Müller, *Ethik und Recht,* p. 74.

[23] Cf. Müller, *Ethik und Recht,* pp. 71-74.

was presupposed.[24] According to this view moral guilt was found in the fact that the delinquent had engaged in an illicit act.

There were several canons in the *Decretum* which lent themselves to this interpretation. One of these was taken from St. Augustine [25] who declared that what had been done *propter bonum et licitum* could not be imputed even if an injury resulted therefrom. And the Council of Worms (868) decreed that the woodchopper who accidentally killed a man while engaged in an *opus necessarium,* was not obliged to perform the penance prescribed for homicide.[26] In neither of these canons is it stated that by engaging in an *opus illicitum* or *non necessarium* one would become liable for the penalty. But the Decretists drew this conclusion from them, and thus arrived at the principle that he who engages in a forbidden action must be held accountable for even the unforeseen results of that action.[27]

Not only was the doctrine of *versari in re illicita* accepted by later canonists [28] but was employed by several papal decrees and so found its way into the *Corpus Iuris.*[29] From Canon Law the doc-

[24] "Imputatur . . . in penitentiam; est igitur peccatum."—Rufinus, *Summa, ad* c. 44, D. L, *v.* "si autem non voluntate"—ed. Singer, p. 127; "Ubi . . . penitentia indicitur, culpa affuisse monstratur."—*Summa Coloniensis, ad* C. XV, q. 1—Müller, *ibidem,* p. 79.

[25] *Ad Publicolam,* Epistola 47—c. 8, C. XXIII, q. 5.

[26] C. 50, D. L.

[27] Simon of Bisignano, *Glossa, ad* c. 13, C. XV, q. 1: " . . . et quidem credimus, quod si rei licite dabam operam . . . , quod michi non debet imputari; . . . si vero illicite rei dabam operam . . . , est quod michi debeat imputari . . . "—Kuttner, *Schuldlehre,* p. 204, note 3. For the details of this development, cf. *op. cit.*, pp. 200-213.

[28] V. gr., *Glossa Ordinaria, ad* cc. 10, 19, X, *de homicidio voluntario vel casuali,* V, 12; Hostiensis, *Commentaria,* cc. 8, 13, *de homicidio voluntario vel casuali,* V, 12; Sylvester, *Summa Summarum, v.* "homicidium," n. 2; Fagnanus, *Commentaria,* lib. V, tit. XII, cap. XII, n. 19.

[29] Thus, in several cases of homicide the fact that the individual was not engaged in an illicit aaction was taken into consideration. V. gr., c. 13, X, *de homicidio voluntario vel casuali,* V, 12 (Innocent III): " . . . quum idem capellanus (who had killed a child when the horse he was riding broke out of control) nec voluntate nec actu homicidium perpetravit, nec dedit operam illicitae rei, non impedias, quo minus divina possit officia celebrare." C. 23,

trine of *versari in re illicita* spread, chiefly through the medium of the Roman Law Glossators,[80] into Italian jurisprudence. In fact, scarcely a modern legal system has not been influenced by the doctrine of liability for the effects of an *opus illicitum*. It has spread even to German Law [81] and to the English Common Law.[82]

It is not at all surprising that an opinion, however inadequate for the determination of criminal liability for unintended results, with the weight of so much authority behind it should have lasted as long as it did. It is one of the achievements of the Moral Theologians of the School of Salamanca to have defined more accurately the limits of the *voluntarium indirectum*.[83]

Among the jurists, who must be accredited with refuting the doctrine of criminal liability for unintended effects resulting from an illicit action, Covarrubias (d. 1577) is perhaps the most out-

X, *h. t.* V, 12 (Honorius III): "Nos igitur attendentes, quod dicto sacerdoti, qui dabat operam rei licitae (a boy had been killed through the fall of a bell which the priest was ringing), nihil potuit imputari . . ." Cf. also c. 25, X, *h. t.* V, 12 (Gregory IX).

80 Müller, *Ethik und Recht*, p. 101.

81 Müller, *ibidem*, pp. 102-104.

82 Cf. Bodenstein, "Phases in the Development of Criminal *Mens Rea*"—*South African Law Journal*, XXXVI (1919), 335-349. The principle still seems to be applied in American Criminal Law. In speaking of the instances in which mistake does not negative the criminal mind, Keedy ("Ignorance and Mistake in the Criminal Law"—*Harvard Law Review*, XXII [1908-1909], p. 83) mentions the case in which "the defendant, while engaged in a commission of one criminal act, does another criminal act under ignorance or mistake of fact. Here the criminal mind is carried over from the first act." The frequently cited example of Coke (*Institutes* [London, 1797], III, 56) closely resembles those given by Canonists. "As if A, meaning to steale a deere in the park of B, shooteth at the deere, and by the glance of the arrow killeth a boy that is hidden in a bush: this is murder for that act was unlawful, although A had no intention to hurt the boy, nor knew not of him." Modern decisions generally limit the application of the principle to criminal effects resulting from engaging in *mala in se* to the exclusion of those flowing from *mala prohibita*. Cf. Clark-Marshall, *A Treatise on the Law of Crimes* (4. ed., Chicago: Callaghan and Co., 1940), pp. 92-93.

83 Cf. Müller, *ibidem*, pp. 233-240; Montes, "La ignorancia en el derecho penal"—*Ciudad de Dios*, CXLIX (1927), 220-221.

standing.[34] Covarrubias limited responsibility for effects flowing from an *opus illicitum* to those which must necessarily be foreseen as the natural consequences of the illicit act. This is practically equivalent to saying that the very placing of the *opus illicitum* is at least negligence so far as the unintended effects are concerned. In other words, applying the doctrine to ignorance, the delinquent must be considered morally responsible in not foreseeing the evil or injurious results of his conduct.[35]

Hence, the mere fact that a person violates a law in ignorance while engaging in an illicit act does not make him responsible in regard to unforeseen effects. With this the distinction between the ignorance of a person engaged in illicit conduct and one not engaged in illicit action is no longer of any practical value, because no juridical consequences follow from it.[36]

Article II. The Distinction between Medicinal and Vindicative Penalties, and its Results

The developments peculiar to this period in regard to the principles of ignorance occur almost exclusively in regard to censures. The present article will deal with the causes of this development and its primary result, namely, the admission of *ignorantia solius poenae*

[34] Cf. Löffler, *Schuldformen des Strafrechts* (Leipzig, 1895), p. 161.

[35] " . . . homicidium casuale tunc demum ad irregularitatem imputandum fore danti operam rei illicitae, quando actus ille illicitus est ordinatus sua propria natura ad mortis laesionem, vel ad homicidium . . . aut quoties homicidium illud procedit ab illo actu illicito, per se quidem, et necessario, non per accidens . . . aut saltem, ubi illicitum illud opus per se volitum est periculosum ex natura, sua, aut saltem saepe inde mors sequatur, aut frequenter."—*In Clementis Quinti Constitutionem*, "Si Furiosus," *de Homicidio*, pars II, par. IV, n. 10.

[36] Cf. Suarez, *De Censuris*, disp. IV, sect. VIII, n. 13; Sanchez, *De Matrimonio*, lib. IX, disp. XXXII, n. 24; Pirhing, *Ius Canonicum*, lib. V, tit. XXXIX, sec. II, n. 42; Reiffenstuel, *Ius Canonicum Universum* (Parisiis, 1864-1870), lib. V, tit. XII, nn. 191-201; Thesaurus-Giraldi, *De Poenis Ecclesiasticis* (Romae, 1831), P. I, cap. XV, q. II. An exception is often made in regard to irregularities, v. gr., that incurred by a cleric who, while engaged in illicit chase, kills a man. This was considered an exception based upon positive law. Cf. Sanchez, *ibidem*, n. 25.

as an excuse from censures. The following article will review briefly the general principles applicable to censures, especially in the internal forum, with a view to describing the legal status of the question as it existed at the time of the Codification of Canon Law.

Although the declaration of Innocent III at some time between 1198 and 1205 fixed the term "censure" as applying only to excommunication, suspension and interdict,[37] it was not until the fifteenth and sixteenth century that the concept of a censure as spiritual and medicinal penalty was fully developed.[38]

The special characteristic of censures, so far as ignorance is concerned, is that these penalties require contumacy on the part of the delinquent in order that they can be inflicted or incurred. It is only when this principle was admitted that *ignorantia solius poenae* was recognized as a sufficient reason for excuse from censures.

The principle that censures could be inflicted only upon the contumacious delinquent arose because of the law which prescribed proper canonical warnings before censures could be imposed.[39] The necessity of canonical warnings was at first required by law only for excommunication. There are numerous instances in the *Decretum Gratiani* in which canonical warnings were prescribed at least in regard to particular crimes.[40] The Decretists generally insisted upon the necessity of a canonical warning, especially in regard to

[37] C. 20, X, *de verborum significatione,* V, 40.

[38] Cf. Wernz, *Ius Decretalium,* VI, 149; Hinschius, *Kirchenrecht,* V, 641; Francis Moriarty, *The Extraordinary Absolution from Censures,* The Catholic University of America, Canon Law Studies, n. 113 (Washington: The Catholic University of America, 1938), pp. 4-5.

[39] From a purely doctrinal or legal viewpoint the rule would today be stated conversely, namely: canonical warning is necessary because censures can be inflicted only upon the contumacious. Historically, the principle that contumacy is required for censures developed out of the necessity of the canonical warnings. This is another instance of how a rule of substantive law evolves from adjective law.

[40] V. gr., a triple canonical warning was prescribed before excommunication could be inflicted, for refusal to render the *decimae*—c. 5, C. XVI, q. 7; for violation of the *privilegium canonis*—c. 23, C. XVII, q. 4; for the refusal to answer a *vocatio in synodum*—c. 2, C. V, q. 2. The practice of requiring a triple warning is based on Christ's instructions in regard to fraternal correction. Cf. c. 23, C. XVII, q. 4; Matt. XVIII, 15-17.

excommunication,[41] but in practice the rule must have been violated frequently; so much so, that the Third Lateran Council (1179) could speak of the prevailing abuse of inflicting excommunication without proper canonical warning.[42] The Council then proceeded to impose the obligation of giving a canonical warning before inflicting excommunication and suspension.[43] The Fourth Lateran Council (1215) repeated the prohibition to excommunicate without canonical warning and imposed an *interdictum ab ingressu ecclesiae per mensem* upon those who violated this law.[44] The First Council of Lyons (1245) renewed the penalty imposed by the Fourth Lateran Council and added a suspension *a divinis*. Furthermore, it extended the provisions regarding the necessity of proper canonical warning not only to suspension but also to interdict.[45]

Because it was necessary that the canonical warning be violated by the delinquent before he could be punished with a censure (at first only in regard to excommunication), it was natural enough that the Roman Law concept of procedural *contumacia* was applied to this case. There is much similarity between the contempt of the canonical warnings and the refusal to appear in court upon the summons of a judge. In Roman Law contempt of a magistrate's command to appear in court was called *contumacia*, and like the canonical warning it had to be threefold or at least one peremptory

[41] Cf. *Glossa Ordinaria ad* c. 5, C. XVI, q. 7, *v.* "admoneantur"; c. 21, C. XII, q. 2, *v.* "admonitio." In the latter text of the *Decretum* there is a general statement to the effect that a warning must precede punishment: "De quibus (i. e., those who usurp ecclesiastical property) tanta debet esse prouisio, ut uindictam ammonitio precedat, . . ." To this the *Glossa* (*loc. cit.*) remarks: ". . . admonitio semper praecedat uindictam . . . Sed verum est cum agitur ad poenam excommunicationis: quia nemo excommunicandus est nisi praecedat admonitio trina . . . Item et in illis criminibus praecedet admonitio ubi ad brachium saeculare est recurrendum. . . ."

[42] C. 6—Schroeder, *Disciplinary Decrees of the General Councils*, p. 552.

[43] C. 26, X, *de appellationibus*, II, 28.

[44] C. 47 (c. 48, X, *de sententia excommunicationis*, V, 39)—Schroeder, *op. cit.*, pp. 576-577.

[45] C. 7 (c. 1, *de sententia excommunicationis, suspensionis et interdicti*, V, 11 in VI°—Schroeder, *op. cit.*, p. 593.

command.[46] Hence, the refusal to heed the canonical warning came to be known as *contumacia* or, especially in older writings, *contemptus.*

In general the Decretists admit the necessity of *contumacia* for excommunication, though not as an absolutely universal rule. Some require *contumacia* for an *ab homine* excommunication but do not see its necessity in the case of a *latae sententiae* excommunication.[47] However, the insistence of the Holy See upon the necessity of a canonical warning, not only for excommunication, but also for interdict and suspension, naturally led to the conclusion that contumacy was a necessary requisite for the inflicting or incurring of any censure.

The necessity of contumacy for the incurring of any censure led to the admission of *ignorantia solius poenae* as an excuse from *latae sententiae* censures.[48] Again the opinion that ignorance of penalty alone excuses was advanced first in regard to excommunication. When it was first proposed, however, it was discussed under a different aspect. It was asked, namely: Whether ignorance of the statute of a bishop imposing excommunication upon something al-

[46] "Contumacia eorum, qui ius dicenti non obtemperant, litis damno coercetur. 1. Contumax est, qui tribus edictis propositis vel uno pro tribus, quod vulgo peremptorium appellatur, litteris evocatus praesentiam sui facere contemnet."—D. (42, 1) 53. Cf. also D. (3, 1) 1, 3; D. (11, 1) 11, 4; D. (37, 6) 1, 10; D. (42, 1) 2; D. (48, 19) 5, *pr.;* D. (43, 5) 3, 14.

[47] *Glossa Ordinaria ad* c. 23, C. XVII, q. 4, *v.* "praemissa": " . . . aut excommunicatur quis pro contumacia, aut pro delicto. . . . Certe semper excommunicatur quis pro contumacia, sed illa quandoque provenit ex delicto, . . . nisi ipso iure incidat in canonem latae sententiae, . . ."; *Glossa Ordinaria* (Joannes Teutonicus) *ad* c. 8, C. XI, q. 3, *v.* "minimis": " . . . nonne pro sola contumacia est quis excommunicandus? . . . ad hoc dicunt quidem, quod ab homine non est aliquis excommunicandus nisi pro contumacia, sed a canone [*i. e., latae sententiae*] bene; . . . hoc non est verum: quia quandoque excommunicatur aliquis pro contumacia: quandoque pro crimine . . . Sed certe illa decre[ta?] dicit, quod pro offensa sit aliquis excommunicandus, cum non vult satisfacere: et ita pro contumacia, quare alia distinctio est melior." Cf. also Laurentius, *Glossa Palatina, loc. cit.*—Kuttner, *Schuldlehre,* p. 35, note 2.

[48] Theoretically the same is true of *ferendae sententiae* censures. However, the case is hardly possible because of the canonical warning which must precede.

ready forbidden by the natural law excused from the excommunication? [49] In support of their opinion the earlier authors (*i. e.*, generally before Suarez) appealed to the *c. Ut Animarum*, which ordered that the statutes of bishops did not bind the ignorant and in the very next sentence spoke of a crime forbidden already by all positive laws as well as the natural law itself.[50] Yet, the very way in which the problem was presented hindered its general acceptance, because it fell within the doctrine of *versari in re illicita*. Accordingly it was argued that one who knowingly violated a natural law or a positive canon law, ignorant only of the local statute imposing the excommunication, should not be excused because he was engaging in an *opus illicitum*.[51]

At this same time, however, the doctrine of *versari in re illicita* was being refuted especially by the Spanish Moralists. Nevertheless, Covarrubias, who had a great share in the final overthrow of the doctrine of *versari in re illicita,* strenuously opposed the opinion which admitted excuse for ignorance of penalty alone.[52] Once more the question was not presented in its proper perspective; because Covarrubias discussed the general problem, whether ignorance of penalty alone excuses from any penalty even those *ferendae*

[49] The opinion was first advanced in the commentaries of c. 21, X, *de sententia excommunicationis*, V. 39, which declared that a general sentence of excommunication imposed by a particular statute upon *furtum* bound only the subjects of the particular territory. Note the similarity of this case to the *c. Ut Animarum* (*supra*, p. 47). Possibly this suggested the interpretation, for the *c. Ut Animarum* is expressly cited. Cf. Hostiensis, Felinus, Panormitanus in their *Commentaria, loc. cit.;* Sylvester, *Summa Summarum, v.* "excommunicatio," X, 3; Barbosa, *Collectanea Doctorum* (Lugduni, 1637), c. 21, X, *h. t.*, V, 39.

[50] Cf. *supra*, pp. 48-50.

[51] Cf. Hostiensis, *Commentaria*, c. 21, *de sententia excommunicationis*, V, 39, n. 1.

[52] In reference to this opinion he writes: "Non me latet, hanc controversiam satis esse difficilem, et tamen libere quid hac de re sentiam minime verebor exponere, constanti animo professus, errorem esse admodum manifestum, quo iuris utriusque Doctores in hac disputatione utuntur, censentes non posse puniri poena legis vel statuti eum, qui huius poenae inscius et ignarus sit, etenim aut ipse fallor, aut haec est maxima, ne dicam pudenda, oscitantia."—*Alma Mater*, Pars I, par. X, nn. 8-9.

sententiae.[53] Perhaps Covarrubias was right in his castigation of an opinion which admitted ignorance of penalty alone to be an excuse from all criminal punishment. Certainly, the arguments in favor of such a view were weak and could easily be refuted. Yet Covarrubias failed to see any reason why ignorance of penalty alone should be accepted as an excuse from excommunication[54] and arrived at the conclusion that only the ignorance which excused from grave guilt exempted from excommunication.[55]

Apparently Suarez, who is largely responsible for the clarification of the concept of a censure, was the first to offer a solution which definitely settled the question of *ignorantia solius poenae* in regard to censures. Suarez admitted that there was no legal text to be found, from which excuse from censures on account of *ignorantia solius poenae* could be deduced.[56] He based his whole argument upon the principle that censures can be imposed only upon the contumacious.

First of all, Suarez argued, it is necessary that the delinquent know the precept of the Church to which the censure is attached, otherwise he would not be *contumax respectu Ecclesiae.*[57] More than that, a censure is a penalty which requires a peculiar kind of contumacy or disobedience that is not present in one who is ignorant of the censure even though he knows the law. For, in order to incur a censure it is necessary that a canonical warning containing a threat of censure precede. Hence, the delinquent who is ignorant of the censure is not sufficiently warned by the law.[58] Finally,

53 "Haec scientia (*i.e.*, of penalty) aut exigitur, ut legis transgressor vere dicatur criminis reus; vel ut is poenae legis visus sit consentire, quo rectius puniri valeat, et iustius."—*ibidem,* n. 9.

54 ". . . sed ipse non video, qua ratione possit excommunicationis poena distingui ab aliis: nec enim est necessarium . . . quod qui ea ligandus est, huius poenae scientiam habeat . . ."—*ibidem,* n. 11.

55 *Ibidem,* n. 7.

56 *De Censuris,* disp. IV, sect. IX, nn. 14-15.

57 *Ibidem,* sect. VIII, n. 20.

58 "Potestque fundari in hoc, quod censura est talis poena, quae peculiarem modum contumaciae et inobedientiae requirit, qui non invenitur in eo, qui ignoravit censuram, quamvis legem noverit. . . . nam ad censuram incurrendam,

Suarez noted that the authors before him had admitted excuse for ignorance of penalty alone solely in regard to excommunication. However, since the reason he gave held equally well in the case of suspension and interdict, Suarez concluded that ignorance of penalty excused from all censures. He admitted at the same time that the opinion was more certain in regard to excommunication, just as it was more necessary.[59]

The argumentation of Suarez was accepted by canonists and moralists alike, and after his time the opinion has never seriously been called into question.[60]

Before concluding, it may be remarked that once it had been settled that *ignorantia solius poenae* excuses from censures because of their peculiar nature the question was also solved in regard to other penalties. In penalties other than censures the rule obtained: whatever does not exclude grave guilt does not exempt from penal liability.

One or other noteworthy exception to this rule may be mentioned. Shortly before Suarez a slightly different criterion had been suggested to determine when ignorance of penalty alone excused. Navarrus (Martinus de Azpilcueta, d. 1586) taught that ignorance of penalty alone excused if the penalty was extraordinary or exorbitant. As an example of an extraordinary penalty, Navarrus men-

necessarium est, ut praecedat monitio, non qualiscumque, sed sub comminatione censurae, . . . ille autem, qui sola lege admonetur, si invincibiliter ignoret, censuram legi annexam esse, reipsa non admonetur sub comminatione censurae; ergo non satis admonetur, ut possit censuram incurrere."—*ibidem*, sect. IX, n. 2.

59 "Et ideo extendendam censeo hanc doctrinam ad censuram, quatenus talis est; quamquam non negaverim in excommunicatione rem esse magis certam, sicut etiam in eadem magis est necessaria."—*ibidem*, n. 19.

60 Cf. v. gr., Sanchez, *De Matrimonio*, lib. IX, tit. XXXII, nn. 20-22; Pirhing, *Ius Canonicum*, lib. V, tit. XXXIX, sect. II, par. V, n. 45; Salmanticenses, *De Censuris* (*Cursus Theologiae Moralis* [Venetiis, 1714], tract. X, vol. II), cap. I, punct. XV, n. 193; Wernz, *Ius Decretalium*, VI, 32, note 81; Reiffenstuel, *Ius Canonicum*, lib. V, tit. XXXIX, nn. 30-32; Kober, *Kirchenbann*, p. 205; Ferraris, *Bibliotheca Canonica Iuridica Moralis Theologica*, *v.* "ignorantia," n. 21; Lehmkuhl, *Theologia Moralis* (5. ed. Friburgi Brisgoviae, 1888), II, 621.

tioned excommunication, but did not determine that concept any further.[61] This view gained relatively few adherents,[62] for, as Suarez remarked of this opinion, it was unfounded in law. As far as guilt before God is concerned, it is untrue, because the sinner need not know the extraordinary character of the punishment attached to his sin in order to become liable for that penalty.[63]

In regard to *latae sententiae* vindicative penalties an exception was sometimes made in those cases where the law by such terms as *praesumpserit* or *scienter* presupposed perfect *dolus* in the commission of the criminal act. In these instances some authors were inclined to admit ignorance of the penalty alone as an excuse from vindicative penalties.[64]

The legal foundation for this opinion must be considered weak. In penalties other than censures the more commonly accepted rule seems to have been that ignorance, whether of law or of fact, excused only when it excluded grave moral guilt.[65] Yet because of the development of the concept of perfect *dolus* as presupposing not only full knowledge of fact but also a clear knowledge of law, this opinion did have some doctrinal foundation. As will be shown in the commentary on the present law, the opinion is at least implicity confirmed by the Code of Canon Law.

Finally, for the sake of completeness some mention should be made of the dispute concerning ignorance of irregularities *ex delicto*. Sanchez, in discussing the extent to which ignorance of penalty alone could be admitted as an excuse, considered it prob-

[61] *Enchiridion,* cap. XXVII, n. 274; *Consilia,* P. I, lib. III, *de sepulturis,* cons. X, n. 5.

[62] V. gr., Alterius, *De Censuris Ecclesiasticis,* lib. III, tit. II, cap. III; Pichler, *Candidatus Iurisprudentiae* (3. and 4. ed., August., 1723-1733), lib. I, tit. II, n. 42. Noldin (*De Poenis Ecclesiasticis* [5. ed., Oeniponte, 1905], p. 23, note 25) went so far as to consider all *latae sententiae* vindicative penalties exorbitant and extraordinary.

[63] *De Censuris,* disp. IV, sect. IX, nn. 21-22. Cf. also Sanchez, *De Matrimonio,* lib. IX, tit. XXXII, nn. 20-21.

[64] V. gr., Schmalzgrueber, *Ius Ecclesiasticum Universum* (Romae, 1843-1845), lib. I, tit. II, n. 40; Smith, *Elements of Ecclesiastical Law,* III (3. ed., New York, 1888), 32-33.

[65] Cf. Wernz, *Ius Decretalium,* VI, 32, note 81.

able that ignorance of irregularity alone excused from an *irregularitas ex delicto*. The whole reason for the doubt and consequent division of opinion arose from the uncertainty which existed concerning the nature of an *irregularitas ex delicto*. Before the Code it was uncertain whether the irregularity should be considered a penalty, and if a penalty whether it was medicinal. If the latter were true then ignorance of irregularity alone should excuse in accord with the accepted doctrine.[66]

Consequently there was a division of opinion regarding the excuse for ignorance of irregularity alone. One view, insisting upon the penal and medicinal character of irregularities *ex delicto*, held that mere ignorance solely of the irregularity did not suffice to excuse from incurring the same.[67] Others, considering irregularities to be rather inhabilities than penalties in the strict sense, held that ignorance of irregularity alone did not excuse from them.[68]

Before the Code of Canon Law the doubt was practically insoluble and both opinions were probable. It remained for the Code to determine the nature of irregularities and to settle the doubt concerning ignorance by expressly declaring that ignorance does not excuse.[69]

Article III. The Degree of Excusing Ignorance in Regard to *Latae Sententiae* Censures

As has already been shown, the development in doctrine of this

[66] Cf. Sanchez, *De Matrimonio*, lib. IX, disp. XXXII, nn. 20-21.

[67] V. gr., Sanchez, *loc. cit.*; Schmalzgrueber, *Ius Ecclesiasticum*, lib. V, tit. XXXVII, nn. 107-109. (The latter admits excuse at least for the internal forum, and his chief argument seems to be based on the fact that he considers irregularities extraordinary penalties.) Lehmkuhl, *Theologia Moralis*, II, 710; S. Alphonsus (*Theologia Moralis* [ed. Gaudé, Romae, 1905-1912], lib. VII, cap. V, dub. III, n. 351) admits the opinion at least as probable.

[68] V. gr., Suarez, *De Censuris*, disp. XL, sect. V, n. 10; Salmanticenses, *De Censuris*, cap. I. punct. XV, n. 195; Thesaurus-Giraldi, *De Poenis Ecclesiasticis*, Pars I, cap. XV, q. I, n. 2; Pichler, *Candidatus Iurisprudentiae*, lib. V, tit. XXXVII, n. 25. For the opinion of other authors for both views see S. Alphonsus, *Theologia Moralis*, lib. VII, cap. II, dub. III, n. 351.

[69] Canon 988. Cf. Vermeersch-Creusen, *Epitome* (vol. I, 6. ed., 1937, vols. II and III, 5. ed., 1934-1936, Romae) II, 171.

period occurred primarily in regard to censures. The multiplication of *latae sententiae* censures in the common law, together with the numerous censures attached to the violation of particular decrees of the Holy See and those introduced by particular law[70] necessarily led to important changes in the legal rules for ignorance. The nature of excusing ignorance has already been considered. It has been shown that ignorance of law and ignorance of fact are now considered according to the same standards of negligence. The identical distinctions are applicable to both and the difference between the principles applicable to ignorance of law and ignorance of fact remains only as a matter of degree. In other words, while there is no substantial difference between ignorance of law and ignorance of fact, the former should be considered more strictly than the latter.[71] The extent to which ignorance of penalty alone can be considered as an excuse was discussed in the previous article.

Consequently to complete the study of this period only the *degree* of excusing ignorance remains to be examined. It would be impossible to go into every angle of the doctrine as it developed in the works of both canonists and moralists. Authors differ widely in their approach to the problem so that to give an entirely complete picture it would be necessary to discuss many of them singly. There was much confusion, both in the matter of divisions employed and of the principles arrived at. This article attempts to summarize the general results achieved, with a view toward presenting some idea of the state of the law at the time of the Codification. It is hoped that this method will contribute toward a better understanding of the legal principles now in force.

On the basis of culpability, the following degrees of ignorance can be distinguished:

[70] Cf. *supra*, pp. 46-47; Hinschius, *Kirchenrecht*, V, 654-657.

[71] Cf. Hollweck, *Die kirchlichen Strafgesetze* (Mainz, 1899), note 2 *ad* par. 16, p. 78. This holds true primarily in the internal forum. In the external forum, because knowledge of law is generally presumed, ignorance of law cannot be admitted as easily as ignorance of fact. Cf. Lega, *De Delictis et Poenis*, pp. 61-66. D'Annibale's statement (*In Constitutionem Apostolicae Sedis Commentarii* [5. ed., Romae, 1909], p. 8, note 23) is undoubtedly true: "Verum ignorantia juris vix admittitur in foro externo."

1. Invincible or inculpable ignorance;
2. Vincible or culpable ignorance, which may be:
   a. either directly sought (affected ignorance);
   b. or indirectly willed because of negligence; the latter can be distinguished into:
      aa. venially sinful ignorance;
      bb. gravely sinful ignorance (*simpliciter culpabilis vel vincibilis*);
      cc. crass or supine;
      dd. *crassa cum temeritate* (*crassissima, supina*).

Of these invincible and venially culpable ignorance offer no difficulty. These always excuse from censures according to the general principle that no grave censure can be inflicted for venial guilt.[72]

On the other hand, affected and crass ignorance are never admitted as an excuse from censures when the law does not presuppose perfect *dolus* by such terms as *scienter* or *praesumpserit*. If, however, the law expressly requires perfect *dolus* gravely culpable ignorance and crass ignorance are commonly admitted as excusing from *latae sententiae* censures. This latter rule must be considered a new principle in Canon Law developed during this period. If one were to consider the legal texts alone, both of the Roman Law as

[72] The principle that no grave penalty can be imposed except for grave sin is universally admitted at least in theory. Cf. Sylvester, *Summa Summarum*, *v.* "excommunicatio," I, 3; Covarrubias, *Alma Mater*, Pars I, par. X, n. 7; Suarez, *De Legibus* (*Opera Omna*, V), lib. V, cap. XII, n. 16; Passerinus, *Commentaria in Sextum Librum*, lib. I, tit. II, cap. II, q. I, art. 17, n. 356. Emphasis must be placed on the fact that this principle says that no *grave* penalty can be inflicted for less than grave guilt. Many authors held that a slight penalty could be imposed for venial guilt. As examples of slight penalties the following are frequently mentioned: Minor excommunication—Suarez, *De Censuris*, disp. IV, sect. IV, n. 6; Thesaurus-Giraldi, *De Poenis Ecclesiasticis*, Pars I, cap. XV, q. 1, n. 1; *Suspensio ab uno vel alio effectu non gravi ad tempus breve*—Passerinus, *Commentaria in Sextum Librum*, lib. I, tit. II, cap. II, q. 1, art. 21; *Suspensio a Missa celebranda per unum vel alterum diem*—Pirhing, *Ius Canonicum*, lib. V, tit. XXXIX, sect. VI, n. 207; Reiffenstuel, *Theologia Moralis* (Mutinae, 1737), tract. XIII, dist. I, q. 2, n. 10; *Interdictum particularis personae, et ad breve tempus, et privando aliquo usu dumtaxat*—Salmanticenses, *De Censuris*, cap. I, punct. X, n. 124.

well as the Canon Law, one would certainly arrive at an opposite conclusion.

The opinion that certain penal laws presuppose express or perfect *dolus* does not seem to be very old.[73] Panormitanus [74] and Felinus Sandaeus [75] are among the first to advance the opinion that the penalty of the law is not incurred for *lata culpa* in those cases where the law expressly or tacitly requires perfect *dolus* as an element of the delict. Upon this basis a distinction grew up between laws which by their express terms penalize only those violations which are performed with formal knowledge and contempt and those laws which inflict penalties upon every morally culpable transgression. When perfect *dolus* is necessary to constitute the crime, there must be formal knowledge or at least its legal equivalent. *Lata culpa* does not suffice to constitute the crime penalized by the law in this instance and hence crass ignorance, which arises from *lata culpa,* excuses.

Suarez was perhaps one of the first who expressly taught that crass ignorance excused when the law presupposes perfect *dolus* in the commission of the delict. If the law stated that only those who *scienter* committed a crime were to be punished, then knowledge is required; and crass ignorance negatived knowledge even though it did result from grave negligence. So also if the law had such terms as *praesumpserit* or *temere,* one who transgressed the law out of crass ignorance did so rather out of negligence than presumption or malice.[76]

Nor was this opinion considered to be contrary to the *c. Ut*

[73] Joannes de Sancto Georgio (d. 1378), Philippus Franchus de Franchis (d. 1471), the *Summa Rosella* (1483), *Summa Sylvestriana* (ca. 1500), *Summa Tabiena* (1515) seem not to be aware of the opinion.—Sanchez, *De Matrimonio,* lib. IX, tit. XXXII, n. 35.

[74] "Et hoc casu dic, quod si statutum requirat dolum expressum, vel tacite, non habet locum in eo, qui fuit in lata culpa (the equivalent of crass ignorance), licet pro modo culpae aliter sit puniendus." As an example he cites c. 29, C. XVII, q. 4 (*Si quis suadente diabolo*) and c. 4, X, *de sententia excommunicationis,* V, 39—*Commentaria,* c. 2, X, *de constitutionibus,* I, 2.

[75] "Et dicitur lata culpa: puta, quia homines loci communiter sciebant . . . Fallit . . . ubi lex requirit dolum expresse, vel tacite . . ."—*Commentaria,* c. 2, X, *de constitutionibus,* I, 2, n. 4.

[76] *De Censuris,* disp. IV, sect. X, nn. 2-3.

Animarum, which expressly excluded crass or supine ignorance as an excuse from penalties; because, it was argued, the *c. Ut Animarum* concerned only the general rule and was not to be applied to those crimes which were fully realized only when they were perpetrated with perfect *dolus.*[77] Penalties, especially *latae sententiae* censures, should be interpreted in favor of the delinquent [78] and, hence, even though crass ignorance is gravely sinful and often considered the equivalent of knowledge by the law, in the strict sense it is not knowledge.[79]

These arguments were accepted by moralists as well as canonists and the opinion became a universally accepted principle.[80]

1. Disputes Concerning Crass Ignorance

On the basis of the *c. Ut Animarum* some authors arrived at the conclusion that gravely culpable ignorance excused from censures, even when the law did not presuppose perfect *dolus,* so long as the ignorance could not be called crass. The argument was as follows: Any ignorance which excused from grave guilt exempted from censures *ex iure naturae.* Hence, the *c. Ut Animarum,* in order to prevent possible danger to souls, evidently intended to grant something over and above the natural law, otherwise it would have been useless.

[77] Cf. Pichler, *Candidatus Iurisprudentiae,* lib. I, tit. II, n. 41; Duardus, *Commentaria in Bullam S. D. N. D. Pauli V Lectam in Die Coenae Domini Anno 1618* (Mediolani, 1620), lib. II, can. I, q. 36, n. 21.

[78] "Odia restringi, et favores convenit ampliari."—Reg. 15, *R. J.,* in VI°; "In poenis benignior est interpretatio facienda."—Reg. 49, *R. J.,* in VI°.

[79] Cf. Pichler, *loc. cit.;* Duardus, *ibidem,* n. 1.

[80] Cf. Passerinus, *Commentaria in Sextum Librum,* lib. I, tit. II, cap. II, q. I, art. 21; Sanchez, *De Matrimonio,* lib. IX, disp. XXXII, n. 22; S. Alphonsus, *Theologia Moralis,* lib. VII, cap. I, dub. IV, n. 47; Salmanticenses, *De Censuris,* cap. I, punct. XV, n. 198; Castropalaus, *Opus Morale* (Lugduni, 1682), tract. II, disp. I, punct. XVIII, n. 1; Laymann, *Theologia Moralis* (Venetiis, 1719), lib. I, tract. IV, cap. XX, n. 2; Hollweck, *Die kirchlichen Strafgesetze,* §§ 15, 28; Lega, *De Delictis et Poenis,* pp. 63-64; Hinschius, *Kirchenrecht,* V, 926.

Therefore, the *c. Ut Animarum* by expressly excluding crass ignorance implicitly included gravely culpable ignorance.[81]

Some authors, moreover, argued that merely grave ignorance was not sufficient to constitute contumacy which was necessary in order to incur any censure.[82]

The difficulty for this opinion arose from the lack of a practical criterion by means of which gravely negligent ignorance could be distinguished from crass ignorance. The opponents of this view defined crass ignorance as that which resulted from gravely sinful negligence, while the supporters of the same required a higher degree of negligence. Crass ignorance was defined by the latter as that which resulted from the highest degree of negligence.[83]

Due to the practical difficulty of distinguishing grave from crass ignorance and to the fact that the basis of the opinion was weak, many rejected the distinction altogether.[84] For this reason the more common opinion before the Codification of Canon Law seems to have been the view of Suarez. His line of reasoning was often repeated [85] and many authorities felt that the opposite opinion was so impractical that it was useless and even that it could not be held as a probable opinion.[86]

[81] Cf. Sanchez, *De Matrimonio,* lib. II, disp. XXXII, nn. 32-33; D'Annibale, *Summula Theologiae Moralis* (5. ed., Romae, 1908), I, 313, note 77; Ballerini-Palmieri, *Opus Morale* (Prati, 1889-1893), VII, 75-76; Lehmkuhl, *Theologia Moralis,* II, 621; Lega, *De Delictis et Poenis,* pp. 65-66.

[82] Pirhing, *Ius Canonicum,* lib. V, tit. XXXIX, sect. II, n. 46.

[83] D. (22, 6) 9, 2 was often cited, namely: "Sed facti ignorantia ita demum cuique non nocet, si non ei summa negligentia obiciatur."

[84] Thus Suarez (*De Censuris,* disp. IV, sect. X, n. 12) pointed out that ". . . talium graduum distinctio, et nullo jure fundata est, et nulla ratione explicari potest."

[85] There was, however, strenuous opposition. Thus A. Ballerini in his edition of Gury's *Compendium Theologiae Moralis* ([3. ed., Romae, 1875], II, n. 939, note a) calls the reason of Suarez *levissimam illam ratiunculam.* Kober (*Der Kirchenbann,* p. 207) preferred the milder view because it was more in harmony with the spirit of leniency which characterized the penal law of the Church. Cf. also *supra,* p. 74, note 78.

[86] St. Alphonsus (*Theologia Moralis,* lib. VII, cap. I, dub. IV, n. 45) said that the opinion " . . . vix esse practice probabilem"; Hollweck (*Die kirchlichen Strafgesetze,* note 5 *ad* § 15, p. 77) criticized the opinion in these words:

Some authors attempted a distinction between the internal forum and the external forum and, oddly enough, arrived at the conclusion that in the internal forum one could not distinguish between grave and crass ignorance. In the external forum, because of the express ordinance of Boniface VIII in the *c. Ut Animarum,* it was necessary to distinguish degrees of criminally culpable ignorance. These degrees, however, were not to be measured entirely according to the quantity of theological or moral guilt [87] but rather according to the degrees of juridical guilt. In the external forum penal imputability was to be fixed accordingly as the delinquent was in *culpa lata, levi vel levissima.*[88] In the internal forum there was only one degree to be considered, namely, crass or grave.

When the law expressly required perfect *dolus* all authors admitted that crass ignorance excused from *latae sententiae* censures. Yet, because an authoritative definition of crass ignorance was wanting, authors sometimes placed restrictions upon this commonly accepted principle. The limitations placed upon the excuse for crass ignorance in these cases generally amounted to limitations of degree. Thus, the excusing ignorance could not be *crassissima* [89] nor could it be so negligent that it would amount to *ingens temeritas.* There was *ingens temeritas* if the delinquent had a serious suspicion *(vehementem suspicionem)* that a penal law existed, yet, despite the suspicion, performed the act without doing anything to find out. To violate the law in this manner was considered to be the equivalent of temerity or presumption and hence the penalty was not avoided.[90]

". . . scheint praktisch nützlos. Wer kann solche Feinheiten noch fassen!" Cf. Salmanticenses, *De Censuris,* cap. I, punct. XV, n. 197; Téphany, *Constitution Apostolicae Sedis* (Tours, 1883), p. 42; Wernz, *Ius Decretalium,* VI, 31, note 79.

[87] Lega, *De Delictis et Poenis,* 65.

[88] Passerinus, *Commentarium in Sextum Librum,* lib. I, tit. II, cap. II, q. I, art. 6, n. 146.

[89] S. Antoninus according to Sanchez, *De Matrimonio,* lib. IX, disp. XXXII, n. 39.

[90] Sanchez, *De Matrimonio,* lib. IX, disp. XXXII, n. 39; *Opus Morale in Praecepta Decalogi* (Romae, 1723), tom. I, lib. II, cap. II, n. 38; Maschat-

2. The Dispute Concerning Affected Ignorance

When the law required perfect *dolus* all authors agreed that the crime as defined by the law was not committed unless the transgression were directly voluntary and deliberate. The doubt as to whether or not affected ignorance excused arose largely out of the theological and moral difficulty concerning the effect of directly procured ignorance upon imputability. The early Scholastics [91] and Decretists held that affected ignorance, rather than diminishing guilt, increased it. St. Thomas adopted this view, though it seems that in doing so he was influenced rather by traditional opinion than by his own general principles. According to St. Thomas's principle of the *voluntarium,* an act which resulted from voluntary ignorance must be considered voluntary.[92] Yet, this *voluntarium* carried with it an *involuntarium secundum quid* and consequently an act performed even out of affected ignorance ought logically to have been considered less voluntary than the deliberate act.[93]

Later writers, especially Suarez [94] and Arriaga [95] pointed out that the motive of affected ignorance need not necessarily be contempt of law or a desire to sin more freely, but that it could be directed to the physical act itself. To illustrate by an example, sup-

Giraldi, *Institutiones Canonicae* (Romae, 1757), P. II, lib. IV, tit. III, q. IX, n. 27; Duardus, *Commentaria in Bullam Coenae Domini,* lib. II, can. I, q. 36, n. 18.

[91] Cf. Müller, *Ethik und Recht,* p. 205.

[92] ". . . si ipsa ignorantia reputatur voluntaria, dum homo eam non vult vitare sicut tenetur, consequens est quod nec illud quod per huiusmodi ignorantiam fit, involuntarium iudicetur."—*Commentaria in X Libros Ethicorum ad Nicomachum* (*Opera Omnia,* XXV), lib. III, lect. III.

[93] Cf. *Summa,* I-II, q. 6, art. 8. Müller (*Ethik und Recht,* pp. 178-179) calls attention to the fact that St. Thomas in his work *De Malo* (q. III, art. 8) states absolutely: "talis ignorantia . . . magis auget." On the other hand, in the I-II, q. 76, art. 4 of his *Summa* (which Müller thinks was written after the treatise *De Malo*—cf. *op. cit.,* p. 176 with note 28) St. Thomas hesitates somewhat and states that affected ignorance *videtur augere.*

[94] *Tractatus ad Primam Secundae D. Thomae,* tract. II, *De Voluntario et Involuntario* (*Opera Omnia,* IV), disp. IV, sect. II, n. 9.

[95] *Disputationes Theologicae in I-II D. Thomae* (Lugduni, 1647), disp. XII, sect. XII, subs. 4, n. 31. Cf. Müller, *op. cit.,* pp. 206-207.

pose a man directly seeks ignorance concerning a book which he suspects of being a forbidden book. His motive in remaining ignorant is not so much contempt of authority as his desire to retain or read this particular book. He feels that if he knew he would have to get rid of the book or discontinue his reading. This man can scarcely be said to despise the law but rather to respect it. Hence, affected ignorance in this instance can hardly be considered a factor which increases guilt.

Quite naturally the dispute concerning the moral imputability of an act performed out of affected ignorance resulted in a sharp division in opinion concerning the penal imputability in case of affected ignorance. Even Suarez, who contributed towards the development of a milder view, regarded the diminution of imputability so slight in case of affected ignorance that he did not consider it an excuse even in cases where the law requires perfect *dolus*.[96] Hence, even though many admitted that affected ignorance did not increase guilt they did not consider it sufficient to justify any excuse from censures. This would seem to have been the better view before the Code, at least so far as ignorance of law was concerned; and it was adopted by a great number of both moralists and canonists.[97] Many authors, however, insisting upon the strict interpretation of penal law, argued that even affected ignorance could not properly be considered knowledge and hence excused when the law required it expressly by such terms as *scienter* or *praesumpserit*. Neither could the delinquent be considered to have the necessary

[96] "Hoc primo certissima est de ignorantia affectata, (viz. no excuse) quia haec fere aequivalet scientiae, et vel nihil, vel parum minuit culpam, et contemptum. Item diximus . . . in illis legibus, quae habent particulas exaggerantes culpam, aut modum peccandi. . . ."—*De Censuris*, disp. IV, sect. X, n. 4.

[97] Pirhing, *Ius Canonicum*, lib. V, tit. XXXIX, sect. II, n. 46; Passerinus, *Commentaria in Sextum Librum*, lib. I, tit. II, cap. II, q. I, art. 21, n. 411; Heiner, *Katholisches Kirchenrecht* (5. ed., Paderborn, 1909), II, 86. St. Alphonsus (*Theologia Moralis* lib. VII, cap. I, dub. IV, n. 48) calls this view *communior* and accepts it, though he hesitated to call the opposing view improbable. For a list of authors who held this opinion, cf. St. Alphonsus, *loc. cit.*; Salmanticenses, *De Censuris*, cap. I, punct. XV, n. 198; Gury-Ballerini, *Compendium Theologiae Moralis*, II, 934-936.

presumption or temerity in these cases if he violated the law out of ignorance.[98]

Before the Code this opinion had sufficient reason and authority to support it, both in regard to ignorance of law and ignorance of fact, to make it at least a probable opinion.[99]

Shortly before the Code a number of authors made a distinction between those laws requiring perfect *dolus* by expressly demanding knowledge (namely by employing the terms *scienter* or *consulto*) and those which did not demand knowledge expressly (namely, by using the terms *temere, praesumere, audere*). Only in the former instance did affected ignorance excuse because the law requiring explicit knowledge was not perfectly fulfilled.[100]

Résumé of the Historical Development

The basic principles of moral imputability for actions performed through ignorance are to be found in the works of the an-

98 Sanchez, while apparently one of the first to advance this opinion expressly, seems to contradict himself. In *De Matrimonio* (lib. IX, disp. XXXII, n. 40) he writes: "Ignorantia affectata . . . numquam excusat ab his poenis scientiam ac praesumptionem exigentibus." In his *Opus Morale in Praecepta Decalogi* (tom. I, lib. II, cap. X, n. 38) he writes concerning the *scienter legentes libros prohibitos*: "Quia, nimirum, quis affectavit nescire cujus Authoris sit liber aut qua de re tractet ut liberius legat. Quia re vera non dicitur hic scienter legere. Nec est ingens temeritas: nisi quando vehementem suspicionem habuit malitiae libri." The apparent contradiction can be solved very easily by pointing out that in the first case Sanchez is speaking of ignorance of law, while in the second instance he is considering ignorance of fact.

99 The Salmanticenses (*De Censuris,* cap. I, punct. XV, n. 199) call this opinion *probabilior;* St. Alphonsus (*Theologia Moralis,* lib. VII, cap. I, dub. IV, n. 48) hesitated to call this view improbable but inclined to the other because it was the more common. Hollweck (*Strafgesetze,* note 7 *ad* par. 15, pp. 77-78) admitted the opinion but restricted its application to the internal forum. Wernz (*Ius Decretalium,* VI, 31, note 79) at least implicitly admitted the opinion for censures on account of their peculiar nature. It was defended also by Duardus, *Commentaria in Bullam Coenae Domini,* lib. II, can. I, q. 37; Bucceroni, "De ignorantia a censura excusante"—*Analecta Ecclesiastica,* XIII (1905), 319.

100 Lehmkuhl, *Theologia Moralis,* II, 621; D'Annibale, *Summula Theologiae Moralis,* I, 314; Lega, *De Delictis et Poenis,* p. 64.

cient Writers and Fathers of the Church. Yet, in actual practice it seems that penances and punishments were inflicted with little regard for subjective imputability. There was some excuse allowed for ignorance in the commission of crime, but such excuse was limited to specific cases. The excuse admitted for ignorance did not flow from any general principle.

The Penitential Books were influenced in a marked degree by the primitive penal systems in use among the nations where these Books were composed and employed. In them we find that crimes are dealt with by a minute scale of fixed compensations. Penalties are precisely determined in the Penitential Books themselves for crimes when committed in ignorance.

The Decretists laid the foundations for a scientific doctrine or systematized body of principles governing the imputability of delicts committed through ignorance. The doctrine developed under the influences of the Scholastic Theologians and the Roman Law Glossators. The result was that a more equitable system of principles was developed, which was better suited to the evaluation or measuring of human responsibility.

Under the Decretists and early Decretalists ignorance of law was admitted as an excuse only to a very limited degree. However, as ignorance of law gradually came to be judged according to the degree of negligence from which it sprang, it was more and more admitted as an excuse from penalties.

A notable change in doctrine occurred in the sixteenth and seventeenth centuries due to developments in Moral Theology and especially to the introduction of the distinction between vindicative and medicinal penalties. Since the latter were inflicted only upon the contumacious, even ignorance of the mere penalty of the law was admitted as an excuse from all censures.

The doctrine was completely developed by the time of Suarez. After the seventeenth century no essentially new principles in regard to ignorance were proposed. There were of course disputed opinions and gradual shifts of authority in one direction or the other. But from this time onwards, both canonists and moralists were content to repeat the traditional doctrine and support one or the other side in the disputed opinions. Without the intervention of legislative authority it seems that further progress would have been impossible. The materials with which canonists and moralists labored had been exhausted.

Because of disputed opinions in important matters there existed a great deal of doubt and uncertainty. Yet, so far as actual practice was concerned there was little difficulty, because in practically all the disputes authors granted that both opinions—for and against a certain rule—were to be considered probable. This too hindered further progress, since authors often appealed to mere extrinsic authority. The consequence was that in the century immediately preceding the Code, argumentation dwindled into little more than a nice balancing of opposing authorities.[101]

[101] Cf., v. gr., Gury-Ballerini, *Compendium Theologiae Moralis*, II, 932-935.

PART II

CANONICAL COMMENTARY

CHAPTER V

IMPUTABILITY OF CRIME

ARTICLE I. THE ELEMENTS OF A DELICT

BEFORE one proceeds to a detailed analysis of ignorance in relation to penal imputability and responsibility, it will be necessary to review briefly some preliminary notions regarding the essential elements of crime in general and the subjective element in particular. These considerations form the necessary basis for the principles and legal rules regarding the influence of ignorance in penal law. In fact, the interpretation of these legal rules depends to a great extent upon the views adopted in regard to penal responsibility as such.

A crime must necessarily comprise three elements. These essential elements of a delict are clearly enunciated in the introductory definition of the first canon in the Fifth Book of the Code of Canon Law. They are: the objective element, or actual concrete violation of the law; the juridical element, or the penal sanction; the subjective element, or imputability.[1]

The objective element is the actual or concrete violation of the law, the individual or particular injury to the social order. Canon 2195, §1, speaks of this element simply in the words: *externa* . . .

[1] For a detailed study of this subject, see Roberti, *De Delictis et Poenis,* I, 53-55; Michiels, *De Delictis et Poenis,* I, 56-59; Latini, *Iuris Criminalis Philosophici Summa Lineamenta* (Romae: Marietti, 1924), pp. 67-71; Berutti, *Institutiones Iuris Canonici,* VI, *De Delictis et Poenis* (Romae: Marietti, 1938), pp. 3-5. The same is true in the Common Law. Cf. Blackstone, *Commentaries on the Laws of England* (ed. Cooley, 4. by Andrews, Chicago, 1899), IV, 21: "So that to constitute a crime against human laws [1], there must be, first, a vicious will [2]; and, secondly, an unlawful act [3] consequent upon such vicious will."

legis violatio.[2] The concrete violation of the law forms the basis or foundation of every question regarding penalties. It is the violation of law and order which prompts the legislator to make the penal law and which brings the individual subject under the hand of the criminal court for trial and punishment. Without it there can be no possibility of just penalties, because there is no social and juridical order to be restored, or no injury of the law to be righted. The nature of the law which is violated determines the quality of the delict and together with subjective imputability also the quantity of the delict.[3] Consequently, it is also the first measure or standard to be applied in the application of a canonical penalty.[4]

In order to constitute an injury to the social order the violation of the law must be external.[5] The legislator does not consider all transgressions of the moral or ethical order as crimes, but only such which as a matter of public policy are considered to constitute a danger or *damnum* to the social order. It is this disturbance of the external, social order, or the violation of public rights, which penal laws strive to prevent. When prevention has proved fruitless, then penal laws seek to reinstate and restore the social order. Though the violation of the law must be existing in fact, it need not always be consummated in the same degree. Sometimes the mere attempt to violate the law constitutes a crime,[6] while at other times the delict must be completely consummated.[7]

Yet, not every external violation of the social order constitutes a crime. There must be a second element, called the juridical element. This latter consists in the penal sanction or penalty placed

[2] The law, as well as a precept, may be either universal or particular. Cf. canon 2195, § 2. Throughout this study, unless otherwise specified, whatever is said of law in general applies also to a particular statute and a precept.

[3] Canon 2196.

[4] Canon 2218, § 1.

[5] "Cogitationis poenam nemo patitur."—c. 14, D. I, *de poenit.*—D. (48, 19) 18. " . . . quod, si excessus eorum esset ecclesiae manifestus, quae non iudicat de occultis, poena essent canonica feriendi."—c. 33, X, *de simonia et ne aliquid pro spiritualibus exigatur vel promittatur,* V, 3—Pope Innocent III in letter to the Abbot of Gemblaux (1199)—Potthast, n. 820.

[6] Cf. canons 2212; 2213.

[7] Canons 2228; 2242, § 1.

by the lawgiver or commanding authority upon the violation of the law.[8] The penal sanction is sometimes specifically determined; sometimes, however, it consists merely in a general threat of punishment. It is even considered sufficient that the law empower proper authority to inflict a penalty in some specific instances.[9]

There remains a third essential element of crime, namely the subjective element. Since this study will be concerned exclusively with the subjective element of crime, it will be necessary to consider this subject in some detail.

Article II. The Subjective Element of Crime or Imputability in Particular

The law punishes with canonical sanctions only human acts, that is, acts which proceed from a free human agent and, moreover, only in so far as these acts arise from a free principle and can be attributed to the latter as their author and master. The definition of crime given in canon 2195 refers to this element in the words: *moraliter imputabilis legis violatio.*

The Code has no uniform technical term to express this element of crime.[10] Most frequently it uses the term *imputabilitas* [11] which seems to be technical in this connection.[12] Despite this fact and the particular technical meaning of the term *culpa,*[13] the latter [14] together with the derived forms *culpabilitas* [15] and *culpabilis* [16] are employed quite frequently to connote imputability in general.[17]

[8] Canon 2195, § 1: " . . . legis violatio cui addita sit sanctio canonica . . . "

[9] Canon 2222, § 1.

[10] Cf. Moersdorf, *Die Rechtssprache des Codex Juris Canonici* (Paderborn: Schöningh, 1937), p. 372.

[11] Canons 2196; 2197, n. 4; 2199; 2201, § 4; 2202, §§ 1, 2; 2203, §§ 1, 2; 2204; 2205, §§ 3, 4; 2206; 2209, §§ 3, 4, 5, 6, 7; 2213, §§ 1, 3.

[12] Cf. the inscription of Title II: *De imputabilitate delicti, de causis illam aggravantibus vel minuentibus et de iuridicis delicti effectibus*; canon 2199.

[13] Canon 2199.

[14] Cf. canons 829; 1455, n. 2; 1476, § 2; 1644, § 3; 1737; 1553, § 1, n. 2; 2147, § 1; 2193; 2322, n. 1; 2324; 2325; 2331, § 1.

[15] Cf. canons 2208, § 2; 2209, § 1, § 5.

[16] Cf. canons 2209, § 2; 2213, § 2; 2184; 2354, § 2.

[17] To complicate matters still more, some authors employ the term *dolus*

For the sake of clearness and uniformity it would seem better indicated to use the term "imputability" to designate the necessary subjective element of crime in general, and to employ *culpa* and *dolus* only in their specific and technical meanings according to canon 2199.

1. The Nature of Imputability [18]

The literal meaning of the word *imputare* (from *in* and *putare* —to reckon or compute) is: to bring into the reckoning, to enter into the account.[19] When applied to the moral order *"imputare"* has the general meaning of attributing to or ascribing to the account of someone, and generally is used in an unfavorable or bad sense.[20]

To impute, therefore, means to ascribe something to someone or to something as to its cause. Imputability is a judgment in the abstract, whereby something is ascribed to a cause.

In a loose signification one can speak of physical "imputability" in the sense that an effect is ascribed to a physical agent as its efficient cause. In this sense, for example, light and heat are "imputable" to fire. Strictly considered, imputability bespeaks a moral relationship of causality. In this sense, an action, event or effect, can be ascribed or imputed only to free and intelligent beings, acting with knowledge and deliberation. This is the meaning of *imputabilis* in canon 2195, § 1. There is, however, another form of

to designate imputability in general. This term should be reserved for a very special form or degree of imputability, as will be shown later.

[18] Cf. Berutti, *De Delictis et Poenis*, pp. 14-49; Michiels, *De Delictis et Poenis*, I, 82-100 (pp. 87-98 give an excellent historical synopsis of imputability in canon law); Pistocchi, "Nature e divisione del delitto"—*Mon. Eccl.*, XLVI (1934), 19-23; Roberti, *De Delictis et Poenis*, I, 86-87; for a detailed historical study see Müller, *Ethik und Recht.*

[19] " . . . eos dumtaxat sumptuum societati imputabit qui in eam rem impensi sunt . . . "—D. (17, 2) 52, 15; see also D. (35, 2) 91. Cf. Forcellini, *Lexicon Totius Latinitatis* (ed. Furlanetto, Corradini, Perin, Patavii, 1864), *v.* "imputo."

[20] "Stari autem debet sententiae arbitri, quam de ea re dixerit, sive aequa sive iniqua sit: et sibi imputet qui compromisit."—D. (4, 8) 27, 2; "Si quidem non postulavit a praetore, ut promatur pecunia . . . sibi imputet."—D. (27, 4) 3, 6.

imputability, which presupposes moral imputability but does not coincide perfectly with it. This is juridical or political imputability.[21] Canons 2199 to 2213 deal with juridico-criminal imputability.

It was stated above that juridical imputability presupposes moral imputability, because by her penal laws the Church punishes only those anti-juridical acts which flow not only from a free being but from a free being acting freely; it punishes those acts over which a man exercises dominion, those actions over which he is master.[22] It was stated, furthermore, that juridico-criminal imputability differs from moral imputability. The principles of moral imputability are derived from reason, they are philosophical or ethical. The rules governing juridical imputability are dictated by public policy to meet the peculiar circumstances of social life and consequently need not always be perfectly logical. Some rules are, from a rational point of view, more or less arbitrary; as, for example, the presumptions of the external forum[23] or the norms of canon 2229 which are dictated by a spirit of mildness.[24]

[21] Roberti (*De Delictis et Poenis,* I, 87) distinguishes between *politica* and *iuridica imputabilitas.* The former is determined by the legislator when he defines that the author of certain acts must be held responsible before society. The latter is determined by the magistrate when he decides that the author of a crime must be held accountable in a concrete case. There seems to be little advantage in making this distinction and consequently authors generally use the two terms in the same signification. Cf. Coronata, *Institutiones Iuris Canonici,* IV, 8; Michiels, *De Delictis et Poenis,* I, 98-100.

[22] "Quorum igitur nos sumus domini, eorum principia extrinsecus non requiramus . . . sed agnoscamus ea, que proprie nostra sunt."—c. 6, C. XV, q. 1.

[23] Canons 2200, § 2; 2201, § 2; 2204.

[24] The distinctions of imputability made by Latini (*Iuris Criminalis Philosophici Summa Lineamenta,* p. 69) are hardly tenable. He writes: "Ex elemento formali (dolo) oritur ratio imputabilitatis moralis; ex elemento materiali (facto) oritur ratio imputabilitatis politicae; ex elemento legali (lege) oritur ratio imputabilitatis legalis." In this division Latini employs the term "imputability" in an equivocal sense. Imputability, though it presupposes a fact, yet it does not arise from the material fact of a violation of law. The material fact is the thing imputed, but it is in no sense convertible with imputability itself. The same holds good for the legal sanction. The legal sanction determines how the delinquent shall be held responsible before society, or in what way he shall restore the social order. But it does not give rise to imputa-

Imputability, therefore, denotes a relationship between an agent and his act. It is a causal relationship of a particular kind. Mere physical causality is not enough to establish imputability;[25] it must be a relationship of moral causality. Responsibility, on the other hand, bespeaks a relationship between the agent and some third party. Thus, a crime is imputable to the delinquent, but the delinquent is responsible to society.[26] In penal law, responsibility is the opposite of excuse from penalty; and it means that the delinquent is answerable to society and must, therefore, pay the penalty imposed by law.

Responsibility and imputability are not only different concepts, referring to vastly different relationships, but they need not always coincide or be present at the same time in a given concrete instance. This distinction will be of considerable importance in considering excuse from penalty. It may, therefore, be usefully illustrated by a few examples. Canon 2228 presupposes a distinction between imputability for a crime and responsibility for a determined penalty. This canon ordains that the penalty determined by law is not incurred unless the crime be perfectly consummated according to the strict wording of the law. Thus, if a law demands perfect knowledge [27] and this perfect knowledge is not had, there is no responsibility for the determined penalty, though there may be imputability according to the rules of Title II of the Fifth Book.[28] Another instance of this distinction is found in canon 2242, § 1, in which the elements of a crime punishable with censure are described. Because of the gravity of the penalty, the legislator requires an especial degree of imputability, namely *contumacia,* before censures can be inflicted or incurred.[29]

bility, which is, on the contrary, presupposed before legal sanctions can be applied.

[25] Canons 2203, § 2; 2205; 2206.

[26] To use the example of Roberti (*De Delictis et Poenis,* I, 87), the creative work of God is imputable to Him, but He is responsible to no one.

[27] Canon 2229, § 2.

[28] Cf. Michiels, *De Delictis et Poenis,* I, 113.

[29] Cf. canons 2229, § 4; 2230; 2233, § 2; 2242.

2. The Elements of Imputability

Two elements are necessarily involved in imputability, namely, deliberation and free will. Crime, as every violation of law, is formally constituted by the will. It is the free volition of the delinquent which is the cause of crime. This is frequently brought out in the terminology of the legal texts, in which the subjective element or imputability is called *animus* [30] or *voluntas*,[31] or is qualified by the word *sponte* [32] and other similar expressions, which will be discussed below in the consideration of *dolus*.

However, knowledge is a prerequisite for every free act. There cannot be any question of a deliberate and free act, and consequently, also, of any free anti-juridical act, unless there was previous knowledge on the part of the agent. Sometimes the law lays particular stress upon this element of imputability in using such terms as *deliberatio*,[33] *scienter*, and the like. Anything which partially hinders the action of the intellect correspondingly lessens the degree of imputability. Anything which totally impedes the exercise of the intellect precludes at the same time the knowledge essentially requisite for imputability and consequently obliterates all imputability.

In this study only the diminution or exclusion of imputability on the part of the intellect will be studied. Yet, not every defect of

[30] C. 45, D. L; *animus simoniacus*—canon 728; *animus malitiosus*—canon 644, § 2.

[31] C. 46, D. L; " . . . crimen enim contrahitur, si et voluntas nocendi intercedit."—c. 47, D. L; c. 5, C. XV, q. 1; c. 3, X, *de his, qui filios occiderunt*, V, 10; c. 13, X, *de homicidio voluntario vel casuali*, V, 12; *perversa voluntas*—canon 657; *studiosa voluntas*—canon 727, § 1; *mala voluntas*—canon 2185; *deliberata voluntas*—canon 2200, § 1.

[32] " . . . quoniam non tua sponte id fecisse cognosceris, inde canonice nullo modo iudicaris."—c. 38, D. L; "De his, qui sponte homicidium uel casu faciunt."—c. 44, D. L (the title); "Cum minister iudicis occidet eum, quem iudex iussit occidi, profecto, si id sponte facit, homicida est, etiamsi eum occidat, quem scit a iudice debuisse occidi."—c. 14, C. XXIII, q. 5; " . . . si clericus alicui sponte duellum obtulerit . . . "—c. 1, X, *de clericis pugnantibus in duello*, V, 14; canons 2339; 2390, § 2.

[33] Cf. c. 3, X, *de sententia excommunicationis*, V, 39; *deliberata voluntas*—canon 2200, § 1.

knowledge will be considered. The defective knowledge of the infant, of the insane person, of the mentally defective, of the unconscious or drunken person do have an important bearing upon subsequent imputability for crime. While with reference to all these mental states one can speak of ignorance, at least in a broad sense of the term, still they are factors which offer a special subject for study in themselves and will not be discussed in these pages. Here physical ability to attain knowledge is presupposed and the defective knowledge or ignorance of only such persons is considered as are both habitually and actually able, so far as physical aptitude is concerned, to acquire the necessary knowledge.

3. Degrees of Imputability

The quantity or gravity of a crime and the consequent severity of the penalty depend not only upon the gravity of the law violated and the damage inflicted but also upon the subjective guilt of the individual delinquent.[34] The subjective guilt varies greatly according to the circumstances of each concrete case, which affect the intensity of the anti-juridical will and the consciousness and the knowledge of the delinquent. The Code distinguishes two degrees of imputability, *dolus* and *culpa.*[35] This division of imputability corresponds, in a general way, to the distinction of the *voluntarium* into *voluntarium directum* and *voluntarium indirectum.*[36]

A. *Dolus*

The term *dolus* has a variety of meanings in legal language. In the Roman Law *dolus* was employed in both civil and criminal matters and had a different meaning in each instance.[37] In Canon Law, also, the term *dolus* has several meanings. In other than penal laws *dolus* retains the Roman Law meaning of cunning, deceit and

[34] Canons 2196 and 2218, § 1.

[35] Canon 2199.

[36] Cf. Pistocchi, "Il dolo"—*Mon. Eccl.*, XLVI (1934), 40; Michiels, *De Delictis et Poenis*, I, 101.

[37] Cf. *supra*, pp. 3-7.

deliberate deception.[38] Thus, *dolus* is used to designate a deceitful non-use of a rescript[39] and has about the same meaning as *fraus.*[40] Similarly, *dolus* is employed in the sense of deliberate deceit in regard to various juridical acts.[41] To cite some particular examples, *dolus* with regard to the vote of an elector,[42] the renunciation of an office,[43] and religious profession[44] may be noted.

Even in penal laws the term does not always retain its technical meaning, as defined in canon 2200, § 1. Thus canon 2387 uses the term in defining the crime of a religious who has deliberately and deceitfully entered into an invalid profession. Canon 2353 uses it to describe the deceitful abduction of a woman. The use of *dolus* in the identical meaning as found in canons 52 and 48, § 2, appears also in canon 2361 in its definition of the crimes committed in deceitfully assigning false causes or in omitting necessary facts when applying for a rescript.

The technical definition of *dolus* for the Fifth Book of the Code is found in canon 2200, § 1, viz., *deliberata voluntas violandi legem.* A crime committed with deliberate will to violate a law is called a *delictum dolosum.*

According to the definition, two things are necessary for *dolus* or a *delictum dolosum*: direct will to violate the law and deliberation. For the purposes of this study it is not necessary to dwell upon the nature of the volitional act. It need only be pointed out that a direct will (*voluntarium directum*) to violate the law does not imply a direct intention to commit a crime. It is sufficient that the action by which the law is violated be directly willed, provided one have knowledge that the same is prohibited. For instance, a

[38] Cf. Bieter, "The Canon Law on Deceit"—*ER,* LVI (1922), 42-51; Badii, "Il dolo nel Codice di Diritto Canonico"—*Il Diritto Ecclesiastico,* XL (1929), 305-326.

[39] Canon 48, § 2.

[40] Canon 52.

[41] "Actus positi . . . ex dolo, valent, nisi aliud iure caveatur."—canon 103, § 2.

[42] Canon 169, § 1, n. 1.

[43] Canon 185.

[44] Canon 572, § 1, n. 4.

person need not commit abortion with the specific intention of violating the law; it is enough that he will the abortion, knowing that it is forbidden.[45]

On the part of the intellect, there must be knowledge of the law against which the delinquent offends. It is to be noted that canon 2200, § 1, does not say: *deliberata voluntas violandi legem poenalem,* but simply *deliberata voluntas violandi legem.* Knowledge of the penalty is not necessary for *dolus,* and hence it is possible to have a *delictum dolosum* without any knowledge of the penal character of the violated law. Much less is it necessary for the constitution of *dolus* that one have knowledge of the specific penalty imposed by the law.[46]

It is, however, not sufficient that the delinquent have a habitual knowledge of the law; he must also have actual advertence to the law which is violated and to the fact that the action he is now placing is in reality the one contemplated by the law as a violation. This does not mean that the delinquent must have an explicit consciousness of transgressing the law during the entire duration of the act or acts by means of which he violates the law. This would be necessary for formal *dolus.* It is sufficient to have virtual *dolus,* that is, the delinquent must be aware of his own action and of its anti-juridical character at some time before or during the act of committing the crime. If a man were aware of the law at the time he resolved to commit the crime, or even at any time while he was deliberating upon his course of action, even though he did not actually advert to the fact while he was placing the anti-juridical action, he would still be guilty of a *delictum dolosum.* The knowledge must be had at a time when it can be said to be at least morally connected with the action.

[45] This point is well illustrated in the *dicta* of an American court. "In the popular mind intent and motive are not infrequently regarded as one and the same thing. In law there is a clear distinction between them. Motive is the moving power which impels to action for a definite result. Intent is the purpose to use a particular means to effect such result."—People *v.* Molineux (1901), 61 N. E. 286, 296.

[46] Michiels, *De Delictis et Poenis,* I, 102; Wernz-Vidal, *Ius Canonicum,* VII, 58; *contra* Berutti, *De Delictis et Poenis,* p. 15.

It is not necessary for the purpose of this study to review all the divisions of *dolus* generally given by canonists.[47] The distinction between simple *dolus* and perfect *dolus* is of special importance for the proper understanding of the legal principles regarding the effects of ignorance upon imputability and the knowledge of this distinction is especially necessary for the practical application of these principles to specific laws.

There is a considerable amount of uncertainty about this distinction. The terminology is still in a stage of development; the distinction is not clearly defined; its application to specific laws is not always certain. These points, therefore, merit some attention.

1. The Existence and Nature of the Distinction

In the first place, it is necessary to show that there is really a distinction between *dolus* as defined by canon 2200, § 1, and the *dolus* of canon 2229, which requires *full* knowledge and deliberation. Before the Code the question of *dolus* received comparatively little attention. The distinction between *dolus* and *culpa* was not clearly defined,[48] and hence it is not surprising that no sharply defined distinction was made between *dolus* and perfect *dolus*. The distinction gradually evolved in the doctrine of canonists concerning the excuse of crass and supine ignorance relative to the incurring of censures.[49]

In general, canonists were content simply to make the distinction between penal laws which had such terms as *praesumpserit, scienter, consulto egerit,* and laws which did not have these terms, without defining the nature of the subjective element required by the former.[50] Frequently these terms were interpreted to mean merely that *dolus* was *expressly* required by the particular law which

[47] Cf. Michiels, *De Delictis et Poenis,* I, 103-105; Roberti, *De Delictis et Poenis,* I, 90-91.

[48] Cf. Hinschius, *Kirchenrecht,* V, 921-928.

[49] Cf. *supra,* pp. 72-74.

[50] Cf. Suarez, *De Censuris,* disp. IV, sect. X, nn. 2-3; Sanchez, *De Matrimonio,* lib. IX, disp. XXXII, nn. 35-38; Lehmkuhl, *Theologia Moralis,* II, 621; Wernz, *Ius Decretalium,* VI, 31, note 79.

incorporated one of these terms and consequently that *lata culpa* did not suffice for the penalty imposed by law. Apparently, therefore, no distinction was made between *dolus* in general and the *dolus* stipulated by these laws.[51]

A number of authors seem to have understood these expressions to mean more than that *dolus* was expressly supposed by the law. According to the latter, laws which contained the above mentioned expressions demanded a *voluntarium directum* and *perfectum*[52] or at least required an actual knowledge of fact and of law in order that the penalty be incurred.[53]

Hollweck distinguishes between *dolus* in the strict sense (*Vorsätzlichkeit*) and *dolus* in a broader sense (*Freiwilligkeit*). In the strict sense *dolus* means a greater degree of freedom and a stronger adherence of the will to the forbidden object. Consequently, in order to have strict *dolus* it is necessary that the intellect have ample time to consider the matter and thus form a clear idea of the delict. *Dolus* in the broad sense (*voluntas* and *voluntarie* in the sources) is more than *culpa,* but does not imply any higher degree of guilt.[54]

Substantially this seems to be the doctrine or theory of *dolus* presupposed by the Code. However, the Code does not distinguish between *dolus* in a strict sense and *dolus* in a wider sense; but it does distinguish between *dolus* in general and perfect *dolus. Dolus* is expressly defined in canon 2200, § 1; while perfect *dolus* is nowhere defined but is implied or presupposed in canon 2229, § 2.

A study of the actual use of the words *praesumere, audere, scienter, temerarie,* and others of less frequent use, such as, *de industria, contemnere, sponte, pertinaciter, malitiose,* and *suadente diabolo,* which are now considered as technical terms demanding

[51] Sanchez, *De Matrimonio,* lib. XI, disp. XXXII, n. 35; after the Code, Eichmann, *Lehrbuch des Kirchenrechts* (2. ed., Paderborn: Schöningh, 1926), 670.

[52] Kober, *Der Kirchenbann,* p. 206; Konings, *Theologia Moralis* (4. ed., New York, 1880), II, 311; Gury-Ballerini, *Compendium Theologiae Moralis,* II, 934.

[53] Suarez, *De Censuris,* disp. IV, sect. X, n. 2; Heiner, *Katholisches Kirchenrecht,* II, 86.

[54] *Die kirchlichen Strafgesetze,* note 5 *ad* par. 13, p. 75.

perfect knowledge, points to the conclusion that originally, when the laws were actually written, no special meaning was attached to these expressions. In fact, no less an authority in penal laws than Hollweck points out that until the Constitution *"Apostolicae Sedis"* of Pius IX (1869) these terms had no fixed legal meaning.[55] The most commonly employed terms, viz., *praesumere, audere, scienter* and *temerarie,* occur so frequently in the more important papal decretals and canons of councils that it can scarcely be maintained that these terms were purposely chosen to indicate a special degree of knowledge as a requisite for incurring the threatened penalties.

Some examples will help to illustrate and establish this contention. Familiar to all is the conclusion to the solemn papal bull, in which three of the terms occur:

> Nulli ergo omnino hominum liceat hanc paginam . . . infringere, vel ei ausu temerario contraire. Si quis autem hoc attentare praesumpserit . . .

Praesumere was frequently used at the close of a decree or canon when penalties were threatened for those who would violate the prescriptions of that particular decree or canon.[56] In the same way other expressions, such as *temerarie*[57] and *audere*[58] are sometimes employed, either alone or in various combinations.

[55] *Die kirchlichen Strafgesetze,* note 3 *ad* par. 29, pp. 96-97. The majority of these terms are employed already by the Decretists to express criminal intent or *dolus* in general. An accurate definition of *dolus* is not to be found in the writings of the Decretists. This was to develop chiefly through the discussions on ignorance and error. Cf. Kuttner, *Schuldlehre,* pp. 74-76.

[56] Cf. c. 11, C. XVI, q. 7—c. 7, Conc. Later. I (1123); c. 3, X, *de privilegiis et excessibus privilegiatorum,* V, 33—c. 9, Conc. Later. III (1179); Comp. V, c. 2, *de excessibus praelatorum et subditorum,* V, 10; c. 6, X, *de baptismo et eius effectu,* III, 42—c. 4, Conc. Later. IV (1215); c. 24, X, *de privilegiis et excessibus privilegiatorum,* V, 33—c. 57, Conc. Later. IV; c. un., *de iudaeis et sarracenis,* V, 2 in Clem.; cc. 7, 8, 18, 22, Conc. Later. I—Mansi, XXI, 283-286; cc. 2, 6, 9, 14, 16, 19, 22, 24, 27, Conc. Later. III—Mansi, XXII, 218-233; cc. 29, 31, 32, 33, 34, 37, Conc. Later. IV—Mansi, XXII, 1018-1023.

[57] V. gr., c. 1, *de iudaeis,* V, 2, in Extravag. com.; c. 1, *de sententia excommunicationis, suspensionis et interdicti,* V, 11, in VI°; c. 3, *de poenis,* V, 8, in Clem.; c. un., *de immunitate ecclesiarum,* III, 13, in Extravag. com.

[58] C. 1, *de iudaeis,* V, 2, in Extravag. com.; c. 8, Conc. Constantinop. IV (869-870)—Mansi, XVI, 17.

Often the terms seem simply to have been employed to add solemnity to the decree or canon, to emphasize the gravity of the crime and to point out the seriousness of an abuse prevalent at the particular time when the law was passed. Hence the terms would refer rather to the objective gravity of the crime than to the special degree of subjective imputability required on the part of the delinquent in order to incur the threatened penalty. These reasons seem to explain the frequent appearance of the terms under discussion in connection with such crimes as heresy,[59] simony,[60] abuse or usurpation of authority,[61] violation or disregard for an ecclesiastical penalty,[62] or the violation of the *privilegium canonis.*[63]

[59] Thus, for example, *praesumere* is found in c. 8, X, *de haereticis,* V, 7; Comp. III, c. 1, *de haereticis,* V, 4; c. 11, X, *de haereticis,* V, 7; c. 1, *de haereticis,* V, 3, in Clem.; *audere* in c. 7, *de haereticis,* V, 7, and *temerarie* in c. 12, X, *de haereticis,* V, 7.

[60] V. gr., *praesumere* is used in c. 8, X, *de simonia, et ne aliquid pro spiritualibus exigatur vel promittatur,* V, 3; c. 29, *eod. tit.;* Comp. III, c. 3, *de simonia et ne aliquid pro spiritualibus exigatur vel promittatur,* V, 2; *ausu temerario* in c. 16, X, *de simonia, et ne aliquid pro spiritualibus exigatur vel promittatur,* V, 3.

[61] In this connection *praesumere* is employed in c. 1, X, *de excessibus praelatorum et subditorum,* V, 31; cc. 11, 12, *eod. tit.;* c. 3, *de privilegiis,* V, 7, in Extravag. com.; *temerarie* in c. 1, X, *de clerico non ordinato ministrante,* V, 28; c. 11, X, *de poenis,* V, 37.

[62] In connection with this crime a variety of expressions are to be found, v. gr., *pro ausu tantae temeritatis*—c. 3, X, *de clerico excommunicato, deposito vel interdicto ministrante,* V, 27; *temere violavit . . . non absque praesumptione temeraria*—c. 18, X, *de excessibus praelatorum et subditorum,* V, 31; *temere*—cc. 11, 20, *de privilegiis et excessibus privilegiatorum,* V, 33; *scienter*—c. 8, *de privilegiis,* V, 7, in VI°; *praesumptione damnabili violare praesumunt*—c. 1, *de sententia excommunicationis, suspensionis et interdicti,* V, 10, in Clem.

[63] By way of example the following phrases may be noted: *temerarias manus praesumit iniicere*—c. 24, X, *de sententia excommunicationis,* V, 39; *pro temeraria manuum iniectione*—Comp. II, c. 3, *de sententia excommunicationis,* V, 18; *temerarias manus iniiciunt*—cc. 19, 25, X, *de sententia excommunicationis, suspensionis et interdicti,* V, 39; *quantae praesumptionis et temeritatis exsistat in rectores ecclesiae manus iniicere violentas*—c. 47, X, *de sententia excommunicationis, suspensionis et interdicti,* V, 39; *ausu diabolico*—c. 10, X, *de poenis,* V, 37; *suadente diabolo*—c. 29, C. XVII, q. 4; c. 1, *de poenis,* V, 8, in Clem.

Finally, it might be pointed out that *scienter* is used frequently in reference to crimes in which an error of fact might easily occur.[64]

An important rule of interpretation results from this brief study of the use of the words—now understood to indicate special subjective guilt—in pre-Code law. Although, according to canon 6, nn. 2, 3 and 4, the laws of the Code are to be interpreted according to previous law, it is not a valid argument to appeal to the use of these terms in the former legislation in order to establish that special *dolus* is required in some doubtful case in the Code. The reason is now evident, namely, these words did not always have the meaning given them at the present time. This holds good up to the time of the Constitution "*Apostolicae Sedis*" (1869). It is not to be forgotten, however, that these terms did actually occasion the interpretation now given them.[65] It was this interpretation of individual laws which was adopted by the Code. Hence, a safe guide to pre-Code interpretation is the writings and opinions of the canonists of those times.

The Code clearly makes a distinction between *dolus* in general and the *dolus* stipulated for the incurring of penalties regarding which the law has such terms as *praesumpserit, ausus fuerit,* and the like. Canon 2200, § 1, defines *dolus* as the *deliberata voluntas violandi legem,* while canon 2229, § 2, speaks of a *dolus* in which full knowledge and deliberation is necessary and which is not had when any diminished action either on the part of the intellect or of the will is present. Even culpable ignorance of the penalty alone excludes this form of *dolus.*[66]

This is also the common interpretation of canonists since the Code. In commenting upon canon 2229 they generally point out

[64] Thus, conferring benefice upon censured cleric—c. 7, X, *de clerico excommunicato, deposito vel interdicto ministrante,* V, 27; use of false decretals—c. 11, X, *de excessibus praelatorum et subditorum,* V, 31; c. 1, *de sententia excommunicationis,* V, 10, in Extravag. com.; frequently with regard to forbidden *communicatio*—c. 10, X, *de purgatione canonica,* V, 34; c. 16, C. XI, q. 3; cc. 15, 18, 29, 30, X, *de sententia excommunicationis, suspensionis et interdicti,* V, 39.

[65] Cf. *supra,* p. 52.

[66] Compare canon 2202, § 2, with canon 2229, § 2.

that a special degree of imputability, differing from the *dolus* defined in canon 2200, § 1, is presupposed by the laws which incorporate the terms mentioned in the former canon. Their terminology is, however, not uniform. A variety of terms, expressing about the same idea, are used, v. gr., "special *dolus*" [67] "perfect and full *dolus*," [68] "perfect *dolus*," [69] "*dolus plenissimus*" [70] or "full and perfect responsibility." [71] In the light of what has been said above the last mentioned expression would seem to be the most accurate. However, the term "perfect *dolus*" will be used, since it is sufficiently accurate and is generally used by canonists.[72]

2. Penal Laws Requiring Perfect *Dolus*

For the practical application of the juridical norms regarding ignorance in reference to penal responsibility it is necessary to know which penal laws require perfect *dolus* and which require simple *dolus*. Hence it will be useful to conclude this discussion with an enumeration of those penal canons which demand perfect *dolus* and those which require simple *dolus* in the delinquent for the incurring of the penalties of the law.

First of all, there can be no doubt that perfect *dolus* is presupposed by those canons which have one of the terms expressly enumerated in canon 2229, § 2. *Praesumpserit* is found in the follow-

[67] Vermeersch-Creusen, *Epitome*, III, 219.

[68] Pistocchi, "De subiecto coactivae potestati obnoxio"—*Mon. Eccl.*, XLIX (1937), 206; Wernz-Vidal, *Ius Canonicum*, VII, 214.

[69] Roberti, *De Delictis et Poenis*, I, 276.

[70] De Meester, *Juris Canonici et Juris Canonico-Civilis Compendium* (Brugis, 1921-1928), III, Pars II, 152; Vermeersch-Creusen, *Epitome*, III, 248. Sipos (*Enchiridion*, p. 965) calls it simply *dolus plenus*.

[71] Cance, *Le Code de Droit Canonique* (5. ed., Paris: Librairie Lecoffre, 1930), III, 335; cf. Berutti, *De Delictis et Poenis*, p. 91.

[72] Chelodi (*Ius Poenale*, p. 31, note 5) objects to the use of the term *dolus* in this connection. His reasons are not stated and it is not clear whether he wished to say that the term *dolus*, used alone and without any qualifying adjective, or even with this qualification, is incorrect. *Dolus*, used alone, would certainly be incorrect. But, if the term be used with a distinctive qualification, it is not clear why any objection could be raised against its use in this connection.

ing canons: 1625, § 2; 1755, § 3; 2321; 2338, § 1; 2346; 2347; 2365; 2366; 2369, § 1; 2372; 2388; 2390, § 2; 2393; 2396; 2399; 2400; 2406; 2410; 2412, n. 1. *Scienter* is used in canons 2316; 2318, § 1; 2319, § 1, nn. 3, 4; 2326; 2338, §§ 2, 3; 2347, n. 3; 2360, § 1; 2362; 2368, § 2; 2371; 2390, § 2; 2391, §§ 1, 2, 3; 2395. *Ausus fuerit* occurs a few times, namely, in canons 2337, § 1; 2339; 2341; 2364; 2365; 2375.

The remaining three terms, *studiose, temerarie* and *consulto,* are not found in any of the penal canons of the Code. However, canon 2369, § 2, has a modified form of *temerarie,* namely, *temere.* This term presupposes perfect *dolus.* This is evident also from the fact the first paragraph of the same canon demands perfect *dolus.* This paragraph deals with the direct violation of the seal of confession by the confessor. The second part of the canon concerns the violation of the sacramental seal by others than the confessor, and should consequently presuppose at least the same degree of subjective guilt.[73]

While *studiose* does not occur expressly in any of the penal canons, it might be considered as implied in canons 2371 and 2392, which deal with simony. This crime according to the definition of simony in canon 727 presupposes a *studiosa voluntas.* Canon 2371 offers no difficulty, since it expressly uses the term *scienter,* and therefore demands perfect *dolus.* The omission of any qualifying term in canon 2392 might seem to indicate that perfect *dolus* is not stipulated as a condition for incurring the penalty of the law. However, in accord with pre-Code interpretation [74] it can safely be held that also canon 2392 requires perfect *dolus.*

An accurate determination of similar expressions requiring perfect *dolus* offers some difficulty. There are four terms which canon-

[73] Cf. Moersdorf, *Die Rechtssprache des Codex Iuris Canonici,* p. 374. The terms mentioned in canon 2229, § 2, are the same as those enumerated by Wernz, except that he mentions *temere* instead of *temerarie.—Ius Decretalium,* VI, 31, note 79. Cf. also canon 1625, § 1.

[74] Cf. Santi, *Praelectiones Iuris Canonici* (New York, 1886), lib. V, tit. III, n. 2.

ists generally enumerate, namely, *pertinaciter,*[75] *malitose,*[76] *fraude et dolo,*[77] and *de industria.*[78]

This enumeration seems to have begun with Chelodi and has been adopted by a number of the best canonists. Recently, however, some doubt has been cast upon two of these terms, namely, *de industria* and *fraude et dolo*. Roberti [79] and Moersdorf [80] are of the opinion that *fraude et dolo* and *de industria* are not to be included among the terms which stipulate a special *dolus* but that these demand *dolus* simply to the exclusion of a *delictum culposum*. This would seem to be the more rational opinion. However, on the basis of external authority it can scarcely be denied that the opinion of Chelodi and others is solidly probable.

3. Canons Presupposing *Dolus* to the Exclusion of a *Delictum Culposum*

Some delicts of their very nature or by the express will of the legislator require *dolus,* to the exclusion, therefore, of a *delictum*

[75] This term is found in canons 2317 and 2331; it is implied in canon 2314 in regard to the crime of heresy by reason of the definition given in canon 1325, § 2.

[76] As it is used in canon 2374, but not in canon 2354. *Dolus* is implied in canon 2385 which deals with apostasy from religion. Apostasy is defined in canon 644, § 2, as *malitiosus animus* (*i. e. non redeundi* or *sese religiosae obedientiae subtrahendi*).

[77] Used in canon 2361.

[78] Found in canon 2351. Cf. Chelodi, *Ius Poenale,* p. 31, note 5; Michiels, *Normae Generales* (Lublin: Universitas Catholica, 1929), I, 359; Cappello, *De Sacramentis,* vol. II, *De Poenitentia* (Romae: Marietti, 1938), n. 534, note 12; Wernz-Vidal, *Ius Canonicum,* VII, 214; Salucci, *Il Diritto Penale* (Subiaco: Tipografia dei Monasteri, 1926-1930), I, 143, note 1; Jorio, *Theologia Moralis iuxta Methodum Compendii Ioannis P. Gury, et Raphaelis Tummolo* (6. ed., Neapoli: D'Auria, 1938-1939), II, 251, note 2; Berutti (*De Delictis et Poenis,* p. 91) admits all except *de industria.*

[79] *De Delictis et Poenis,* I, 277.

[80] *Die Rechtssprache des Codex Iuris Canonici,* p. 374, note 18. It may be noted here that Moersdorf holds that *pertinaciter* means the same as *contumaciter* (*op. cit.,* p. 375) and doubts about *malitiose.* Strangely enough, while clearly distinguishing between *dolus* and perfect *dolus* (*op. cit.,* p. 374, note 18) he enumerates expressions which, as will be seen, presuppose only a simple *dolus.*

culposum, but which do not require the perfect *dolus* of the previous group of crimes.

First of all, there is a group of delicts which include the element of *dolus* in their very definition. They require a direct will (*voluntarium directum*) to commit the action and hence cannot eventuate through mere negligence. In this class are the *procurantes abortum,*[81] the *fabricatores* and *falsarii* of papal rescripts and other ecclesiastical documents,[82] the electors who are *sollicitantes immixtionem* of lay power in a canonical election,[83] the *attentantes* of a civil marriage,[84] and the *iniicientes violentas manus* in violation of the *privilegium canonis.*

In regard to the latter crime, a few words of explanation may be in place. The conclusion that the criminal violation of the *privilegium canonis* presupposes *dolus* is based upon the doctrine of canonists before the Code. The Decretists had already arrived at the principle that *dolus* was necessary in this instance because the crime consisted in *violentas manus iniicere.* They applied the Roman Law concept of *iniuria* (contumely) to this crime and adopted many rules contained in the title of the *Digest* entitled: *De iniuriis et famosis libellis* (47, 10). Since the *animus iniuriandi* was considered a necessary element of an *iniuria,* the Decretists concluded that it was impossible to have a criminal violation of the *privilegium canonis* unless the delinquent struck a cleric *sciens, volens* or

[81] Canon 2350. Cf. Brys, "De Poena in Procurantes Abortum"—*Coll. Brug.,* XXXIV (1934), 42-46; Roberti, *De Delictis et Poenis,* I, 277; Cappello, *De Censuris,* p. 334; Eichmann (*Das Strafrecht des Codex Iuris Canonici* [Paderborn: Schöningh, 1920], p. 69) lists *procurare* as demanding the *dolus* spoken of in canon 2229, § 2. Eichmann apparently does not distinguish between *dolus* and perfect *dolus.*

[82] Canons 2360 and 2362. Cf. Cappello, *De Censuris,* p. 255; Eichmann (*loc. cit.*) and Moersdorf (*ibidem,* p. 374) list the above among the crimes which presuppose perfect *dolus.* The latter does so with some hesitation.

[83] Canon 2390, § 2. Moersdorf (*loc. cit.*) considers perfect *dolus* to be understood by this term.

[84] Canon 2356. Cf. Coronata, *Institutiones Iuris Canonici,* IV (Taurini: Marietti, 1935), 489. Moersdorf (*loc. cit.*) understands perfect *dolus* to be implied by this expression. Cf. also canon 2407.

cum dolo. The principle was often expressed by the sentence: *Violentia sine dolo non committitur.*[85]

Because of the famous phrase of the Second Lateran Council (1139), *si quis suadente diabolo,*[86] a dispute arose among later canonists as to whether this was one of the laws which expressly required perfect *dolus.*[87] After the time of Sanchez almost every canonist and moralist who took up the question of crass ignorance in reference to those laws which presuppose perfect *dolus* devoted special attention to this case. The more acceptable opinion seems to have been that the expression, *si quis suadente diabolo,* did not imply perfect *dolus.*[88]

However, the conclusion that *dolus* is necessary for the criminal violation of the *privilegium canonis* was arrived at on other grounds than the above mentioned phrase, namely, because the very concept of an *iniuriosa violatio* presupposes *dolus.* Hence, the fact that the Code in canon 2343 no longer has the phrase, *si quis suadente diabolo,* implies no change in the principle formulated by the Decretists: *Violentia sine dolo non committitur.*[89]

Finally, it seems that *usurpare,*[90] *conspirare,*[91] and *dolose detrectare*[92] can be included in the classification of expressions which presuppose simple *dolus.* For, it is difficult to understand how one could become guilty of the delicts described and defined by these terms through mere negligence or *culpa.*

[85] Cf. Kuttner, *Schuldlehre,* p. 73.

[86] C. 15—Mansi, XXI, 530—c. 29, C. XVII, q. 4.

[87] Cf. Sanchez, *De Matrimonio,* lib. IX, disp. XXXII, n. 41.

[88] Cf. St. Alphonsus, *Theologia Moralis,* lib. VII, cap. II, dub. IV, n. 275.

[89] Cf. D'Annibale, *In Constitutionem Apostolicae Sedis,* p. 74; Eichmann in his review of Kuttner, *Schuldlehre—Zeitschrift d. Savigny-stiftung, kanonistische Abtlg.,* XXV (1936), 515.

[90] Canons 2322, § 2 (*munia sacerdotalia usurpare*) and 2345 (*bona vel iura usurpare*).

[91] Canon 2331, § 2 (*conspirantes contra auctoritatem*).

[92] Canon 2406, § 2. Vermeersch-Creusen (*Epitome,* III, 378) and Beste (*Introductio in Codicem,* p. 972) affirm that merely grave guilt is indicated by the term *dolose.* This acceptation of *dolose* would render its use in the canon meaningless, because grave guilt is always required for delictual imputability. Cf. Ayrinhac-Lydon, *Penal Legislation,* p. 318.

Reference has already been made to a group of expressions which certainly imply *dolus,* but which have been interpreted by the weight of authority as terms which require perfect *dolus.* Upon extrinsic authority these expressions were included among those signifying perfect *dolus.* There is one term, however, which seems definitely to indicate only simple *dolus* and not perfect *dolus.* The term in question is *sponte* which occurs four times in the Fifth Book of the Code. Twice, namely, in canons 2316 and 2388, § 2, it is used together with *scienter.* In these canons, therefore, perfect *dolus* is certainly presupposed. In canons 2390, § 2, and 2339, however, *sponte* is used alone. In these latter cases it indicates simple *dolus.* This is evident from the fact that the Code adds *scienter* when it requires perfect *dolus.* Moreover, *sponte* was frequently used in pre-Code legislation to express a *delictum dolosum,* especially in regard to the crime of homicide.[93] This signification of simple *dolus,* in contradistinction to perfect *dolus,* seems to have been retained by the Code in its use of *sponte.* The very context of both canon 2390 and canon 2339 seem to postulate this interpretation.[94]

B. *Culpa*

1. The Nature of *Culpa*

The second root or source of delictual imputability according to canon 2199 is *culpa.* Consequently, a crime which is imputable because of *culpa* is called a *delictum culposum.* It is the *voluntarium indirectum* or *voluntarium in alio* of penal law. In other words, in a *delictum culposum* the criminal deed is not directly willed, but is the morally imputable result of a voluntary action. It matters not whether the voluntary act from which the delictual fact results be in itself licit or illicit.[95]

[93] Cf. c. 44, D. L: "De his, qui sponte homicidium vel casu faciunt."; c. 13, C. XXIII, q. 5; c. 110, C. XI, q. 3.

[94] Cf. Roberti, *De Delictis et Poenis,* I, 277; Wernz-Vidal, *Ius Canonicum,* VII, 214.

[95] Concerning the historical question of imputability for all objectively criminal acts committed by a person while he is engaged in an illicit action, cf. *supra,* pp. 59-62; Kuttner, *Schuldlehre,* pp. 200-213; Müller, *Ethik und Recht,* pp. 101-117.

Culpa, as a distinct source of delictual liability, was introduced into Canon Law by the Decretists. It is a Roman private law concept which was developed in connection with the enactment of legal sanctions as applied in the case of wrongful damage done to property.[96] Despite the fact that *culpa* in case of wrongful damage deals with civil or private law matters, the Decretists applied the concept to delictual matters.[97]

In Canon Law sources and literature the idea of *culpa* is expressed in various ways. The terms *imperitia, negligentia,*[98] *neglectus,*[99] *incaute*[100] and *incuria*[101] are frequently used to connote the presence of *culpa.*

The foundation or ultimate reason of delictual imputability for *culpa* is the obligation incumbent upon all to see to it that no harm come to the public good from their actions. This is not a positive but a negative obligation and, hence, is binding always, at every moment, upon every individual of society. It is sometimes said that a *delictum culposum* can be committed by omission as well as by commission.[102] However, this must be understood correctly. The act from which the criminal fact, or violation of the law, arises may be an omission or commission. But *culpa* itself is always an omission: namely, the failure to exercise due care, which will generally consist in a culpable failure to foresee the injurious effects of an action.[103] The formal note of *culpa* as a source of delictual liability is the morally imputable absence of due care or negligence. The basis of *culpa* is therefore moral guilt. It cannot be overemphasized that the *culpa,* spoken of in canon 2199, presupposes theologi-

[96] The *Lex Aquilia* or *damnum iniuria datum*—D. (9, 2). Cf. Gaius, *Institutiones,* 3, 211; Instit. (4, 3), 3; D. (9, 2) 5, 1.

[97] Kuttner, *Schuldlehre,* p. 186.

[98] "Si culpa tua datum est damnum vel iniuria irrogata, . . . aut haec imperitia tua sive negligentia evenerit: iure super his satisfacere te oportet."—c. 9, X, *de iniuriis et damno dato* V, 36; c. 111, C. XI, q. 3.

[99] Cf. c. 49, D. L.

[100] C. 8, X, *de homicidio voluntario vel casuali,* V. 12.

[101] C. 1, X, *de custodia Eucharistiae, chrismatis et aliorum sacramentorum,* III, 44; c. 50, D. L.

[102] For example, Roberti, *De Delictis et Poenis,* I, 93.

[103] Sole, *De Delictis et Poenis* (Romae: Pustet, 1920), p. 16.

cal or moral guilt and not mere juridical guilt. In civil law systems, and to some extent in Canon Law before the Code, this is not always clear. Pre-Code authors must, consequently, be read with care, because they often used the term *culpa* in the sense of juridical imputability in contrast to *dolus,* which latter included every form of moral imputability not excluding *culpa* in the sense explained above.[104]

Finally, it should be noted here that even the Code does not always employ the term *culpa* in the sense described above. Attention was called to this fact in the discussion on imputability in general. It was pointed out that *culpa, culpabilis* and *culpabilitas* are frequently used in the Code in the sense of imputability in general and not with the connotation of a specific form of imputability.

2. *Culpa* and Related Concepts

A comparison of *culpa* with related concepts will serve to ascertain its nature more clearly and exactly. In the first place, attention should be called to the fact that a *delictum culposum* is not the same as a crime of negligence. The latter consists in a failure to perform some specific duty imposed by law or precept under penalty. A crime of omission or the failure to perform a positive duty can be either *dolosum* or *culposum.* In a word, the negligence from which a crime results is not the same as a crime of negligence.[105]

There are numerous examples of crimes of omission or negligence in the Code. In these cases the crime itself does not result from neglect, but the neglect is itself the crime punishable with canonical penalties. The last four titles of the Code deal with a number of crimes of negligence. In these titles penal sanctions are

[104] Jorio, *Compendium Theologiae Moralis,* II, 239, n. 1.

[105] Cf. Moersdorf, *Die Rechtssprache des Codex Iuris Canonici,* p. 375; Latini, *Iuris Criminalis Philosophici Summa Lineamenta,* p. 81; Michiels, *De Delictis et Poenis,* I, 67-68. An instance of a *delictum dolosum* of negligence would be the following: "Quodsi forte in praedicationibus hoc ipsum supra dictis diebus suadere scienter omiserint [*i.e.,* the *solutio* decimarum] . . .—c. 3, *de poenis,* V, 8, in Clem.

enacted against the transgression of positive duties in the administration of the sacraments, or against the violation of duties imposed by one's state of life and by one's tenure of office or position of authority. For example, canon 2378 makes the grave neglect of compliance with the prescribed rites and ceremonies a crime; canon 2382 makes neglect of parochial duties punishable; and culpable neglect to make the profession of faith is punishable according to canon 2403.[106]

Since *culpa* holds a middle position between *dolus* and *casus* it may prove instructive to examine its relationship to both of these concepts. In *dolus* the criminal result is both foreseen and directly willed. In *culpa* the effect is never directly willed; it is either foreseen and, in consequence, culpably permitted, because of a failure in the duty to prevent a foreseen criminal effect; or it is due to negligence in not foreseeing the violation of a law, whether it be that the law remains unknown to the person or that the effects of his actions are not properly weighed by him. If there is no moral guilt either in not preventing the injurious or anti-juridical effect or in not foreseeing the effect there is *casus* or accident in the juridical sense of the word.[107]

Finally, a *delictum culposum* must not be confounded with a *conatus delicti* or a criminal attempt. Both are, indeed, imperfect crimes but under different aspects. A criminal attempt is an imperfect crime because the objective element is deficient; a *delictum culposum* is imperfect in the sense that the subjective element (imputability) is not complete or perfect.[108]

A *conatus delicti* is complete so far as the subjective element is concerned. From a theoretical point of view it is at least possible to have an attempted crime through negligence. Thus, a man may negligently place an action which of its very nature leads to homicide. Yet, either because he changes his mind, or because the in-

[106] For other examples, see canons 2383, 2384, 2398, 2376. The distinction is not always kept in mind by canonists. Cf. v. gr., Wernz, *Ius Decretalium,* VI, 33.

[107] Canon 2203, § 2.

[108] Cf. canon 2212, § 1; Hennemann, *Der Versuch im kirchlichen Strafrecht* (Limburg: Vereinsdruckerei, 1930), pp. 18-26.

strumentality used is not sufficient, the homicide does not actually follow.[109]

According to the Code it seems that a *conatus delicti* can only be a crime *ex dolo* and not *ex culpa* or negligence. As Hennemann [110] points out, the Code in defining *conatus delicti* presupposes a plan (*consilium*) on the part of the delinquent.[111] But a plan, or a purposeful choice of means to an end, presupposes *dolus*, because no one deliberately chooses means to an end which he does not intend. Hence, a *conatus delicti* according to the law of the Code cannot be the result of negligence or ignorance. It is true that the insufficiency or ineptitude of means spoken of by canon 2212, § 1, may be due to ignorance. But the end or the purpose for which the means are employed (namely the delict) must be known and intended.[112]

3. The Necessary Requisites of *Culpa*

From the previous considerations it follows that in order to have imputability on account of *culpa*, two obligations must exist simultaneously. First there must be the duty to foresee or to know (both the law and the facts constituting the crime) and secondly there must be present the duty to prevent the criminal results. If one of these duties is lacking there can be no imputability for *culpa*. Thus, there is no duty to foresee an effect whose very existence and possibility is not so much as suspected, and hence there can be no *culpa* in such an absence of foresight. Again, a criminal effect may be foreseen when one has no duty to prevent it. In this case a man is acting within his rights if he remains passive and there can be no imputability attaching to his lack of intervention to stave off the criminal effect. Thus, if a religious who has no authority sees the law of enclosure violated, he does not commit a crime if he does not

[109] Latini (*Iuris Criminalis Philosophici Summa Lineamenta*, p. 81) goes so far as to consider *conatus delicti* and *delictum culposum* mutually contradictory.

[110] *Op. cit.*, p. 27.

[111] ". . . delictum non consummaverit, . . . quia consilium suum deseruit, . . ."—canon 2212, § 1.

[112] Cf. Michiels, *De Delictis et Poenis*, I, 260; *contra* Noval, "De conatu delicti et eius punitione iuxta Codicem I. C."—*Jus Pont.*, IX (1929), 124.

prevent the imminent violation, even though he could easily or readily do so.

When both of these duties are present at the same time, and only when they are present together, can there be a possibility of a *delictum ex culpa*. The criminal imputability for the effect follows as soon as one of these duties is violated.[113]

Some authors include a third condition, namely, that the effect must be contrary to the dispositions of the law. While this is certainly a necessary condition for the constitution of a *delictum culposum* (because it is an essential element of every delict), it has nothing to do with the subjective element. Insistence upon this condition can imply nothing more than a simple restatement of the necessary inherence of the objective element for every delict, which, of course, here and elsewhere, is always presupposed.[114]

4. The Source and Degrees of *Culpa*

Canon 2199 distinguishes two sources or reasons for criminal imputability which results from *culpa*. The first is the morally imputable violation of the universal obligation to know the law. The neglect of this obligation and the consequent ignorance forms one of the main objects of this study. The second ground for imputability *ex culpa* is the culpable violation of the duty to refrain from injury to society by neglect. Neglect of due care may consist either in not foreseeing (or knowing) the results of an action, or in not preventing them, when there is both the moral possibility and the moral obligation to do so.

For the purposes of this study one important fact must be stressed: the Code does not identify ignorance of law and ignorance of fact. This is evident from the definition of *culpa* itself in

[113] Cf. Michiels, *De Delictis et Poenis*, I, 106; Wernz, *Ius Decretalium*, VI, 33.

[114] V. gr., Wernz-Vidal, *Ius Canonicum*, VII, 62-63; Pistocchi, "La colpa nella imputabilità del delitto"—*Mon. Eccl.*, XLVII (1935), 28. The latter seems to imply that the action from which the criminal effect flows must in itself be contrary to law. The action, on the contrary, need not in itself be illicit. It is sufficient that the action become illicit because of the anti-juridical effect which flows from it.

canon 2199. This point will be discussed again in connection with the general rules touching on ignorance of fact and on ignorance of law. In canon 2202 ignorance of law is made a separate and distinct source of imputability. The canon speaks only of ignorance of law and therefore excludes ignorance of fact in this first source of imputability for *culpa*. Ignorance of fact is included in the general phrase "*omissio debitae diligentiae*," because due care or *diligentia debita* includes a double obligation; the duty to prevent harm by carefully foreseeing (or knowing) the results of an action; and, the duty to prevent, as far as this is possible and obligatory, a foreseen (or known) injury from going into effect. The reason why ignorance of law is brought under a separate category will be seen later on.

A *delictum culposum* may, therefore, arise because of *culpa* in the ignorance of the law and because of negligence in foreseeing the criminal effects of an action or in preventing foreseen criminal effects. The latter two forms of *culpa* constitute a quasi-delict in the strict sense of the word according to the doctrine before the Code.[115] The Code does not employ either the phrase *delictum culposum* or the term *quasi-delictum*. As is evident, the term *quasi-delictum* does not include a *delictum ex culpa in ignorantia legis* and, therefore, is not as broad a term as a *delictum culposum*. The latter includes all forms of delict imputable on account of *culpa*. It is evident from the definition of a delict[116] and from the definition of imputability[117] that a *delictum culposum* is a delict in the strict sense of the word.[118]

[115] Cf. Wernz-Vidal, *Ius Canonicum*, VII, 65.

[116] Canon 2195.

[117] Canon 2199.

[118] Within recent years German criminologists have devised an apt terminology to express the different sources of *culpa*. Thus, *culpa* because of ignorance of law is called by them *Rechtsfahrlaessigkeit*, and *culpa* because of negligence in regard to the facts of the case is termed *Tatssachenfahrlaessigkeit*. Moersdorf (*Rechtssprache des Codex Iuris Canonici*, p. 375, note 21) attributes the origin of this terminology to Beling and notes that it was introduced into Canon Law by Reinhard Frank in his "Ueber das Strafrecht des Codex Iuris Canonici"—*Archiv f. Strafrecht*, LXV (1918), 406. Other canonists have adopted the terminology. Moersdorf in addition (*loc. cit.*) notes Heimberger ("Die Schuld im Strafrecht des Codex Iuris Canonici" — Festgabe für G.

Canonists generally distinguish three degrees of *culpa*: *lata, levis* and *levissima*. This is a very old division of *culpa*, which was introduced from Roman Law into Canon Law by the Decretists. The distinctions developed in the commentaries of the Roman jurists upon two important *leges*: the *Lex Aquilia de damno iniuria dato* (wrongful damage to property) and the *Lex Cornelia de sicariis*. The distinction is found substantially in the *Digest*, which speaks of *levissima culpa*,[119] *culpa* [120] and *lata culpa*.[121] The similarity of the subject matter in the two above mentioned *leges* to canons 48, 49, 50, of Distinction 50 in the *Decretum Gratiani* led to the early introduction of these divisions into Canon Law.[122] The distinction is found in the first commentaries on the Decretum [123] and is used by canonists up to the present day.

For the purposes of this work it is sufficient to note that there are no hard and fast definitions of these three degrees of *culpa* and consequently their practical application is not determined by any inviolable rule. The latter is a matter rather for the judge to de-

Aschaffenburg, *Monatsschrift f. Kriminalpsychologie und Strafrechtsreform* [Heidelberg, 1926], Beiheft, I, p. 12). Michiels (*De Delictis et Poenis*, I, 107) also uses these terms. It is difficult to translate these terms into English, though *juridical* and *factual* negligence, respectively, may render the idea to some extent.

119 "In lege Aquilia et levissima culpa venit."—D. (9, 2) 44, *pr*.

120 "Praeceptores enim nimia saevitia culpae adsignatur."—D. (9, 2) 6; D. (9, 2) 10.

121 "In lege Cornelia dolus pro facto accipitur. Neque in hac lege culpa lata pro dolo accipitur."—D. (48, 8) 7; "Latae culpae finis est non intelligere id quod omnes intelligunt."—D. (50, 16) 223, *pr*.; cf. D. (50, 16) 226; C. (5, 51) 7. Concerning the controversy about the concept and degrees of *culpa* in classical Roman Law, see Lenel, "Culpa lata und culpa levis"—*Zeitschrift d. Savigny-Stiftung, Roman. Abtlg.*, XXXVIII (1917), 263-290; Binding, "Culpa, Culpa lata und culpa levis"—*op. cit.*, XXXIX (1918), 1-35. Without entering upon a technical consideration of *culpa* in Roman Law, it is sufficient to note that in the *Digest culpa* has the meaning of negligence and that possibly two degrees of negligence are distinguished; namely, ordinary negligence (*culpa levis*) and extraordinary or crass negligence (*culpa lata*).

122 Kuttner, *Schuldlehre*, pp. 214-215.

123 V. gr., *Summa Bambergensis ad* c. 50, D. L.—Kuttner, *Schuldlehre*, pp. 219-220, note 5.

termine in each concrete case than for exact definition. D'Annibale gives this description of the three degrees of *culpa*: "Et metitur, quasi e contrario, ex diligentia quam paterfamilias vel prudentissimus, vel solers, vel etiam desidiosus adhibet suis rebus. Itaque illius diligentiae deesse *levissima* culpa est, istius *levis,* huius *lata.*" [124]

Of greater practical value is the application of this ancient canonical doctrine to the present law of the Code. *Culpa levissima* does not fall under the scope of penal law at all. According to the clear provisions of the Code, a crime must not only be morally imputable, but it must be a matter of grave moral guilt. Whatever, therefore, excuses from serious moral guilt simultaneously excludes criminal imputability. As a result, *culpa levissima* is not considered sufficient for the juridical imputability of crime and for the fixing of responsibility relative to any strictly canonical penalty.[125]

Culpa levis is in reality the only degree of *culpa* known to the Code. This degree of imputability is understood when the Code speaks of *culpa.* It is unnecessary to note that *levis* in this connection does not mean slight or venial moral guilt. *Culpa levis* is here taken in a juridical sense, but presupposes grave moral guilt.[126]

Culpa lata is the degree of imputability described by the Code as "*culpa dolo proxima.*" [127] According to the evident wording of the Code in defining *culpa lata* or *culpa dolo proxima,* it can be had in but one of the three cases of *delicta culposa* described above: namely, when the law is known and the effects of one's action are known or foreseen, and when no diligence, or at least not that diligence which every prudent man would use (ordinary diligence), has been employed to prevent the criminal effects of the action. This ex-

[124] *Summula Theologiae Moralis,* I, 285, note 13.

[125] Canon 2218, § 2; cf. Michiels, *De Delictis et Poenis,* I, 105.

[126] There is a certain amount of flexibility in the use of these terms. What is described in the above text as *culpa levis* may be considered *culpa lata.* The *culpa dolo proxima* mentioned in canon 2203, § 2, would then be considered distinct from *culpa lata.*

[127] Canon 2203, § 2.

cludes every case of ignorance, be it of law or of fact, from being considered *culpa dolo proxima*.[128]

5. Conclusion

The imputability of a delict committed *ex culpa* can be expressed in two general principles. The first is: *culpa* is always a sufficient basis for delictual imputability. This principle does not contradict what has been said above[129] concerning those laws which require *dolus* or perfect *dolus* to the exclusion of *culpa*. In those cases the law demands *dolus* for a determined criminal responsibility, namely, in order that the delinquent be held liable for the penalty specified in the law.[130] The law does not thereby make an exception to the rule of penal imputability stated in canon 2199 and thus provide that in that instance the delictual fact is not imputable. The objective violation of the law is imputable, even criminally, but not in a sufficient degree to entail the application of the penalty determined by the particular law.[131]

However, because the law sometimes presupposes *dolus* for the incurring of a penalty, some authors deny the universal imputability of *culpa*, or rather of a delict committed *ex culpa*.[132] This

[128] Cf. Sole, *De Delictis et Poenis*, pp. 16-17; Pistocchi, "La colpa nella imputabilità del delitto"—*Mon. Eccl.*, XLVII (1935), 28-29; Roberti, *De Delictis et Poenis*, I, 94. Berutti (*De Delictis et Poenis*, p. 16) distinguishes *dolus* and *culpa dolo proxima* precisely in the fact that in the former the violation of the penal law is *certainly* known, while in the latter the violation is only *probably* foreseen. This does not seem to be the distinguishing characteristic of *culpa dolo proxima*, because canon 2203, § 1, states simply "quod si rem praeviderit" without any qualification. To read *probabiliter* into the phrase is hardly permissible. The element of imputability which is lacking to make the *culpa dolo proxima* the practical equivalent of *dolus* is the direct and deliberate will to violate the law. The elements superadded to ordinary *culpa* consist in the certain knowledge of the imminent criminal effect which follows and in the lack of even ordinary diligence to prevent an unmistakably foreseen harm.

[129] *Supra*, pp. 92-99.

[130] Canon 2228.

[131] Cf. Michiels, *De Delictis et Poenis*, I, 112-113; Coronata, *Institutiones Iuris Canonici*, IV, 26-28.

[132] This is the opinion of Moersdorf (*Rechtssprache des Codex Iuris Ca-

question may be viewed from two different angles: (1) from the standpoint of the general principles of imputability, and (2) as a matter of the interpretation of a given individual law. Under the latter aspect, it may be said that the law is in reality not violated according to its strict wording and, therefore, there is no delictual imputability under this particular law. This is true and must be admitted. However, the opinion expressed above does seem to be the more logical. To say that the objective criminal fact (presumed to be completely consummated) is not imputable at all seems to be closing one's eyes to obvious facts. The objective violation of the law is imputable, even criminally imputable, although a defect in the subjective element presupposed by the individual law bars the application of the specific penalties provided in that law.

The two opinions arrive at about the same practical result. One difference may, however, be noted. It is that the opinion adopted in these pages leaves the way open for the application of canon 2222, § 1, while the other opinion, to be logical, would have to deny this application. When a law demands *dolus* or perfect *dolus,* and this law has been violated *ex culpa,* the delinquent can rightly maintain that the transgression of which he was guilty had no penal sanction. In this case the superior could still punish with a just penalty in cases of grave scandal or of special gravity of the violation. This is both equitable and warranted by the similar provision of canon 2229, § 4. However, the infliction of a penalty would be impossible if it must be admitted that there was no delictual imputability inherent in the act.[133]

The second principle in regard to delictual imputability and penal responsibility for *culpa* is: A *delictum culposum* is to be punished according to the degree of moral or subjective guilt. Imputability and consequent responsibility for penalty is always less than it would have been had the crime been committed with *dolus.*[134]

nonici, p. 376) who cites Heimberger ("Die Schuld in Strafrecht des Codex Iuris Canonici," *op. cit.,* p. 16) for his view.

[133] Canon 2218, § 2.

[134] If the *culpa* is *proxima dolo* there cannot be much difference. Cf. canon 2203, § 1.

The measure of guilt and consequent penalty is to be determined in each concrete case by the prudence of the judge. In those cases wherein there is no judge to pronounce a mitigated sentence, namely, in cases of *latae sententiae* penalties, the law makes special provisions to protect the individual against a penalty out of proportion with his subjective guilt.[135]

[135] Cf. canons 2203 and 2229.

CHAPTER VI

THE NATURE AND THE DIVISIONS OF IGNORANCE

Before beginning this chapter one may usefully explain the purpose and plan of its two articles. The purpose is to arrive at an exact definition of ignorance and also of those specific kinds of ignorance of which mention is made in the Code. The first article treats of the nature of ignorance in general. It presents an analysis of the various definitions of ignorance and aims to derive therefrom a definition best suited for the proper understanding of the penal law of the Code.

The second article has been divided into two distinct parts. The plan is the same as in the first article. Hence, in the first part, the numerous divisions of ignorance devised by canonists as well as moralists are proposed and reviewed. Not all the divisions are considered, but only those which will serve a useful purpose in penal law and those which serve to illuminate and illustrate those divisions which have been incorporated in the Code. The second part of the article deals specifically with those divisions which are found in the Code. The aim of this section will be to determine as exactly as possible what the Code understands by those species of ignorance which it uses in penal law.

It is scarcely necessary to recall that the Code does not define either ignorance or any of the species of ignorance which it has appropriated from the writings of canonists. These definitions must therefore be sought in the doctrine of canonists. To arrive at an accurate determination of the mind of the legislator on these points the works of canonists before, and especially at the time of, the codification must be studied. This does not mean that canonists who have written after the Code can be neglected. The Code, by not providing authoritative definitions, left the way open for development and progress toward a more perfect doctrinal basis upon which criminal imputability is to be determined. In the historical section it was shown that this was the principal way in which the legal norms were developed and the Church has been content to lay down only a few authoritative norms to guide the future progress toward a more perfect system of juridical rules for determining the imputability of delicts committed in ignorance.

Article I. The Nature of Ignorance

Ignorance, from the Latin *ignorare* (=ἄγνοια, from α + γνο, meaning want of perception, ignorance) signifies a lack of knowledge. In a broad sense it means any absence or negation of knowledge. Thus, in the loose sense, a nonintellectual being might be said to be ignorant. But this is a mere negation of something which cannot be predicated of the being at all. Ignorance in the proper sense of the term is the lack (*carentia* or *privatio*) of something which ought to be possessed by the mind. Therefore, only an intellectual being can be ignorant, because it alone possesses not only the possibility but also the positive aptitude for knowing. Knowledge is a perfection of being which by nature should be present in a human individual. Hence, to be ignorant is to lack something which should naturally be possessed. However, the "should" must be understood in the sense of a natural perfection and not in the sense of a moral perfection or of a moral obligation. Consequently ignorance is defined as the privation of knowledge in a subject naturally capable of and constituted for knowledge.[1] A great number of authors, in order to bring out the idea that ignorance is a privation and not a simple negation, define ignorance as the lack of knowledge which one can and should have.[2]

[1] " . . . ignorantia . . . importat scientiae privationem, dum scilicet alicui deest scientia eorum, quae aptus natus est scire."—St. Thomas, *Summa,* I-II, q. 76, art. 2. Cf. Passerinus, *Commentaria in Sextum Librum,* lib. I, tit. II, cap. II, q. I, art. 1; Brys, "De ignorantia ejusque influxu in actum humanum" —*Coll. Brug.,* XXX (1930), 117; Vermeersch, *Theologiae Moralis Principia* (3. ed., Romae: Universitas Gregoriana, 1933-1937), I, 72; Wernz-Vidal, *Ius Canonicum,* VII, 91; Ferreres, *Institutiones Canonicae* (Barcinone: Subirana, 1920), II, 414.

[2] This definition is also based upon St. Thomas. Cf. *De Malo,* q. 8, art. 1, *ad* 7. Numerous modern authors adopt this definition; v. gr., Ojetti, *Commentarium in Codicem Iuris Canonici* (Romae: Universitas Gregoriana, 1927-1931), I, 127; Blat, *Commentarium Textus Codicis Iuris Canonici,* lib. V, *De Delictis et Poenis* (Romae: Collegio Angelico, 1924), p. 72; Michiels, *Normae Generales,* I, 348; Sole, *De Delictis et Poenis,* p. 21.

The latter definition, while capable of a correct explanation, is less clear for the reason that it is apt to give the impression that ignorance in the strict sense is a lack of that knowledge which one can and is obliged to have. This is not entirely true, because such a definition would not be comprehensive. It excludes all inculpable ignorance, or at least inclines one to consider such ignorance as improperly included in the universal concept. It is capable of a correct interpretation, however, and its proponents explain that the *debet* does not imply a moral obligation, but merely a perfection which should be present *ratione naturae*.[3]

Since the first definition contains all the necessary elements of ignorance and is clear in itself it should be preferred. It is to be noted that the definition speaks only of a subject capable of acquiring knowledge. This means that he not only has the necessary faculty to do so, but that this faculty is habitually and actually capable of acquiring knowledge. Hence, an insane person is improperly said to be ignorant. His imputability is not determined according to the norms for ignorance, but according to special rules.[4] The same holds good for infants in view of their intellectual inability,[5] and for those who act under the influence of intoxicating drink[6] or of passion.[7]

Knowledge and ignorance mutually exclude each other. They are mutually contradictory, that is, they cannot exist in the same subject, at the same time and under the same aspect. The most complete ignorance is that in which the individual has never become aware of the truth at all. The opposite of this is certitude, or the firm assent of the mind to a true proposition. Error may also be a firm assent of the mind, but it differs from certitude in that it is assent to a false proposition. Knowledge and ignorance, on the other hand, can coexist in the same subject relative to the same truth but viewed under different aspects. An object may be partially known and partially unknown. Hence, between the extremes of cer-

[3] Cf. Passerinus, *Commentarium in Sextum Librum*, lib. I, tit. II, cap. II, q. I, art. 1.

[4] Canon 2201, §§ 1, 2, 4.

[5] Canon 2201; and minors—canon 2204.

[6] Canon 2201, § 3.

[7] Canon 2206.

tain assent to truth and complete lack of even the first perception of the truth there are a number of mental states ranging from moral certainty, probability and positive doubt to negative doubt and mere suspicion.

The philosopher finds great differences in these mental states. Psychologically considered only the complete lack of knowledge can be defined as ignorance. The mind is inactive when it is ignorant. In suspicion, opinion and doubt the mind is active; it gives its assent or makes a judgment. Due, however, to lack of complete knowledge the mind is unable to give a firm assent. In suspicion, the mind gives assent, but only with the highest degree of hesitation, fearing that because of its ignorance the opposite of the proposition may be true. In opinion, the mind has sufficient knowledge upon which to base a reasonable judgment, but it does so not without fear of error. In doubt, the mind is wavering between more or less evenly balanced reasons for assent to both sides of a proposition. In the positive doubt there still remains a good reason which would deter a prudent man from giving firm assent. If the motives for assent reach that degree of probability which would justify a prudent man in giving assent to the proposition the mind is said to have moral certainty.[8]

As far as moral imputability is concerned, these mental states must be judged according to the norms given under the general heading of ignorance. In fact, as will be seen in the consideration of the divisions of ignorance, it is impossible to have any form of culpable ignorance without some suspicion, doubt or opinion in the mind concerning the truth which is not known. Ignorance is really the cause of these mental states; for it alone, barring bad faith and prejudice, stands between the mind and firm assent to truth. In practice it very frequently happens that the term "ignorance" is applied to subjective states of mind which strictly considered are

[8] Cf. St. Thomas, *Summa*, II-II, q. 2, art. 1. For a more complete treatment of this subject consult the works of Moral Theologians, v. gr., Noldin-Schmitt, *Summa Theologiae Moralis*, I, *De Principiis* (26. ed., Oeniponte: Rauch, 1939), pp. 219-226.

nothing else than suspicion, doubt or opinion. By metonomy all these are classified under the general term "ignorance." [9]

In order to avoid misunderstanding, it may be necessary to add a few remarks about doubt. In this study doubt is considered only in its relation to imputability and, as has been pointed out, is frequently associated with ignorance and at times identified with it.[10] From this it must not be concluded that ignorance and doubt can always be identified or that the two are always used in the same way in the Code. Thus, the *dubium iuris* and the *dubium facti* of canon 209 are not mere subjective doubts, but demand some objective support in fact. To borrow the words of Miaskiewicz: "Positive and probable doubt postulates more than subjective certitude. It demands, in addition, at least some objective evidence to support and to justify the subjective belief in the existence of the jurisdictional power about which there is question." [11] As is at once evident, the doubt in this sense differs fundamentally from the purely subjective doubt which is sometimes identified with ignorance. A positive and probable doubt, based upon objective reasons, would not only excuse from imputability, but would destroy the very binding force of a penal law.

While the terminology, a *doubt of law* or a *doubt of fact,* may in itself be correctly employed in reference to criminal imputability,

[9] Cf. Passerinus, *Commentaria in Sextum Librum,* lib. I, tit. II, cap. II, q. I, art. 1, n. 60; Romani, "De ignorantia iuris"—*Acta Congressus Internat.,* IV, 81.

[10] " . . . qui dubitat de aliquo de quo debet esse certus, potius dicitur illud ignorare quam scire. . . ."—St. Bonaventure, *Commentaria in IV Libros Sententiarum* (ed. minor, Ad Claras Aquas: Typographia Collegii S. Bonaventurae, 1934-1938), lib. II, dist. XXII, art. 2. Coronata (*Institutiones Iuris Canonici,* I [2. ed., Taurini: Marietti, 1939], p. 42) goes so far as to define ignorance in general as: "status mentis inter duo contraria haerentis ancipitis." While this can scarcely be considered universally true of all forms of ignorance, it shows that ignorance and doubt do have much in common. A negative doubt is in reality little more than ignorance. However, the definition of Coronata does not include total or complete ignorance which is present when a person does not even advert to the truth.

[11] *Supplied Jurisdiction according to Canon 209,* The Catholic University of America, Canon Law Studies, no. 122 (Washington: The Catholic University of America Press, 1940), p. 312, Conclusion 11; cf. also, *ibid.,* 176-220.

it is not only contrary to general usage to do so but can very easily lead to serious confusion. One instance has already been mentioned. Two other cases may be cited in which doubt is used in the sense of an objective doubt, that is, a doubt based upon reasons external to the mind of the individual subject and affecting even those who know the law. The two instances referred to are found in canon 15 and canon 2245, § 4. The latter is merely a specific application of canon 15. It would be wrong, for example, to identify the doubt of law and the doubt of fact considered in canon 15 with the ignorance of law and ignorance of fact mentioned in canon 16 and in the Fifth Book of the Code in general. The doubt referred to in canon 15, as well as in canon 2245, § 4, is an objective doubt in the sense that the law itself is unclear or that the fact from an objective viewpoint is not envisioned as being clearly within the scope of the law.[12] In the case of a doubt of law in this sense the penal law has no recognized existence at all, precisely in view of the existing status of doubt.[13] In case of an objective doubt of fact the penal law cannot be urged, because penal laws must be interpreted strictly [14] and a penalty cannot be incurred or inflicted unless the penal law has certainly been violated.[15] Hence, when Berutti [16] and Michiels [17] in interpreting these canons speak of "an excuse from delictual imputability," they are using "excuse" in a rather broad meaning, because there can hardly be an excuse from an obligation which does not objectively exist.

In this work the only doubt considered is the subjective doubt on the part of the individual delinquent, and for this case the same principles obtain as those which are applied in the case of a violation of the law through ignorance.[18]

[12] Cf. Cicognani, *Ius Canonicum, Commentarium ad Librum I Codicis,* II (Romae, 1925), 107-108.

[13] "Leges, . . . in dubio iuris non urgent . . . "—canon 15.

[14] Cf. canons 19; 2219, § 1; Reg. 15, *R. J.*, in VI°.

[15] This is often stated in the Code, cf., v. gr., canons 2228; 2233, § 1; 1933, § 4; 1939, § 1; 2190; S. R. R., *In Recentiores,* Decis. 274, n. 16.

[16] *De Delictis et Poenis,* p. 19.

[17] *De Delictis et Poenis,* I, 193.

[18] Cf. Perathoner, "Forum internum und Forum externum im kirchlichen Strafrechte"—*LQS,* LXX (1917), 451.

The doubt which is the immediate concern of this study is one, moreover, which exists in the mind of the delinquent before or at the time of the criminal act and not one which occurs after the act is completed. The former alone can influence the imputability of the delinquent.[19]

But ignorance does not always result in merely a less firm assent of the mind to a true proposition. Sometimes it gives rise to a positive denial of truth. This is error or false judgment. There is a great difference between ignorance and error; the former is the mere negation of knowledge while the latter implies positive assent of the mind to a proposition which is contrary to objective truth.[20] Error is always the result of ignorance, except in those cases wherein the mind is influenced by passion or prejudice.[21]

In considering the effect of error upon imputability the canonist rightly identifies error and ignorance because the two are generally found together. Error cannot exist without ignorance. Ignorance is in itself a non-entity and can be the cause of human acts only as a *causa removens prohibens,* that is, it takes away that (namely, knowledge) which would impede the illicit act. Not ignorance as such, but error which is ignorance in action [22] can positively influence human conduct. Hence, in the great majority of cases in which

[19] A common example of a doubt occurring after the commission of the crime is that regarding the question of incurring a *latae sententiae* penalty. In this case, namely, when there is a probable and positive doubt as to whether the penalty has been incurred, the doubt must be resolved in favor of the penitent. Cf. "Re-Examining a Doubtful Censure"—*ER,* LXXXVII (1932), 422-423; Miaskiewicz, *Supplied Jurisdiction according to Canon 209,* pp. 217-218.

[20] The distinction is very old. St. Augustine noted it when he wrote: " . . . non tamen est consequens ut continuo erret quisquis aliquid nescit, sed quisquis se existimat scire quod nescit. pro vero quippe approbat falsum, quod est erroris proprium."—*Enchiridion ad Laurentium,* c. 17—*MPL,* XL, 239—c. 11, D. XXXVIII. Cf. Alexander of Hales, *Summa Theologica,* lib. II, P. II, inq. III, tract. I, sect. I, q. II, tit. I, c. 3.

[21] "Ignorantia mater est erroris . . . ".—Maroto, *Institutiones Iuris Canonici,* I (3. ed., Romae: apud *Commentarium pro Religiosis,* 1921), 465; Cicognani, *Jus Canonicum,* II, 113.

[22] Toso, "De Errore Communi"—*Jus Pont.,* III (1923), 150.

moralists and canonists speak of "ignorance" in relation to imputability they are really referring to error in the proper sense of the term. When it is said that an act was performed because of ignorance, what is really meant is that the act resulted from error. There was present at least this implicit error or false judgment: In this case there is no law forbidding or commanding the act. Or, to take a concrete case, which is very often cited as an example of ignorance of fact: A hunter shoots at an object which he believes is an animal. Later on, however, the hunter discovers that the object was in reality a human being. This is a case of an error resulting from ignorance, for the hunter, not knowing the facts, was led to the erroneous conclusion: The object at which I am shooting is an animal.

By common usage the term "ignorance" has acquired a wider meaning in Canon Law than its strict philosophical definition would admit. There is no reason to find fault with this use of the term, because in the final analysis ignorance is the more fundamental notion and the source of all error.[23] For the practical purposes of this study on imputability the two concepts will generally not be sharply distinguished. In fact, ignorance may be said to be the technical term used to designate both ignorance and error. At any event, both ignorance and error are to be governed by the same principles.[24]

By way of illustration it may be pointed out, that the distinction between error and ignorance is generally considered immaterial by the American criminal courts. Professor Keedy in an article appearing some thirty years ago defended a distinction between ignorance and mistake especially in regard to ignorance (mere lack of knowledge) and mistake (misconstruction) of the law.[25] The courts have generally not adopted the distinction,[26] considering it "a re-

[23] Cf. Lega, *De Delictis et Poenis,* p. 58; Latini, *Iuris Criminalis Philosophici Summa Lineamenta,* p. 115.

[24] Canon 2202, § 3.

[25] "Ignorance and Mistake in the Criminal Law"—*Harvard Law Review,* XXII (1908-1909), 75-96; cf. especially p. 90.

[26] Cf. Perkins, "Ignorance and Mistake in Criminal Law"—*U. of Pa. Law Review,* LXXXVIII (1939-1940), 35; Clark-Marshall, *A Treatise on the Law of Crimes,* p. 83.

finement too subtle to be applied to the every-day business of life"[27] and one which "rests upon no solid foundation."[28]

Before concluding, it is necessary to insist that ignorance and error are not universally interchangeable in the entire canon law system, nor for that matter in the whole of the Fifth Book of the Code. Thus, the error spoken of in canon 209 differs from the purely subjective error considered in this study and, moreover, according to the more probable opinion of canonists, does not include mere ignorance.[29] So also in the Fifth Book of the Code ignorance and error can be confounded only when there is question of imputability. To cite a specific instance in which the contrary is true; the ignorance, mentioned in canon 2247, § 3, in reference to a confessor absolving from a reserved censure, is not entirely the same as error on the part of the confessor. In a word, what this canon determines for ignorance in this instance is not universally applicable to error.[30]

Common experience teaches that man does not remain in conscious possession of all the truth that he has once acquired. The mind is capable of adverting fully to but one matter at a time. Moreover, the faculty of cognition is in itself passive in the sense that it must be acted upon from an outside cause before it moves in any specific direction. Abstracting from divine intervention, the mind cannot consider a specific truth without being moved thereto by the will or some sensible perception or, finally, by its own consideration of some related truth (association of ideas) which is but the mediate influence of an outside cause. The intellect is consequently in constant and unconscious possession of a great fund of knowledge to which it does not actively advert.

In the moral order some advertence is necessary for an imputable act. Advertence may be complete or incomplete. It is com-

[27] Schlesinger *v.* United States (1863), I *Court of Claims Reports,* 16, 25.

[28] Champlin *v.* Laytin (1837), 18 *Wendell's Reports, New York Supreme Court,* 407, 416.

[29] Cf. Miaskiewicz, *Supplied Jurisdiction according to Canon 209,* pp. 151-156.

[30] Cf. Galtier, "De ignorantia et errore in censurarum specialissimo modo reservatarum absolutione"—*Periodica,* XVII (1928), 55-68.

plete when the mind adverts not only to the physical character and effects of the act which is being performed, but also to its moral implications. It is incomplete when the mind is conscious only of the physical nature of the act. Complete advertence may be distinct or confused; that is, a man may realize the specific moral quality of his action, or he may be aware in an obscure way that it is right or wrong, but not that it is in accord with or offends against this or that specific law.

In order to have an imputable moral act the agent must not only be in possession of the necessary knowledge but he must also advert to this knowledge. The advertence need not be the most perfect. For example, a man need not actively, by a reflex action, appreciate the specific moral implications of his act. The necessary and sufficient advertence for imputability can be described as having the following qualities:

1. It must be complete, that is, not only the physical but also the moral nature of the act must be consciously realized;

2. It suffices that advertence be confused, that is, the specific malice of the act need not be known so long as it is realized that the act is wrong in general;

3. It must at least be virtual, that is, the advertence must have existed at some time and, even though it now no longer exists, it must have some moral connection with the act performed.[31]

It is by no means asserted that every advertence which has these qualities suffices for the imputability of the crime, and much less for the responsibility presupposed by the penalty of the law. This question will be considered in the following chapter. At present only the nature of inadvertence is considered.

Inadvertence is a lack of attention on the part of the mind to the physical act itself or to the morality of that act. Inadvertence presupposes that the mind has sufficient knowledge to evaluate the act correctly but that this knowledge is not applied. Ignorance is a permanent defect of knowledge and implies that the necessary

[31] Cf. Prümmer, *Manuale Theologiae Moralis* (8. ed., Friburgi Brisgoviae: Herder, 1935-1936), I, 32-34; Noldin-Schmitt, *Summa Theologiae Moralis,* I, 55-56; 287-288; 312-313.

knowledge was never possessed at least up to the time of the act under consideration. Inadvertence, on the other hand, is a temporary defect or lack of knowledge and necessarily implies that the knowledge was once possessed at some time previous to the act. In contrasting ignorance and inadvertence authors often call the former "habitual ignorance" and the latter "actual ignorance." [32] This terminology brings out the important point of contrast between the two concepts, but is in itself inexact; for, inadvertence is not ignorance in the strict sense, since on the contrary it presupposes knowledge. On the other hand, ignorance in the proper sense is not a habit nor does it have anything to do with a habit; it is a state of mind and nothing more. Furthermore, it is actual in the same sense that inadvertence is actual, for both exist at the moment of the act under consideration.

Inadvertence may arise from various causes. Some of these are purely physical, while others are within at least the remote or mediate control of the agent. According to the nature of its origin inadvertence can be had in various forms. These can be considered as separate species under the general notion of inadvertence, for all have this in common, namely, the present non-application of knowledge which is permanently possessed by the mind.

1. At times this state of mind may be the result of a habitual disregard for law and the consequences of one's actions. This is sometimes called *incuria*.[33]

2. Again, inadvertence may result from a simple lapse of memory. This is a natural defect to which all men are subject in different degrees, and is in itself not imputable. This form of inadvertence is referred to as *oblivio* or *oblivio actualis*.[34]

3. Finally, preoccupation with other affairs can absorb the at-

[32] V. gr., Cicognani, *Ius Canonicum,* II, 111; Romani, "De ignorantia iuris"—*Acta Congressus Internat.,* IV, 81; Suarez, *De Censuris,* disp. IV, sect. VIII, n. 5; Hollweck, *Die kirchlichen Strafgesetze,* note 3 *ad* par. 13, p. 75.

[33] Cf. c. 7, X, *de poenitentiis et remissionibus,* V, 38: *ex incuria ipsorum* is contrasted to *ipsis procurantibus vel studiose negligentibus.*

[34] Cf. Cicognani, *Ius Canonicum,* II, 111; Van Hove, *De Legibus Ecclesiasticis,* p. 239; Lega, *De Delictis et Poenis,* p. 66; Suarez, *De Censuris,* disp. IV, sect. VIII, n. 5.

tention of the mind and prevent or hinder a consideration of an act actually being placed. Thus, a doctor, intent upon the technical side of his task, may inadvertently perform a criminal operation. Such inadvertence is often spoken of as preoccupation, inattention, absent-mindedness or the Latin *inconsideratio*.[35]

Article II. The Divisions of Ignorance

1. General Theoretical Considerations

Thus far the nature of ignorance and what may be called the modes of ignorance have been considered. Error, suspicion, doubt, opinion and inadvertence are generally not considered divisions of ignorance. They are modes rather than species of ignorance, because in reality they represent the various ways in which ignorance appears in concrete circumstances. All can be resolved into ignorance and, barring a few exceptions to be considered later, what is said of ignorance may also be applied to these mental states. Error, suspicion, doubt and opinion are but the results of ignorance, while inadvertence is temporary ignorance. Hence, for both practical and theoretical reasons they should not be classified as species or divisions of ignorance.

It would serve no useful purpose to collect a list of all the divisions of ignorance which have been delineated in the course of time. Many have only historical importance and, therefore, have been reviewed in the historical section of this study. The divisions presented in this chapter have become the common property of both canonists and moralists and are well known to all. They are discussed here for two reasons: because a proper understanding of these distinctions is necessary for the correct evaluation of criminal imputability and, secondly, because the divisions in themselves throw light upon problems involved in the interpretation of the Code.

In the historical synopsis it was observed that from about the time of Suarez (d. 1617), canonists have quite generally identified four sets of divisions, namely: antecedent-(concomitant)-consequent, involuntary-voluntary, invincible-vincible and inculpable-culpable. These four divisions will be considered for the purpose of

[35] Cf. Pellé, *Le Droit Pénal de l'Église* (Paris: Lethielleux, 1939), p. 13.

illustrating their interrelation, particularly their specific points of difference. The ultimate reason for undertaking a detailed analysis of these divisions is to prepare the way for the solution of two practical difficulties. The first of these has to do with the nature of the ignorance necessary for penal imputability. The second is concerned with the reason which prompted the selection of the inculpable-culpable division in the Code and with the practical conclusions to be deduced from this choice.

The tripartite division of antecedent-concomitant-consequent ignorance is based upon the relation of ignorance to the will. Historically this division developed from an older one which was based upon a purely *temporal* relationship of the will to ignorance. In the doctrine of the later Scholastics this relationship developed into one of causality. In their teaching it was carried beyond the correlation of merely temporal elements. By the time of St. Thomas the doctrine was traditional in the schools and the expression given to the division by the Angelic Doctor may be considered the classical one.[36]

The division can scarcely be more clearly explained than by citing the text of St. Thomas. He writes:

> . . . ignorance has a threefold relationship to the act of the will: in one way, *concomitantly;* in another, *consequently;* in a third way, *antecedently.—Concomitantly,* when there is ignorance of what is done; but, so that even if it were known, it would be done. For then, ignorance does not induce one to wish this to be done, but it just happens that a thing is at the same time done and not known . . . And ignorance of this kind . . . does not cause involuntariness, since it is not the cause of anything that is repugnant to the will: but it causes *non-voluntariness,* since that which is unknown cannot be actually willed. Ignorance is *consequent* to the act of the will, in so far as ignorance itself is voluntary: and this happens in two ways . . . First, because the act of the will is brought to bear on the ignorance: as when a man wishes not to know, that he may have an excuse for sin, or that he may not be withheld from sin . . . And it is called *affected ignorance.*—Secondly, ignorance is said to be voluntary, when it regards that which one can and ought to know: for in

[36] For the historical development, cf. *supra*, pp. 56-59.

> this sense ***not to act*** and ***not to will*** are said to be voluntary . . . And ignorance of this kind happens, either when one does not actually consider what one can and ought to consider; this is called *ignorance of evil choice,* and arises from some passion or habit: or when one does not take the trouble to acquire the knowledge which one ought to have . . . Accordingly, if in either of these ways ignorance is voluntary, it cannot cause involuntariness simply. Nevertheless it causes involuntariness in a certain respect, inasmuch as it precedes the movement of the will towards the act, which movement would not be, if there were knowledge. Ignorance is *antecedent* to the act of the will, when it is not voluntary, and yet is the cause of man's willing what he would not will otherwise . . . Such ignorance causes involuntariness simply.[37]

From a logical viewpoint this division is defective, because it is based upon two different terms of comparison. It is true that the division is made on the basis of the relation of ignorance to the will, but a closer examination reveals that in reality *two entirely distinct acts* of the will are made the bases of the division.

1. In concomitant ignorance the relation of ignorance to the act of the will to violate the law (the crime itself) is considered. Hence, this member of the division concerns the effect of ignorance upon the crime.

2. In the second and third members of the division the relation of ignorance to the will as the origin of the ignorance is considered. Hence, these members concern the origin of the ignorance or the voluntariness of the ignorance itself.

Since there are two terms of comparison (*rationes divisionis*) there are in reality two distinct sets of divisions, each having two members. To complete the first division the following member should be added: "when there is ignorance of what is done; but, if it were known, it would not be done." This stands in opposition to concomitant ignorance, which is had "when there is ignorance of

[37] *Summa,* I-II, q. 6, art. 8—*English Translation by the Fathers of the English Dominican Province* (2. ed., London: Burns, Oates & Washbourne, 1927).

what is done; but, so that even if it were known, it would be done." The former is frequently called antecedent ignorance.[38]

This division is of little service for the evaluation of penal imputability and it would be better for the clarity of canonical doctrine if it were dropped entirely. In the first place, the term "antecedent ignorance" is ambiguous; because, as has been shown, it can be defined in two ways. Thus, it can be considered as an ignorance which does not depend upon the will; in which sense it is synonymous with involuntary ignorance. Or, it may be defined as ignorance in which the state of mind of the delinquent is such that he would not violate the law if he knew.[39]

Furthermore, one member of this division is of no consequence so far as penal imputability is concerned and its use can easily lead to a false conclusion. As to the first point, it has been settled long ago that concomitant ignorance does not suffice for criminal imputability. The reason is to be found in the fact that this ignorance does not make the external violation of the law imputable. An example will make this clear. Someone is about to strike a man. He suspects that the person he is about to strike is a cleric. But he is unable to find out and therefore acts in invincible ignorance. However, he is so minded that he would strike even if he did know. Of what is he guilty? The answer is that he is liable only for an internal sin; more specifically, he has a sinful intention. But is he guilty of an external and morally imputable violation of the law? The answer must be in the negative, because no one can be made morally responsible for an effect which he could not foresee.[40]

[38] Cf. Vermeersch, *Theologiae Moralis Principia*, I, 74-75; Prümmer, *Manuale Theologiae Moralis*, I, 37. In regard to the division as it is given by St. Thomas in the text above it is to be noted that he makes the last two members (antecedent and consequent) "antecedent" in the sense that in neither would the act occur if the agent knew the truth.

[39] Cf. Van Hove, *De Legibus Ecclesiasticis*, pp. 239-240. To complicate matters still more some use the term to express the mere time factor; viz., antecedent ignorance is defined as that which results from some former neglect (v. gr., during the time of studies now long past). The correlative member of this division is *actual* ignorance, resulting from present negligence. Cf. Bouquillon, *Theologia Moralis Fundamentalis* (2. ed., Brugis, 1890), p. 345.

[40] Cf. *supra*, pp. 58-59; Suarez, *De Censuris*, disp. IV, sect. VIII, nn. 8-10; Lega, *De Delictis et Poenis*, p. 58; Montes, "La ignorancia en el derecho

Furthermore, if it were true that concomitant ignorance does not excuse, then in every instance of inculpable ignorance the question would have to be asked: "Would you have committed the crime had you known?" Obviously, this would not only be an extremely difficult question to answer in many cases, but would act as an unfounded restriction upon the clear principle of the Code that inculpable ignorance of law excuses from penal imputability.[41]

The second part of this division with the correlative members of antecedent and consequent ignorance does express an indispensable distinction. However, there are three other divisions which achieve about the same practical results and are free from ambiguity. It is true that this division expresses an element not stressed in the three divisions about to be discussed, namely, that the act would not have happened but for the ignorance. However, this element is of no concern in penal imputability which is concerned only with imputability for external acts. The jurist does not speculate as to what the delinquent would have done under other circumstances. As long as the external violation is *de facto* imputable it makes no difference whether or not the crime would have been prevented had the culpable negligence not been present.[42]

It is not surprising, therefore, that canonists have for practical purposes generally adopted one of the three following divisions:[43]

penal"—*Ciudad de Dios,* CL (1927), 42-47. Many authors, especially moralists, hold a person responsible who acted with concomitant ignorance but made this express intention: *Volo hunc occidere etiamsi sit clericus.* Cf. Suarez, *loc. cit.*, n. 20; Salmanticenses, *De Censuris,* cap. II, punct. I, n. 202; St. Alphonsus, *Theologia Moralis,* lib. VII, cap. I, dub. IV, n. 43. In this case it must be conceded that there is an internal sin. Yet it is difficult to see how the external act can be imputed to the agent even in this case, because one cannot be liable for that which one does not know. *Nihil volitum quin praecognitum.* Since the external fact is *de facto* not known it cannot be willed. At best there is a constructive or interpretative intention or will so far as the external act is concerned, viz., the delinquent *would* perform the act *wilfully* if he knew.

[41] Canon 2202, § 1.

[42] Canons 2195, § 1; 2199.

[43] Cf., v. gr., Passerinus, *Commentaria in Sextum Librum,* lib. I, tit. II, cap. II, q. I, art. 5; Romani, "De ignorantia iuris"—*Acta Congressus Internat.*, IV, 81.

1. Of less frequent use is the voluntary-involuntary division of ignorance. Ignorance is voluntary if it can be ascribed to the free choice of the will; it is involuntary if it cannot be attributed to the will. In itself the division does not imply that the ignorance is morally imputable in a bad sense. Thus, the perfectly voluntary ignorance regarding penal law is not necessarily a moral defect in an astronomer. In itself the distinction, therefore, fails to bring out an important element, necessary in all imputability for ignorance, namely, that there must be an obligation to know before ignorance can become morally imputable.

2. Perhaps the most frequently used division is that which, on the basis of the objective possibility or difficulty of acquiring the corresponding knowledge, distinguishes ignorance into vincible and invincible ignorance. Ignorance may be invincible because either of physical or of moral impossibility to overcome it.

If the genuine meaning of the division be retained it must be considered unsatisfactory, because the difficulty or possibility of acquiring necessary knowledge is but one element in determining imputable ignorance. The mere possibility of gaining knowledge is but a necessary condition for every imputable act. There must be objective freedom. But another and more important factor is overlooked in this division, namely, that there must be a duty or obligation to overcome the ignorance.[44] Thus, a mechanic may be vincibly ignorant of all the penal laws of the Church, and, nevertheless, not guilty of the slightest negligence. On the other hand, it is possible according to the strict meaning of this division to have ignorance which is invincible at the present moment, but is nevertheless culpable. For instance, one can posit the case of the individual who neglects investigation until it is too late. He now finds himself confronted with the necessity of acting and yet in all truth he can claim that he has invincible ignorance. All moralists will, of course,

[44] It must be admitted that those who use this division understand it to refer only to knowledge which is obligatory. This is true especially of those authors who make no distinction between consequent, voluntary, vincible and culpable ignorance. Cf. Navarrus, *Consilia,* P. I, lib. I, *de constitutionibus,* cons. I, n. 2; Passerinus, *Commentaria in Sextum Librum,* lib. I, tit. II, cap. II, q. I, art. 5.

hold the man responsible for his neglect of foresight, but the vincible-invincible division does not aid in solving the problem.

2. Definition of the Divisions found in the Code

A. Division Based on Subjective Culpability

At the time of the codification of the law there was no uniformity in the use of the three distinctions considered above and the one now to be studied, namely, culpable-inculpable. Despite the fact that the culpable-inculpable division has been adopted in the Code, many authors continue to use one or other of the divisions considered above. The most frequently employed distinction is vincible-invincible.[45]

Roberti goes even further and criticizes the Code because of the adoption of the culpable-inculpable division.[46] The criticism offered by the learned canonist is not wholly without foundation. He points out that the use of the term "culpable" in this connection does not make for clarity, because the same term has another and more technical meaning in the Code. *Culpabilis* should be retained as the technical term to designate a violation of the law *ex culpa* in contradistinction to a violation *ex dolo*. The *ignorantia culpabilis* of which the Code speaks is not *ignorantia ex culpa* in contrast to *ignorantia ex dolo,* though the crime which may result from such ignorance is a *delictum ex culpa.*[47] *Culpabilis* here points to a morally imputable ignorance, no matter how the moral imputability arises. The Code itself frequently uses *culpa*[48] and *culpabilis*[49] to designate moral imputability in general and not the specific form of delictual imputability defined in canon 2199. But the use of the term in connection with ignorance is sufficiently clear to avoid mis-

[45] Sometimes it is used exclusively and sometimes together with the culpable-inculpable division and as practically synonymous with it. Cf., v. gr., Cipollini, *De Censuris Latae Sententiae,* p. 21; Chelodi, *Ius Poenale,* p. 31; Pistocchi, "De subjecto coactivae potestati obnoxio"—*Mon. Eccl.,* XLIX (1937), 207; Sole, *De Delictis et Poenis,* pp. 23, 80.

[46] *De Delictis et Poenis,* I, 106, note 2.

[47] Canon 2199.

[48] V. gr., canons 829; 1455, n. 2; 1737; 1553, § 1, n. 2; 2147, § 1; 2322, n. 1; 2324; 2325; 2331, § 1; 2390, § 1; 2395; 2406, § 1.

[49] V. gr., canons 2213, § 2; 2184; 2354, § 2.

understanding, even though this be done at the sacrifice of strict uniformity.

By selecting this terminology the Code has placed the evaluation of ignorance on a strictly subjective or moral basis: that is, imputability for a crime committed in ignorance is to be determined according to the subjective guilt of the individual delinquent. Only such ignorance can become the basis of imputability *ex culpa* as measures up to the various degrees of moral culpability required by law. Far from adopting another terminology, one should retain the one adopted by the Code itself, not merely because it is sufficiently satisfactory, but especially because it is in reality the best suited method for distinguishing incriminating from non-incriminating ignorance.

The imputability of a crime committed through ignorance is determined entirely by the culpability of the ignorance.[50] Hence, it is of fundamental importance to have an exact definition of culpable ignorance and to know the conditions under which culpable ignorance is to be judged a sufficient basis for criminal imputability.

Culpable ignorance may be defined as a morally imputable lack of necessary and possible knowledge, in consequence of which the delinquent foresees that he is exposing himself to the proximate danger of violating a penal law. This definition contains four necessary elements which will be examined in detail.

1. The knowledge must be *necessary*. In other words there must be a moral obligation to know either the law or the facts which are actually not known. Moral guilt in the absence of any violation of duty or of any transgression against obligation is wholly unthinkable.[51] The obligation to know some law or fact can arise, to use

[50] Canon 2202, § 1.

[51] " . . . nec ignorantia te excusat, si scire debuisti . . . "—c. 9, X, *de iniuriis et damno dato,* V, 36. " . . . dicendum quod ignorare non dicitur esse culpa culpa, nisi eatenus qua quis tenetur scire quod ignorat."—St. Bonaventure, *Commentaria in IV Libros Sententiarum,* lib. II, dist. XXII, art. II, q. 2 *ad* obj. 5. This condition is often expressed by saying that the ignorance must be voluntary not only in a physical but also in a moral sense. Thus, Passerinus (*Commentaria in Sextum Librum,* lib. I, tit. II, cap. II, q. I, art. 5, n. 116) writes: " . . . . ignorantia ex hoc est involuntaria, quod vel est invincibilis, vel est ejus, quod quis scire non tenetur . . . "

the language of Theologians, either *propter se* (*i. e.*, because the truth in itself must be known) or *propter aliud* (*i. e.*, because of an act about to be placed).[52]

An example of truths which must be known *propter se* are the fundamental truths of the Faith. The obligation considered in this work arises not in itself, but because of an act which is about to be performed. Fundamentally this obligation arises from the basic duty incumbent upon all of using due diligence to prevent harm to society from their free actions. This is true both for ignorance of law and for ignorance of fact. In both instances the ignorance becomes culpable because knowledge of the particular law or fact is necessary for the proper performance or the complete avoidance of an act. Laws are the norms which safeguard the public good. If they are to achieve this purpose they must be known and observed. The obligation to know the law, therefore, does not arise of itself but because of the obligation to observe the law. Nor can it be said that there is a moral obligation binding upon all subjects to know all the penal laws of the Church. The obligation becomes actual in the individual subject when the other conditions, described below, are fulfilled.

With regard to knowledge of facts it is self-evident that, of itself no one is obliged to have this knowledge. For instance, there is no moral or legal duty to know that this particular house is a convent with papal enclosure, or that this individual is a cleric. The obligation begins, so far as penal law is concerned, at the moment when the individual plans to do something whereby the law protecting the enclosure or the cleric is in danger of being violated.

2. The obligation must be not only physically but also *morally possible of fulfillment*. In other words, the ignorance must be mor-

[52] Cf. Billuart, *Tractatus de Peccatis* (*Summa S. Thomae Hodiernis Academiarum Moribus Accommodata*, vol. II [Parisiis, *s. d.*]), dissert. V, art. II. The fact that the general principles of the natural law and the duties of one's state in life or of one's office were included among the laws which must be known *propter se*, explains to some extent why ignorance of the primary principles of the natural law was often held to be inexcusable and why ignorance of a cleric in matters pertaining to his office was generally considered crass.

ally vincible by the use of such diligence as would be employed by a prudent man under the facts and circumstances. Hence, invincible ignorance is always inculpable, provided there is no previous negligence which made the present invincibility culpable. The same principle which forbids negligence in general also forbids the lack of due care whereby it becomes impossible to observe the law at some future time.

3. Since it is physically impossible to comply with an unknown obligation, it follows that ignorance cannot become culpable unless the delinquent *realizes* that he is ignorant. The delinquent must foresee, at least in a confused way, that his conduct may result in a criminal violation of the law because he has not the necessary knowledge. From this it follows that culpable ignorance is always accompanied by some suspicion or doubt to the effect that possibly there is a law forbidding or commanding the action or that the act about to be placed may result in a violation of the law. Otherwise the ignorance is purely antecedent to the will and consequently cannot become culpable.[53]

4. Precisely the obligation to know on account of the act about to be placed must actually be violated. This principle is best illustrated by two examples. A cleric has been gravely negligent during his years of study. He has not, of course, intended to commit any delict, and only in a general way has he foreseen that his culpable ignorance would expose him to the danger of violating the laws of the Church. Later, while engaged in the sacred ministry, he com-

[53] The necessity of this condition for all forms of culpable ignorance was not always recognized. There are evidences of controversy about this point at the time of Vasquez (d. 1604). After showing that advertence is necessary for culpable ignorance, Vasquez registers a somewhat vehement protest against his opponents. "Id quod nunc diximus, . . . nempe tunc esse ignorantiam, vel inconsiderantiam invincibilem, quando nulla subiit cogitatio, aut ratio dubitandi, primum docuimus in nostro Collegio Complutensi anno Domini 1581, quod quamvis aliquibus viris doctis paulo post primo aspectu visum fuerit difficile, tandem, re bene perspecta, et rationibus expensis, non solum probarunt, sed etiam scripto docuerunt, et tanquam propriam doctrinam tradiderunt: ut vel inde discant, non nisi maturo judicio aliorum opiniones notare."—*Commentaria ac Disputationes in Primam Secundae Sancti Thomae* (Lugduni, 1631), disp. CXXIII, cap. II, n. 6. Cf. canon 2203, § 2.

pletely forgets his former negligence. In present good faith he commits a crime. A similar example is that of the doctor who has been careless during his medical studies. In the course of his practice he is called upon to render medical services to a friend. He does everything within his power to effect a recovery, and yet, because of his ignorance, he is guilty of malpractice. Are these two persons guilty of a crime because of their culpable ignorance? Suppose that both have repented and, furthermore, have done all in their power to remedy their defective knowledge and now conscientiously believe that they are capable of fulfilling their respective offices. Neither of them can be considered liable for the crimes which they have materially performed. It cannot be denied that both had culpable ignorance. But, the law which they violated was not the criminal law in question. At the time of their transgressions both were in good faith and foresaw nothing wrong in their present conduct. The law does not make neglect of studies criminal, and this is the only transgression for which they can be held liable.

It is somewhat difficult to state this condition in a general principle. The following proposition, while true, may not prove very informing: The culpability of the ignorance must be morally connected with the objective violation of the law. This is rather a matter to be decided by the prudence of the judge upon the merits of each individual case.

From these considerations it must not be concluded that in a violation of the law through culpable ignorance there are two specific sins: the culpable ignorance and the violation of the particular law to which the penalty is attached. There was a time when moralists disputed whether or not there was a double sin in the violation of the law through ignorance.[54] There is but one specific moral guilt and it consists in the omission of due care with reference to the particular law which the delinquent foresees as likely to be violated because of his ignorance. Moralists speak of the iden-

[54] Cf. Gabriel a S. Vincentio, *De Remediis Ignorantiae* (Romae, 1671), disp. I, dub. III, "An ignorantia sit peccatum distinctum a re contra quam peccatur." Gabriel answers the question in the negative.

tical question when dealing with the moral guilt of actions performed with a practically dubious conscience.[55]

The moral imputability of the external transgression is determined *specifically* by the nature of the law whose violation is foreseen [56] and *quantitatively* by the degree of culpability manifest in the ignorance.[57] Hence, it is not the end-result which gives the moral guilt its specific and quantitative character; guilt is complete at the moment when the act which results in the violation of the law is placed, even before the actual criminal result has materialized. For example, a man is about to throw a stone into a street. At the moment he throws the stone the morality of the act is determined and complete. He actually foresees probable harm to people who may be in that street. The fact that later on he finds that he actually killed or merely wounded someone does not change the nature of the crime committed. As far as the subjective guilt of the individual is concerned, it makes no difference whether the practical doubt turns out to be true or false. The guilt, in the example given above, would be the same if any or no people were in the street. The crime may best be described as the negligent throwing of a stone.

The result, however, is vastly important in penal responsibility, because mere subjective guilt is not in itself punishable without an external and concrete violation of the law. But, whether this external violation is or is not to be imputed depends upon the subjective guilt of the delinquent.[58]

B. *Degrees of Culpable Ignorance*

The elements of culpable ignorance are extremely variable. The

[55] Cf. Noldin-Schmitt, *Summa Theologiae Moralis,* I, 221-224; Müller, *Ethik und Recht,* 208-213.

[56] " . . . qui cum dubio practico antecedente operatur, eodem peccato se inquinat, quo scienter peccans juxta communem theologorum . . .".—Reiffenstuel, *Ius Canonicum,* lib. V, tit. III, n. 321.

[57] Canon 2196.

[58] This is, of course, theoretical and perfectly applicable only to the internal forum. In the external forum the result is important because *dolus* is presumed upon proof that a law has been violated by this individual. Cf. canon 2200, § 2.

gravity of the obligation itself to investigate the truth depends upon the nature of the law which is in danger of being violated, upon the difficulties to be encountered and upon the strength of the suspicion or doubt which brings the existing ignorance to the notice of the delinquent. Finally, the seriousness of the actual omission to investigate the truth is proportionate in inverse ratio to the amount of diligence employed. Consequently the culpability of the resulting ignorance has in reality innumerable degrees. It is humanly impossible to measure subjective imputability with mathematical exactitude. Human justice cannot be more than an approximation to absolute justice. The law, however, attempts to approach ideal justice as closely as possible and for practical purposes distinguishes four distinct degrees of culpable ignorance and predicates important juridical consequences upon the basis of this fourfold distinction.[59]

In practice it is difficult to fit the extreme variety of human conduct and factual circumstances into their proper legal category. The more refined the legal categories become, the more difficult will it be to determine under which of these the concrete case under consideration is to be included. For this reason the law leaves the refinements of evaluating and balancing guilt and penalty in the hands of the prudent judge.[60] The penal law of the Church is unique in that it contains penalties which do not need the sentence of a judge before they go into effect. The law itself passes the sentence to be executed by the conscience of the delinquent immediately upon the transgression of the law.[61] For this reason the delinquent and also the confessor, when he is called on to absolve the penitent delinquent, must be able to determine the degree of culpability if the transgression occurred through ignorance.

The Code expressly mentions only two degrees of ignorance, affected and crass or supine ignorance. Since two other degrees are implied in the law, it follows that four degrees are to be distinguished. Affected ignorance is mentioned in canon 2229, § 1. Crass or supine ignorance is spoken of in § 3, n. 1 of the same canon.

[59] Cf. canons 2202; 2229; 2223, § 3, n. 3.
[60] Canons 2203, § 1; 2229, § 4; 2223.
[61] Canons 2217, § 1, n. 2; 2232, § 1.

The same number mentions a degree of culpable ignorance which is sufficient for incurring a vindicative penalty, but which is not crass or supine. Since no penalty can be inflicted or incurred for anything less than grave imputability [62] it follows that there is a gravely culpable ignorance which is not crass or supine.[63] Both canon 2202, § 1 and canon 2229, § 3, n. 1, taken in relation to canon 2218, § 2, presuppose a fourth degree of culpable ignorance, namely venially or slightly culpable ignorance. This latter includes all degrees of culpability which are not sufficient for strict penal liability as defined by canon 2218, § 2.

Both the doctrine of moral theology and the pastoral practice in the care of souls are witness to the difficulty of distinguishing in a concrete case between grave and venial sin. The disputes of moral theologians and the doubts of penitents and confessors alike prove this to be beyond question. Small wonder then, that the canonist encounters difficulty in attempting to draw a clear line of demarkation between three degrees of grave guilt.

Theoretically, perhaps, it can be accomplished in a general way. The oft repeated formulae are familiar to all. Affected ignorance is directly procured ignorance. Crass ignorance results from the highest degree of negligence. Grave ignorance holds a middle position between crass and venial ignorance; if some diligence has been used, but it falls markedly short of the measure which a prudent man would use under the facts and circumstances, then the ignorance is grave; otherwise it is venial.

The practical application of these general definitions offers no small difficulty. Since the Code, very little has been done towards solving the questions which necessarily arise, for, a definite and clear criterion is lacking by which the several degrees of ignorance can be determined in the varied concrete circumstances of life. Modern authorities have done little more than reproduce one or the other of the traditional formulae, leaving the solution of individual cases to pastoral prudence. Perhaps nothing more can be attained. The

[62] Canon 2218, § 2.

[63] The Code, therefore, authoritatively solved the dispute which existed formerly concerning the distinction between crass and grave ignorance. Cf. *supra*, pp. 74-76.

following paragraphs are submitted in the hope that at least the practical difficulties will be brought to notice by reopening questions which engaged the careful attention of former canonists and theologians. Possibly some suggestions will be offered which will aid towards the eventual solution of the problems involved.

a. Affected Ignorance

The Latin word *"affectata"* is the participial adjective of the verb *affectare* or *adfectare,* which signifies "to exert oneself to obtain" or "to strife after."[64] In the literal sense affected ignorance is that which one exerts oneself to obtain. It is not merely voluntary, but is the result of a direct effort on the part of the will.[65] Affected ignorance is correctly compared to a *delictum dolosum* in that both are directly voluntary. But affected ignorance is not *dolus,* nor is the resulting crime a *delictum dolosum.* In affected ignorance there is no deliberate will to violate the law, because the law is not known. Deliberation and ignorance mutually exclude each other. There is a deliberate will not to investigate the law but not a deliberate will to violate the law.

It must be emphasized that affected ignorance is *real* ignorance and not merely simulated or pretended ignorance. A man who pretends ignorance or pleads ignorance in court contrary to fact is not ignorant at all. He is merely trying to deceive others.[66]

[64] The meaning of *affectare* is rendered by such Latin synonyms as *aggredi, adoriri, temptare, cum studio expetere.—Thesaurus Linguae Latinae* (Lipsiae: Teubneri, 1900-), *v.* "affecto." Cf. D. (48, 10) 18, 1: " . . . suspectus esse praesumitur, quod ultra tutelam videbitur affectasse . . .".

[65] Some authors derive the term *"affectata"* from *"affectus"* because, as they say, in affected ignorance there is an *affectus ad peccatum.* Cf. Cocchi, *Commentarium in Codicem Iuris Canonici,* lib. I (5. ed., Taurinorum Augustae, 1938), n. 116. This is hardly true, because the will tends directly to the ignorance and the *affectus ad peccatum* is not essential for affected ignorance.

[66] A number of authors, writing in English, have incorrectly substituted the word "pretended" as a synonym for affected ignorance; v. gr., Woywod, "The Requisites for incurring the Penalty of the Law"—*HPR,* XXXVI (1936), 839; Ayrinhac-Lydon, *Penal Legislation* (New York: Benziger, 1936), p. 41; Cicognani, *Canon Law* (Translation by O'Hara and Brennan, Philadelphia: Dolphin Press, 1935), p. 596. While these authors define affected ignorance

Affected ignorance can, therefore, be defined as a directly voluntary lack of obligatory knowledge, which is procured by positive effort and from a wrongful motive. Three points in this definition must be emphasized.

The first point is that the ignorance must be directly voluntary. This point has already been discussed and is, moreover, clearly brought out in practically all the definitions given by authors. The direct voluntariness of the ignorance is expressed in various ways: for example, by defining affected ignorance as that which is *directe et per se voluntaria,*[67] or which arises *ex proposito non inquirendi,*[68] *data opera*[69] and *de industria.*[70]

Besides the direct voluntariness of the ignorance another element is necessary, namely, the positive will to remain ignorant must in some way be manifest. The desire to remain ignorant may exist concomitantly with an ignorance that results from sheer neglect and

correctly, yet they mislead the reader by employing "pretended" as a synonym for affected ignorance. The English word "affected" is more properly employed in the sense of "assumed artifice" or "pretense." The word is used here in the original meaning of the Latin term *"affectata."* This use of the term is now obsolete in general usage. Cf. Webster, *New International Dictionary of the English Language* (2. unabridged ed., Springfield: Merriam, 1935), *v.* "affected." It is admitted that affected ignorance was at one time defined as "simulated" or "pretended" ignorance. Cf. *supra,* pp. 42-43. This meaning of the term was lost when affected ignorance became a subdivision of voluntary ignorance, and distinguished from all other forms of voluntary ignorance in that it was *directly* willed.

[67] St. Thomas, *Summa*, I-II, q. 76, art. 4; Passerinus, *Commentaria in Sextum Librum,* lib. I, tit. II, cap. II, q. I, art. 6, n. 141.

[68] Lega, *De Delictis et Poenis,* pp. 64-65.

[69] Noldin-Schmitt, *Summa Theologiae Moralis,* I, 59; Van Hove, *De Legibus Ecclesiasticis,* p. 244.

[70] Ferreres, *Institutiones Canonicae,* II, 413-414. While the substance of these numerous definitions is about the same in all, the variety of expressions used to delineate the idea points to the fact that a good technical definition has not yet been found. The same variety of expression is found in works written in the modern languages. Cf. Woywod, "Requisites for Incurring the Penalty of the Law"—*op. cit.,* p. 840; Cance, *Le Code de Droit Canonique,* III, 335, note 2; Mothon, *Institutions Canoniques* (Paris: Desclée, 1922-1924), II, art. 2785; Pistocchi, "De subiecto coactivae potestati obnoxio"—*Mon. Eccl.,* XLIX (1937), 204.

hence something more must be required for affected ignorance. Thus, a person who makes a serious effort to discover the truth may at the same time desire to remain ignorant.[71] There must be some *positive effort to avoid the discovery* of the unwanted and troublesome truth. The man who merely remains inactive, though his inaction be deliberate, has crass ignorance; but he who takes deliberate precautions to prevent the information from reaching him has affected ignorance. The effort need not be of prolonged duration or one involving much external activity. For instance, it would be sufficient to close a book deliberately because one notices that the unwanted information is to be found in the next pages; or deliberately to turn aside from a public notice; to avoid a person who will make the undesired disclosure; or even to try deliberately and positively to distract one's mind in order to beguile its attention away from the truth.

It must be admitted that this element is not clearly enunciated in the well known definitions given by the authorities. But it seems to be an element demanded by a sort of legal necessity. Since the Code it is certain that there are three degrees of grave ignorance. If a merely grave ignorance requires a high degree of negligence, then crass ignorance must imply that no diligence has been used or only so small an effort has been made that it is practically negligible. Hence, the mere failure to do anything (even from an evil motive) is not of itself sufficient to connote affected ignorance, otherwise there would be no sure norm for distinguishing affected and crass ignorance.

It might be objected that a practical criterion for distinguishing the two can be found in the motive which prompts the omission of diligence. In affected ignorance the will tends directly towards the ignorance, while in crass ignorance the will tends directly to the negligence or to one's ease, and mediately to the ignorance. This

[71] Hence, those definitions which make affected ignorance the result of mere negligence, even from a bad motive, are hardly satisfactory. For example, Ojetti (*Commentarium,* I, 128) defines affected ignorance as that which is had "quando quis media ad deponendam ignorantiam voluntarie et consulte negligit." Cf. also Hinschius (*Kirchenrecht,* V, 923), who gives about the same definition.

latter statement is fully correct, but it must still be insisted that the criterion would not be sufficient for arriving at anything like well founded certainty. Experience teaches that men do not carefully analyze the motives of their actions. As a rule the actual facts and actions can be discovered, at least in the internal forum. But about all that a confessor, for example, will be able to find out is that either no diligence was used or that the penitent positively attempted to prevent the information from reaching him. The motive will often remain obscure. Unless, therefore, one is satisfied to leave the matter to guesswork and hazy presumptions or mere subjective suspicions, it will be necessary to include the ascertainable fact of positive avoidance in the definition of affected ignorance.

To illustrate this point and to show that the view is not without doctrinal foundation, it will not be out of place to reproduce several definitions of affected ignorance which do at least imply the use of positive means to prevent knowledge from coming to the notice of the ignorant person. Thus, Lehmkuhl defines affected ignorance as that which "ex industria non depellatur, sed *studiose foveatur.*" [72] Cerato says about the same: Affected ignorance is that "quam quis affectu seu studio tenet, refugiendo a veritate inquirenda." [73] Others, for example, Eichmann,[74] Sole [75] and Salucci [76] speak of a voluntary or malicious refusal to employ the necessary means to discover the truth. This refusal implies more than mere inactivity coupled with a direct will to remain ignorant. Others use synonyms for affected ignorance which justify the inference that they understood affected ignorance as that which was procured through special precautions. Donatus calls affected ignorance *pro-*

[72] *Theologia Moralis,* II, 621, note 2; cf. Reiffenstuel, *Tractatus de Regulis Iuris,* cap. II, reg. XIII, n. 7: " . . . data opera scire quis non vult, vel scire *cavet* . . . "

[73] *Censurae Vigentes Ipso Facto* (2. ed., Patavii: Typis Seminarii, 1921), p. 50.

[74] *Das Strafrecht,* pp. 38 and 69.

[75] *De Delictis et Poenis,* p. 80.

[76] *Il Diritto Penale,* I, 140.

curata,[77] Barbosa refers to it as *ignorantia adscita,*[78] while Montes speaks of the same ignorance as that which is *aceptada o procurada de proposito.*[79]

The third and final element of affected ignorance is the wrongful motive. In itself affected ignorance is not morally wrong, but is something indifferent and may become something praiseworthy or even obligatory through circumstances in a given case. Thus, to turn the mind away from a consideration of immoral and dangerous ideas is an affected ignorance which can only be commended. When the Church forbids a book it becomes an obligation to have "affected ignorance" of the contents of the book, at least so far as a reading-knowledge is concerned. Even the affected ignorance of penal laws cannot of itself be considered morally wrong. Such ignorance becomes morally wrong only when the conditions for culpable ignorance are fulfilled. In the latter event it is indeed morally wrong directly to will to remain ignorant. The evil or malicious motive need not be the same in each instance. In fact, the numerous definitions of affected ignorance offer no end of variety in assigning the motive for this form of ignorance. Examples of such motives are: contempt of authority, the facility to commit sin more freely, the possession of a false excuse for the violation of the law, the desire to be unhindered by the law which one suspects to be binding or the enjoyment of a false freedom of action.

For the present it is sufficient to remark that the very desire to remain ignorant when the obligation to investigate arises and is realized constitutes a wrongful motive. Furthermore, the concept of affected ignorance does not demand that the ignorance be willed for the express purpose of sinning more freely or of violating the law with greater subjective impunity. Hence it is not exact to bring any one of these particular motives into the definition. At least from a legal point of view such a definition is too narrow, because

[77] *Rerum Moralium ac Regularium* (Neapoli, 1661), tit. IV, tract. I, q. 25.

[78] *Collectanea Doctorum, ad* c. 3, X, *de clandestina desponsatione,* IV, 3, n. 11.

[79] "La ignorancia en el derecho penal"—*Ciudad de Dios,* CL (1928), 41.

it excludes other possible motives.[80] Finally, the gravity of the affected ignorance depends, *ceteris paribus,* upon the gravity of the motive on account of which the ignorance is directly sought.

b. Ignorance Resulting from Negligence

In contradistinction to affected ignorance are the three degrees of ignorance which result from the mere omission of due care. The phrase *ignorantia negligentiae*[81] expresses the essential character common to crass, grave and venial ignorance. Substantially the only distinguishing note in the three is the greater or lesser degree of the negligence through which they are caused.

At the sacrifice of strict logical order, the distinction between venial and grave ignorance will be disposed of first. Venially culpable ignorance comprises all degrees of moral guilt which do not offer a sufficient basis for criminal imputability according to canon 2218, § 2. In a word, when the subjective moral guilt of the delinquent must be judged slight or venial according to the principles of moral theology, the ignorance will be considered as an excuse from all strict canonical liability.[82]

[80] Following St. Thomas (*Summa,* I-II, q. 76, art. 4) many insert the motive, *ut liberius peccet,* into the definition of affected ignorance. Cf., for example, Roberti, *De Delictis et Poenis,* I, 106; Salucci, *Il Diritto Penale,* I, 140. Montes (*loc. cit.*) states the motive correctly and comprehensively when he writes that affected ignorance arises *de proposito y con fin reprobable.* Cf. Passerinus, *Commentaria in Sextum Librum,* lib. I, tit. II, cap. II, q. I, art. 6, n. 142.

[81] The phrase is used in this meaning by St. Thomas (*De Malo,* q. 3, art. 8) and forms the second member of another tripartite division: *ignorantia affectata, ignorantia negligentiae* and *ignorantia per accidens.* The latter (*ignorantia per accidens*) is ignorance which results from a state of mind in which mental activity is impossible or at least impaired, v. gr., from drunkenness, insanity, passion. The penal imputability of these mental states is not judged according to the principles of ignorance but according to separate and distinct norms. Thus insanity is treated in canons 2201, §§ 2, 4; 2229, § 3, n. 2; drunkenness in canons 2201, § 3, and 2229, § 3, n. 2; and passion in canons 2206 and 2229, § 3, n. 2.

[82] Strictly considered venially culpable ignorance in the moral sense is *inculpable* ignorance so far as penal law is concerned. It does not give rise to *imputabilitas ex culpa* as defined in canon 2199. "De minimis non curat Praetor, et in levia vix animadvertitur." Cf. Michiels, *Normae Generales,* I, 359.

The distinction between venially culpable and gravely culpable ignorance is not difficult to comprehend in comparison with the distinction between the latter and crass or supine ignorance. It will be recalled that before the Code many of the best canonists, as for example, Wernz, Hollweck, Suarez, St. Alphonsus and others [83] rejected this latter distinction simply because no clear and practical criterion could be discovered whereby grave and crass or supine ignorance could be distinguished in practice. Even after the Code some authors, for example, Prümmer,[84] Cipollini [85] and Pighi [86] apparently do not admit the distinction. Salucci, while admitting that the Code does make the distinction, maintains that it is rather speculative than practical. He finds that the Code by making the distinction only increases the difficulties of superiors and judges in applying the law, because there is no way of determining crass ignorance.[87]

It is true that the Code by simply affirming that the distinction exists does not contribute directly to the solution of the problem. However, it does provide a firm basis for a practical solution if the law is studied in its entire context. In the first place, the Code shows an extremely liberal attitude toward crimes committed in ignorance, especially in so far as *latae sententiae* censures are concerned. Despite this fact, the Code adopts what was the stricter view in regard to affected ignorance of law.[88] For that reason, it seems justifiable to support the rather restricted definition of affected ignorance as explained above and to consider as crass any ignorance which does not have the three characteristics or elements, viz., direct voluntariness, positive effort to procure it and a wrongful motive.

Moreover, while it remains true that crass ignorance must be understood as interpreted by the approved authors before the

[83] Cf. *supra*, pp. 75-76.

[84] *Manuale Theologiae Moralis,* III, 353.

[85] *De Censuris Latae Sententiae,* p. 21.

[86] *Censurae Sententiae Latae et Irregularitates* (7. ed., Verona: Sorores Cinquetti Filiae Felicis, 1922), p. 8.

[87] *Il Diritto Penale,* I, 141-142, note 2.

[88] Canon 2229, § 1.

Code,[89] nevertheless, by affirming the distinction between crass and grave ignorance the Code implicitly adopts the definition given by the authors, which contains some characteristic whereby the two can be distinguished in practice. This element must be of an easily ascertainable factual character, otherwise the distinction would be of little, if any, service. In affected ignorance this factual element was found in the positive rejection of all means of arriving at the truth out of a malicious motive. In crass ignorance the distinguishing feature is to be found in the total lack of any effort, when it is realized that no grave or serious effort would be required to dispel the ignorance. Crass ignorance can be distinguished from grave ignorance, then, by two facts:

1. On the subjective side, there is the complete or total absence of any diligence in investigating the truth;
2. On the objective side, the truth is easily ascertainable, a fact which is realized by the delinquent.

A gravely culpable ignorance is, therefore, an ignorance which results from a lack of due care, which lack indeed implies the guilt of mortal sin, but does not simultaneously involve the presence of more than one or the other of the two characteristics (subjective and objective) here predicated for crass ignorance.

The only point in this opinion—which can hardly be said to contain anything completely new—that must be proved is that the law really understands crass ignorance in this way. The rest follows of logical necessity. The evidence submitted must be viewed in the light of what has been said about the interpretation of authors before the Code. If a representative view of *all* authors were presented and it were *merely* a question of balancing authorities, the argument would have very little value. It is freely admitted that not all authors required the degree of negligence which the opinion defended in this study demands. This is especially true of those authors who admitted no distinction between grave and crass ignorance. If the selection of authorities appears prejudiced in favor of the opinion defended, it must be remembered that this is a "prejudice" with a foundation in the law itself which directs the interpreter implicitly to one group of authors.

[89] Canon 6, n. 3.

1. Crass ignorance is a total lack of diligence.

The very terms themselves point to the complete failure to exercise any care. *"Crassus"* in the figurative and moral sense indicates a person who is rude, stupid and clumsy; hence without even the beginnings of knowledge.[90] In like manner, the intensive adjective *"supinus,"* [91] indicates a person who has not enough energy to move from an easy position.[92] The terms were, moreover, understood in this sense by canonists.[93]

The complete and total absence of any serious effort is brought out in three types of definitions. The first, and probably the oldest, designated that ignorance as crass or supine which arose from *lata culpa* and often expressly appealed to Roman Law in order to show that the negligence involved was *dolo proxima.*[94] This definition is sometimes retained by commentators on the Code.[95]

[90] Literally the term means "having weight or density"; hence anything solid, dense, thick or fat. In a figurative meaning it connotes about the same as *hebes, stultus, simplex rusticus.—Thesaurus Linguae Latinae, v.* "crassus."

[91] Despite the fact that the Code separates *crassa* and *supina* by the disjunctive *vel* there is no reason to suppose that it thereby indicates two distinct species of ignorance. In the first place, the Code employs connectives in general quite loosely, consequently no argument can be derived from their strict meaning alone. Cf. Moersdorf, *Die Rechtssprache des Codex Iuris Canonici,* pp. 31-32. In the second place this interpretation would merely complicate matters. There is no criterion at hand whereby crass ignorance could be distinguished from supine ignorance. Finally, the two terms were in the past always associated and were generally considered synonymous. A few authors did attempt to define the two terms separately. The differences consist in factual descriptions based upon the literal meanings of crass (obese and dull or stupid) and of supine (reclining and lazy) rather than differences either in species or degree of culpability. Cf. Salmanticenses, *De Censuris,* cap. I, punct. XV, n. 190.

[92] Literally, it means *sursum versus, i. e.,* lying with the face or belly turned upwards. In its figurative meaning it signifies *otiosus, ignarus, negligens, delicatus* " . . . hujusmodi enim supini jacere diu aut sedere solent."—Forcellini, *Lexicon Totius Latinitatis, v.* "supinus."

[93] Cf. Reiffenstuel, *Tractatus de Regulis Iuris,* cap. II, reg. XIII, n. 7.

[94] V. gr., Fagnanus, *Commentaria,* lib. V, tit. XXIX, c. I, n. 19; Barbosa, *Collectanea Doctorum,* lib. V, tit. XXXVIII, n. 3; Durandus, *Speculum Iuris* (Venetiis, 1577), lib. I, Partic. I, *de dispensationibus,* § 4, n. 41. The texts of the *Digest* frequently referred to are: D. (16, 3) 32; D. (17, 1) 29.

[95] Cf. Coronata, *Institutiones Iuris Canonici,* IV, 33.

The second mode of expression insists that the degree of negligence must be the highest. Various superlatives are employed which convey about the same idea, namely, a total lack of diligence, because the highest degree of negligence evidently is that in which no effort is made. Thus, Lehmkuhl calls it *negligentia cum excessu gravi* [96] and Lega, amplifying this notion, defines crass ignorance as that which arises "ex neglectu vehementer gravi . . . unde quis negligentissimus habeatur." [97] If the view represented in these pages be the true one, then this definition should be considered less satisfactory, because it expresses the total lack of all diligence less clearly.[98]

Finally, since the Code a great number of canonists expressly state that the distinction between grave and crass ignorance is to be found in the fact that the latter results from a total absence of all care to investigate the truth. By way of example, Cance,[99] Cerato,[100] Roberti,[101] Ayrinhac-Lydon,[102] Van Hove [103] and Pellé [104] may be mentioned as employing this definition.

2. The truth must be easily ascertainable.

Crass ignorance is, on the subjective side, a complete and total failure to use any effort to fulfill the obligation of knowing the law or the pertinent facts falling under the law. The failure itself may arise from mere sloth, from undue preoccupation with other affairs or from a sinful habit of acting without due consideration of the results of one's conduct. Vermeersch-Creusen are of the opinion that this subjective element should be considered the sole criterion for distinguishing crass and supine ignorance from gravely cul-

[96] *Theologia Moralis,* II, 621.

[97] *De Delictis et Poenis,* p. 64. Cf. Passerinus, *Commentaria in Sextum Librum,* lib. I, tit. II, cap. II, q. I, art. 6.

[98] Many canonists still give this definition, v. gr., Sole, *De Delictis et Poenis,* p. 80; Salucci, *Il Diritto Penale,* I, 140; Woywod, "Requisites for Incurring the Penalty of the Law"—*HPR,* XXXVI (1936), 840.

[99] *Le Code de Droit Canonique,* III, 335, note 3.

[100] *Censurae Vigentes,* p. 50.

[101] *De Delictis et Poenis,* I, 106.

[102] *Penal Legislation,* p. 9.

[103] *De Legibus Ecclesiasticis,* p. 239.

[104] *Le Droit Pénal,* p. 14.

pable ignorance.[105] This does not seem to be entirely correct. Objectively, on the part of the obligatory investigation itself, no serious difficulty need be anticipated. Hence, only the ignorance of those things which might easily be learned can be considered crass or supine. When it is evident that a serious effort would be futile, it is difficult to see how a person could be obliged, so to speak, under the pain of becoming guilty of crass ignorance for not making the sterile effort. For example, a pastor realizes that his ignorance on a point of law may possibly result in a criminal violation of the law. For some reason, v. gr., the seal of confession, he finds it almost impossible to solicit the information from others. Yet to consult moral theology or canon law may involve considerable study. If he makes a serious effort all will grant that he is not guilty of crass ignorance. But is he obliged to make that effort if he foresees that it will be useless? It seems not, because the law does not bind one to the use of ineffectual means under pain of becoming more guilty because of the omission.

Therefore, two conditions must be fulfilled before ignorance can be called crass: on the objective side the truth must be readily available, and on the subjective side the delinquent must fail to use any diligence.[106] Vermeersch himself defends this opinion, giving the following as an example. The man who does not take the trouble to get up from bed to make a few steps to consult a clock has gravely culpable ignorance. The man who does not even look at a watch lying in front of himself has crass ignorance in regard to the time.[107]

[105] *Epitome,* III, 249.

[106] The *Glossa Ordinaria* (*ad* c. 2, *de constitutionibus,* I, 2, in VI°) defined "supina" as "ignorare quod omnes sciunt." This is the old Roman Law definition of the concept, cf. *supra,* p. 9. This was amplified by later canonists: " . . . id evenire, quando quis ignoscat quod omnes sciunt, instar hominis crassi coram oculis proposita minime inspicientes."—Sanchez, *De Matrimonio,* lib. IX, disp. XXXII, n. 33. Fagnanus (*Commentaria,* lib. I, tit. II, c. 5, n. 431) and Panormitanus (*Commentaria,* c. 9, X, *de clerico excommunicato . . . ministrante,* V, 27, n. 3) define crass ignorance as that which is had "quando de facili potuit quis scire, et non indagavit."

[107] *Theologiae Moralis Principia,* I, 73; cf. also "De contumacia quae committendae censurae est requisita condicio"—*Periodica,* XXII (1933), 41*; Van Hove, *De Legibus Ecclesiasticis,* p. 239.

Often the statement is made that ignorance in matters pertaining to one's state in life or office is crass ignorance.[108] There is some foundation for this view. In the first place, knowledge of the affairs of one's office or position is presumably easy to obtain. If a man is not fit for a certain position, v. gr., of judge, confessor or pastor, he is bound to give it up when he realizes this fact, otherwise he will justly be held responsible for his own mistakes. The opinion is deeply rooted in the traditional doctrine of canonists.[109] Crass ignorance is frequently defined by the older canonists as that which results from *lata culpa*. But it is *lata culpa* not to know that which men of the same profession or state in life generally know.[110]

The moral theologians, moreover, listed the duties of one's state in life among the truths which must be known on their own account. Ignorance of such duties consequently was considered to be highly culpable. The opinion remained even after the duties of one's state in life were no longer included among the truths which must be known for their own sakes.[111]

Under the present law there is little foundation for this opinion which would make practically all ignorance of law in a priest, and especially in a confessor, pastor or judge, crass ignorance. It is true that in the external forum the presumption of a knowledge of the law on the part of these persons is so strong that it could scarcely be rebutted. Even if ignorance is proved, it will most probably be considered crass by the court. In the internal forum, however, each

[108] De Meester, *Compendium*, III, P. II, 152, note 1; Berutti, *De Delictis et Poenis*, p. 27; Vermeersch-Creusen, *Epitome*, III, 249; Pellé, *Le Droit Pénal*, p. 60; Coronata, *Institutiones Iuris Canonici*, IV, 33.

[109] The basis for this opinion is found already in the *Decretum Gratiani*. Gratian devotes one entire Distinction (D. XXXVIII) to proving that ignorance is inexcusable in a priest or bishop. His general proposition is: "Cum itaque voluntaria ignorantia omnibus sit noxia sacerdotibus est periculosa."—*Dict. Grat. ad* D. XXXVIII, *pr.*

[110] Cf. Sylvester, *Summa Summarum, v.* "ignorantia"; Navarrus, *Enchiridion*, cap. XXIII, n. 45; Passerinus, *Commentaria in Sextum Librum*, lib. I, tit. II, cap. II, q. I, art. 6, n. 145.

[111] Cf. Billuart, *Tractatus de Peccatis*, dissert. V, art. II; Suarez, *De Censuris*, lib. IV, sect. VIII, nn. 14-15; Montes, "La ignorancia en el derecho penal"—*Ciudad de Dios*, CXLIX (1927), 47-49.

case must be considered on its own merits, for the penal law of the Church cannot be said to be so simple that every case of ignorance concerning it must be judged as crass or supine just because a cleric has had a theological training. Moreover, the connection of the ignorance with the actual violation of the law must also be considered. The mere fact that a cleric was guilty of even crass negligence during the time of his studies does not make him liable in conscience for those transgressions of the law which he did not foresee at all. He may have forgotten or repented of his former crass negligence at the moment when he actually violated the penal law. Finally, a man who is diligent in his studies and has acquired the necessary knowledge may in later life forget what he had once learned. Accordingly, he would be excused on account of inadvertence.

Hence, the universal rule is that only such ignorance can be considered crass which results from a complete lack of diligence when it is known that the truth could easily be discovered. Ignorance which lacks either of these two elements is grave ignorance, provided there is sufficient culpability for the commission of a mortal sin.

C. Ignorance of Law, of Penalty and of Fact

An important legal distinction, made on the basis of the unknown object, is that of ignorance of law and ignorance of fact. The distinction itself is not difficult. If the existence, extent or meaning of the law is not known there is ignorance of law. If the concrete or physical conditions necessary for the application of the law are not known there is ignorance of fact.

Generally it is simple enough to distinguish ignorance of law and ignorance of fact. In more involved instances doubts may sometimes arise. It may happen that one does not know whether a certain fact or action falls under the law because the law itself is not clear. In this case there is a *doubt of law* in the sense of canon 15 (an objective doubt). Or it may be because the law, clear in itself, is not known to this particular individual. This is ignorance of law in the sense defined above.

A doubt may arise when the law is objectively clear and subjectively well known, but the facts are not clearly known. This is ignorance of fact. It is possible that both ignorance of law and ignorance of fact concur in the same case. Thus, a man may not know that the novices of religious communities are protected under the *privilegium canonis,* and at the same time be ignorant of the fact that the person before him is a novice. He would have both ignorance of law and ignorance of fact at the same time.[112]

There is a third distinction to be made on the basis of the unknown object, namely, ignorance of the penalty alone. The latter may be considered as a separate species of ignorance of law, or it may be regarded as an independent distinction.[113] Toso regards ignorance of the penalty alone as ignorance of law if one does not know in what the penalty consists; on the other hand he considers it ignorance of fact, if one does not know that the penalty is attached to the law in question.[114] This is a purely arbitrary distinction and has no basis in the law.

From a logical viewpoint it is hardly correct to consider ignorance of the penalty alone as a subdivision of ignorance of law, since that would amount to creating a new division with but one member, because there is no corelative of ignorance of the penalty alone under this system of division.

While it is admitted that in itself the question is rather theoretical than practical, it seems more correct to consider ignorance of the penalty alone as a separate category on a par with ignorance of law and ignorance of fact. In practice, when there is a question of the application of legal rules, neither the norms for igno-

[112] Keedy gives an instructive definition of "facts" in this connection. He writes: "'Facts' are natural phenomena, which are the subject of testimony, and to which the law is applied by or under the direction of a judicial tribunal."—"Ignorance and Mistake in the Criminal Law"—*Harvard Law Review,*" XXII (1908-1909), 77.

[113] Cf. Noldin-Schmitt, *Summa Theologiae Moralis,* I, 57; Vermeersch, *Theologiae Moralis Principia,* I, 74; Cappello, *De Censuris,* p. 48.

[114] *Commentaria Minora,* I (2. ed., Tiferni Tiberini: ex officina Typographica Vinciana, 1921), p. 39. Before the Code authors sometimes considered ignorance of the penalty alone to be a form of ignorance of fact. Cf., v. gr., Gabriel a S. Vincentio, *De Remediis Ignorantiae,* disp. I, dub. I, n. 6.

rance of fact nor those for ignorance of law can be applied to ignorance of penalty alone. Since ignorance of penalty alone has its own specific norms it is better to consider it as an independent legal category.

In this connection it is worthy of note that the Code does not employ the traditional expressions, namely, *ignorantia iuris* and *ignorantia facti*. In speaking of the former, the Code employs the expression *ignorantia legis* [115] and *ignorantia legum* [116] or *ignorantia circa legem*.[117] The Fifth Book of the Code does not make express mention of ignorance of fact. In canon 16, § 2, when speaking of ignorance of fact, the Code uses the phrase *ignorantia circa factum*.

Finally, attention may be called to one notional difficulty in the division under discussion. It concerns the meaning or, more precisely, the comprehension of ignorance of the penalty alone. Strictly considered, ignorance of the penalty alone can occur in two instances:

a. If the penal character of the law is not known, *i. e.*, the command or prohibition is known, but it is not known that any penalty is attached to the violation of the obligation (*ignorantia poenalitatis*).

b. If the law is known to be penal, but the specific nature of the penalty is not known (*ignorantia naturae poenae*). This latter ignorance may concern the question whether a penalty is medicinal or vindicative; whether or not the censure is reserved; and finally, whether the censure be an excommunication, suspension or interdict. These three cases are mentioned because they alone have any practical importance.

The Code does not define *ignorantia solius poenae* and consequently leaves the determination of the legal content to be settled on general principles. This question will be taken up later in connection with the specific problems which result from the lack of a clear definition of ignorance of the penalty alone.

115 Canon 2229, § 1 and § 3, n. 1.
116 Canon 16, § 1.
117 Canon 16, § 2.

CHAPTER VII

EFFECTS OF IGNORANCE UPON PENAL IMPUTABILITY

ARTICLE I. THE EFFECTS OF IGNORANCE UPON IMPUTABILITY IN GENERAL

BEFORE the Code the legal principles regarding the effects of ignorance upon penal imputability were based upon natural equity, the commonly accepted doctrine of canonists and several analogies of law. The Code contains the first express general legislation for penal imputability in cases of ignorance. The legal principles are now clearly defined, though there remain several specific problems of interpretation.

In this article ignorance of law and of fact is considered in reference to criminal imputability in general. The rules are perfectly applicable to responsibility for vindicative penalties. Censures must be handled separately, because medicinal penalties require a special subjective element, namely, contumacy. The second article will deal with this subject.

1. Imputability of Delicts Committed Because of Inculpable Ignorance

> Violatio legis ignoratae nullatenus imputatur, si ignorantia fuerit inculpabilis; . . .[1]
> Casus fortuitus qui praevideri . . . nequit, a qualibet imputabilitate eximit.[2]

In these two paragraphs the Code defines the limits of the *delictum culposum* in case of ignorance of law or of fact. The Code unmistakably bases penal imputability upon moral guilt. If the criminal transgression is not morally imputable there can be no criminal liability.[3] The fundamental reason for the lack of imputa-

[1] Canon 2202, § 1.

[2] Canon 2203, § 2.

[3] Cf. also, canons 2199; 2200; 2201; 2218, § 2.

bility in the case of inculpable ignorance of law and of fact is the same, though the aspect in the two instances is quite different. In inculpable ignorance of law the physical act in itself may be entirely deliberate and voluntary, but the moral character of the act is not voluntary because it is not known. In the case of ignorance of fact it is the full physical nature of the act, its essential qualities, or its effects that are not known and therefore involuntary.

In admitting ignorance as a defense in criminal law the Church goes much farther than any other legal system. In the civil law systems ignorance of law is generally not admitted as an excuse from penalties for reasons of public policy. In the language of the Supreme Court of North Carolina:

> "Ignorantia legis neminem excusat." Every one competent to act for himself is presumed to know the law. No one is allowed to excuse himself by pleading ignorance. Courts are compelled to act upon this rule, as well in criminal as civil matters. It lies at the foundation of the administration of justice. And there is no telling to what extent, if admissible, the plea of ignorance would be carried, or the degree of embarrassment, that would be introduced into every trial, by conflicting evidence upon the question of ignorance . . . To allow ignorance as an excuse would be to offer a reward to the ignorant.[4]

The general rule in American criminal law is that ignorance of law does not excuse.[5] In theory ignorance of law should be admitted as an excuse, because *mens rea* or "guilty mind" is a necessary element of most criminal offenses,[6] yet, for reasons of public policy arising from the difficulty of proving ignorance in court, the law does not admit ignorance as a defense.

[4] State *v.* Boyett (1849) 32 N. C. 336, 343-344.

[5] The rule is variously stated. Sometimes it is said that knowledge of law is conclusively presumed. This is equivalent to saying that ignorance of law does not excuse. Cf. Perkins, "Ignorance and Mistake in Criminal Law" —*U. of Pa. Law Review,* LXXXVIII (1939-1940), 36-41; Keedy, "Ignorance and Mistake in the Criminal Law"—*Harvard Law Review,* XXII (1908-1909), 77-96. There are, however, several important exceptions to this general rule, some of which will be noted in the course of the present chapter.

[6] In some statutory crimes the legislatures dispense with the necessity of *mens rea.* In these cases absence of criminal mind, or good faith, is no defense. Cf. Clark-Marshall, *A Treatise on the Law of Crimes,* pp. 86-87.

The paragraphs of canons 2202 and 2203 which deal with inculpable ignorance are in themselves sufficiently clear. Since the nature of the *delictum culposum* and the question of inculpable ignorance have already been considered little remains to be said. One point may be cleared up here and that is the meaning of the expression "violatio legis ignoratae" of canon 2202, § 1. What is to be understood by *lex* in this connection? [7] Does it mean ignorance of ecclesiastical law alone, or ignorance of any law? The answer to this question is fairly clear from the context. The word *inculpabilis* itself suggests the answer, for, in canon 2202, § 1, it evidently connotes a lack of moral guilt. Hence, as long as there is moral guilt in the violation of the law there is also penal imputability. Consequently where the law imposing the penalty is purely ecclesiastical, ignorance of this law excuses. If the penal law of the Church is merely an expression of an already pre-existing divine law, ignorance of the former does not excuse from moral guilt and hence neither from penal imputability.[8]

It is true that there must be an ecclesiastical law defining that the transgression of the moral law is a delict. This is the juridical element of a delict. Moreover, precisely *this* law must be violated, otherwise the necessary objective element of the delict would be wanting.[9] But nowhere is it stated that knowledge of this law is a necessary element of a delict.[10] Moreover, the Code itself indicates that the Church punishes crime as a violation of the *moral order* which results in an injury to the public good. Thus, canon 2198, in

[7] The same question can be asked in regard to canon 2199, which changes the expression somewhat because of the context. In speaking of the sources of penal imputability the canon refers to *ignorantia legis violatae*. Canon 2229 says simply *ignorantia legis*, while canon 16, § 2, uses the expression *ignorantia circa legem*. The meaning of all these expressions is the same.

[8] *Contra*, Coronata, *Institutiones Iuris Canonici*, IV, 34, with note 1. What Coronata here affirms is true of responsibility for censures but not of penal imputability in general. His reason for assuming a change in the law by the Code is not convincing.

[9] Canon 2195: A delict is " . . . legis violatio cui addita sit sanctio canonica . . . "

[10] Cf. canon 2200, § 1, which defines *dolus* simply as the *voluntas violandi legem*.

defining the limits of ecclesiastical jurisdiction over the punishment of crime, vindicates for the Church penal jurisdiction over all crimes *ratione peccati.*[11] This indicates that the Church intends to punish crime as a sin against the moral order and not merely as a deliberate violation of the positive ecclesiastical law.

Finally, ignorance of the ecclesiastical law alone differs very little from ignorance of the penalty alone. The two concepts are not identical, but practically resolve themselves into the same thing. Thus, a man who knows that abortion is forbidden by the natural law may not know that the Church specifically forbids it. He has ignorance of the penalty, to be sure, but the fact that he does not know the law of the Church does not in itself lessen the crime. The positive law does not impose a specifically new obligation, but merely affirms an existing duty and sanctions it with a penalty.[12]

2. The Imputability of Crimes Committed Because of Culpable Ignorance

> Imputabilitas [violationis legis ignoratae] minuitur plus minusve pro ignorantiae ipsius culpabilitate.[13]
> Ignorantia solius poenae imputabilitatem delicti non tollit sed aliquantum minuit.[14]
> Si quis legem violaverit ex omissione debitae diligentiae, imputabilitas minuitur pro modo a prudenti iudice ex adiunctis determinando . . .[15]

In defining the notion of culpable ignorance the conditions necessary for culpable ignorance were fully analyzed. A more detailed application of these rules belongs rather to practical jurisprudence and pastoral experience than to canonical doctrine. Here it is sufficient to repeat that the culpability of the ignorance itself is the

[11] " . . . delictum quod unice laedit legem societatis civilis, iure proprio . . . punit civilis auctoritas, licet etiam Ecclesia sit in illud competens ratione peccati . . . "

[12] Cf. Wernz, *Ius Decretalium,* VI, 32; Pirhing, *Ius Canonicum,* lib. V, tit. XXXIX, n. 44; Suarez, *De Legibus,* lib. V, cap. XII, n. 7; D'Annibale, *Summula Theologiae Moralis,* I, 314-315.

[13] Canon 2202, § 1.

[14] Canon 2202, § 2.

[15] Canon 2203, § 1.

measure of delictual imputability when a law is violated through ignorance.[16] The culpability of the ignorance may have different degrees according to the circumstances of the case. All the elements of the ignorance must be considered in order to arrive at a just conclusion: namely, the gravity of the law foreseen as likely to be violated, the degree of probability of the transgression, the difficulties to be encountered in acquiring the necessary knowledge and, finally, the extent to which the law is not known.

Two general rules for judging the imputability of culpable ignorance may be noted. The first rule is that a crime committed in ignorance is not criminally imputable if the ignorance itself is not at least gravely sinful. Therefore, no strict canonical penalty can be inflicted for a violation of penal law which is merely venially sinful.[17] Before the Code it was commonly admitted that a grave penalty could not be inflicted for less than a mortally sinful violation of law.[18] The Code has authoritatively confirmed this rule. However, as before the Code, the rule must be restricted to the application of strict canonical penalties. A penal remedy or penance can be imposed in case of lesser guilt, because these do not necessarily presuppose a crime at all. Penal remedies are used by the proper authority to "prevent the occurrence of evil, forestall scandal, remove voluntary occasion and all proximate cause of delinquency." [19]

Canons 2202 and 2203 seem to justify another universal rule,

[16] "Imputabilitas delicti pendet . . . vel *ex* . . . *culpa in ignorantia* legis aut in omissione debitae diligentiae . . . "—canon 2199.

[17] Canon 2218, § 2. Canon 2372 contains an apparent exception to this rule. This canon prohibits the exercise of an order received in good faith from a bishop who has been excommunicated, suspended or interdicted after a declarative or condemnatory sentence, or a bishop who is a notorious apostate, heretic or schismatic. Since the cleric receiving the orders is in good faith, or in other words, in inculpable ignorance of fact, there can be no question of grave moral guilt. The prohibition to exercise the order thus conferred cannot be considered a penalty. It is a mere prohibition or a sort of irregularity *ex defectu*. Cf. Ayrinhac-Lydon, *Penal Legislation*, p. 282; Cappello, *De Censuris*, p. 453.

[18] Cf. *supra*, p. 72.

[19] S. C. Ep. et Ref., instr. 11 iun. 1880, n. 2—*ASS*, XIII (1880), 324-336; *Fontes*, n. 2005; canons 2307-2308. Cf. Prümmer, *Manuale Theologiae Moralis*, I, 39.

namely, that every form of ignorance, no matter how culpable, diminishes delictual imputability. This principle offers no difficulty as far as crass and grave ignorance are concerned. *Culpa* always denotes a lesser degree of imputability than *dolus,* and even crass ignorance does not exceed juridical *culpa.* Even ignorance of the penalty alone lessens imputability. Since knowledge of the penalty of the law is not necessary for *dolus,* it must be admitted that ignorance of the penalty alone does not make the crime a *delictum culposum.* Despite this, ignorance of the penalty alone, no matter how culpable, does diminish imputability to some extent. The reason is that the delinquent in this case does not act with the same open contempt of the law as one who violates a penal law with full knowledge of its penal results. Moreover, in some cases the ignorance of the penalty may lead the delinquent to suppose that the law itself does not bind with such severity, or that it does not bind under grave guilt. In the latter instance the ignorance of penalty becomes also ignorance of law and would obviate criminal imputability.

Affected ignorance, however, offers some difficulty. Before the Code this form of ignorance occasioned a great deal of controversy. The doctrine of earlier canonists, adopted by St. Thomas, held that affected ignorance augmented rather than diminished imputability.[20]

Another opinion, current both before and after the Code, identified a *delictum dolosum* and a delict committed out of affected ignorance so far as imputability was concerned.[21] According to this opinion affected ignorance would not diminish imputability at all.

[20] Cf. *supra,* pp. 77-78. The view of St. Thomas was apparently adopted in a decision of the Sacred Congregation of the Propagation of the Faith.—instr. (ad Vic. Ap. Fokien.), 13 sept. 1760—*Coll. S. C. P. F.,* n. 435. The opinion is still defended today, v. gr., by Prümmer (*Manuale Theologiae Moralis,* I, 35) and Cocchi (*Commentarium in Codicem,* lib. V, n. 43). Ojetti (*Commentarium,* I, 129, note 8) still calls this opinion the more common view of theologians.

[21] Cf. Barbosa, *Collectanea Doctorum, ad* c. 3, X, *de clandestina desponsatione,* IV, 3, nn. 8-11; Perathoner, *Das kirchliche Gesetzbuch* (3. ed., Brixen: Weger's Buchhandlung, 1923), pp. 573-574, note 4; Pellé, *Le Droit Pénal,* p. 14; Pistocchi, "Influsso dell' ignoranza e della inavvertenza nella imputabilità del delitto"—*Mon. Eccl.,* XLVI (1934), 212; Beste, *Introductio in Codicem* (Collegeville: St. John's Abbey Press, 1938), p. 894.

Since the time of Suarez (d. 1617) and Arriaga (d. 1667) a great number of canonists and moralists distinguish the imputability of affected ignorance on the basis of the motive or reason why the ignorance itself is willed or desired. Hence, affected ignorance diminishes or aggravates guilt accordingly as the motive is less or more sinful than the delict itself.[22]

A fourth opinion maintains that, in accord with the general rule for culpable ignorance, affected ignorance diminishes imputability.[23] This seems to be the better view and the one presupposed by the Code.

In regard to the controversy it must be recalled that affected ignorance was not always defined in the same way. This accounts in no small way for the divergence of opinion in regard to its influence upon imputability. Moreover, it must be admitted that the motive of the ignorance must be considered in determining the *whole* moral guilt of the delinquent. Sometimes the motive may be more serious than the crime itself. This is especially the case when a person desires to remain ignorant out of formal contempt of the law and authority. Such contempt is more sinful than, for example, grave neglect of the rites and ceremonies in the sacred ministry,[24] or the refusal of a priest to attend a deanery conference.[25] Yet, even in this case the general rule of canon 2202, § 1, holds good, namely, imputability is diminished. It is true that in many cases the diminution will be so small that the law will not take it into account,[26] but there is no reason for holding that affected ignorance is an exception to the general rule that ignorance diminishes culpability.

No matter how sinful the motive of the affected ignorance may be, the crime which results therefrom is always less imputable than

[22] Cf. Müller, *Ethik und Recht*, pp. 206-208; Van Hove, *De Legibus Ecclesiasticis*, p. 244.

[23] Cf. Lega, *De Delictis et Poenis*, pp. 64-65; D'Annibale, *Summula Theologiae Moralis*, I, 314, note 81.

[24] Canon 2378.

[25] Canon 2377.

[26] Thus canon 2229, § 1, does not admit it as an excuse from any *latae sententiae* penalties when there is affected ignorance of the law.

if it were deliberately done.[27] Penal law considers only the imputability of the external act and not the accompanying motives or desires. Contempt of authority or a desire to sin more freely without remorse of conscience are in fact very serious sins but they are extraneous to the crime. They are internal acts, which have not become externalized by the fact that a specifically different crime has resulted therefrom, but are simply the manifestation of a strong inclination or intense desire to do the act forbidden by the law.

Neither is canon 2229, § 1, an exception to or an argument against this view. Apparently the canon does not admit ignorance among the *"quaelibet imputabilitatis diminutiones"* of the second paragraph. This may be true, but all that the first paragraph necessarily implies is that affected ignorance does not effect *enough* diminution of imputability to justify excuse from *latae sententiae* penalties.

Hence the universal rule stands that all ignorance diminishes imputability. It remains for the judge to decide whether the diminution justifies a smaller penalty in accord with the rules of canon 2223. But as long as the ignorance is gravely sinful or does not destroy grave delictual imputability (as, for example, inculpable

[27] " . . . perversus et iniquus est [in schismate baptizari] et tanto perniciosius, quanto scientius."—c. 40, C. XXIV, q. 1. Cf. Pellé, *Le Droit Pénal,* p. 15. Already St. Bonaventure had set up the general proposition that "omnis ignorantia aliquo modo excusat peccatum. Et ratio huius est, quia minuit de ratione voluntarii, minuit etiam de ratione contemptus. Ceteris enim paribus, magis contemnit qui peccat ex industria quam qui ignoranter peccet."—*Commentaria in IV Libros Sententiarum,* lib. II, dist. XXII, art. II, q. 3. Concerning affected ignorance, it is interesting to note that St. Bonaventure applies this distinction only to ignorance of law and in regard to its effect upon imputability he says: " . . . et ista sic ex una parte excusat quod ex alia parte magis aggrevat . . . " (*ibidem, ad* obj. 5.) Possibly St. Bonaventure was influenced by traditional doctrine to make this exception to the general rule stated above. In itself, to say that affected ignorance excuses and augments the identical guilt at the same time would be a contradiction. However, his position can very well be understood if explained in the sense of the text above, viz., affected ignorance as such diminishes the imputability for the external act; the bad motive, on the other hand, may give rise to greater internal sin than the actual external violation of the law.

ignorance of the penalty alone), the judge is justified in applying the full sanctions of the law.[28]

There is no justification for placing affected ignorance on a par with drunkenness or passion deliberately sought for the purpose of violating the law.[29] Under one aspect there is a similarity, namely, in that the ignorance, drunkenness and passion are directly and deliberately sought or aroused. But affected ignorance differs in this important aspect, namely, that the law itself is not deliberately violated because it is not known. In the other cases the law is directly and deliberately violated, even though the delinquent at the precise moment of the transgression is unaware of the fact. The drunkenness and passion are but means which are used by the delinquent to effectuate his criminal intentions. They are but cowardly devices to still the warning voice of a clear and unmistakable conscience. In case of affected ignorance, however, conscience is at least doubtful and uncertain about the eventual violation of the law. This much is consequently certain: affected ignorance cannot be considered as an aggravating circumstance, that calls for the infliction of a more severe penalty.[30]

3. Relative Imputability of Ignorance in its Nature as Ignorance of Fact, of Law and of the Penalty Alone

Before entering upon this subject one may well point out just where the Code deals with ignorance of fact. The Code does not use the expression *ignorantia facti* when treating of a delict performed in ignorance. Many authors seem to believe that the Code identifies ignorance of law and ignorance of fact and that the latter

[28] This is a statement of general principle, which admits of an exception, as will be seen in the following chapter.

[29] Cf. canons 2201, § 3, and 2206. Thus, Coronata, *Institutiones Iuris Canonici,* IV, 113.

[30] Compare the imputability of drunkenness and passion with the imputability of ignorance in reference to *latae sententiae* censures.—canon 2229, § 3, nn. 1-2. Grave ignorance excuses while drunkenness and passion do not if the violation of the law is still gravely sinful.

is treated in canon 2202, despite the fact that only ignorance of law and ignorance of penalty alone are expressly mentioned.[31]

A careful analysis of canon 2203 shows that culpable ignorance of fact is included in the general notion of the omission of due diligence. This appears from the fact that the second part of the first paragraph begins with the words: *quod si rem praeviderit.* Hence, the first part of the paragraph must provide for the case in which the delinquent does *not* foresee. The first section of the paragraph deals with that defect of prevision which results from negligence, either in not foreseeing the effects of one's action or in not properly investigating the circumstances before placing the act. This is culpable ignorance of fact. The second paragraph of canon 2203 speaks of *casus fortuitus qui praevideri nequit.* This is a good definition of invincible and, therefore, inculpable ignorance of fact.

Canon 2203 is an amplification of the second source of *culpa,* referred to in canon 2199 as the *omissio debitae diligentiae.*[32] The latter can arise in two ways; either from a lack of prudent diligence in preventing a foreseen harm from taking place, or from a want of due care in investigating the facts. The latter gives rise to ignorance of fact, and it is only with this form of *culpa* arising from the omission of due diligence that the present study is concerned.

It is important to know that the Code does not identify ignorance of law and ignorance of fact. Consequently, it is not correct to understand ignorance of fact to be included every time that the Code uses the term *ignorantia legis.* To identify ignorance of law and ignorance of fact is not only contrary to pre-Code doctrine and

[31] V. gr., Michiels (*De Delictis et Poenis,* I, 192-193) says that the Code is silent on the subject, but that the principles are self-evident and must be accepted as admitted in pre-Code law in accordance with the norms of canon 2202, § 1. Moersdorf (*Rechtssprache des Codex Iuris Canonici,* pp. 376-377, note 28) agrees with this opinion. Berutti (*De Delictis et Poenis,* p. 28) finds the norms for ignorance of fact provided for in the third paragraph of the same canon, which says that whatever is determined for ignorance holds also for error. He identifies *error iuris* with *ignorantia facti,* as was sometimes done before the Code.

[32] A crime resulting from negligence in general (not from ignorance of law) was and still is frequently called a quasi-delict. Cf. Wernz-Vidal, *Ius Canonicum,* VII, 65; Beste, *Introductio in Codicem,* p. 880.

the legal systems in general since the time of Roman Law, but also contrary to sound general principles.

The entire historical development of the principles regarding the influence of ignorance upon penal imputability points unmistakably to the conclusion that ignorance of fact diminishes imputability more than does ignorance of law. The reason for this is the general obligation to know the law, which is incumbent upon all subjects. Moreover, the law can be discovered very frequently before the necessity for acting arises, while facts must often be investigated at the time of the act and on the scene of the crime. Hence, ignorance of fact will be less culpable and more readily admissible also in the external forum.[33]

Ignorance of the penalty alone has the least influence upon the diminution of criminal imputability, as is self-evident even apart from its being so expressed in canon 2202, § 2.

In order that ignorance obviate penal imputability it must relate to a substantial element of the law or of the fact. For this reason ignorance of the penalty alone merely diminishes imputability and ignorance of the reservation of a penalty does not diminish imputability at all.

These considerations quite naturally suggest several interesting questions regarding ignorance of fact. The fact must be essential for the constitution of the specific crime contemplated by the law in question. Thus, the fact that a man is either married or single will be accidental so far as the crime of murder is concerned, but substantial in regard to adultery. The fact that a man be a cleric or a religious is essentially prerequisite if an attack upon him is to constitute a violation of the *privilegium canonis*.

A simple error in regard to personal identity is accidental. Thus it is immaterial whether the man who is murdered be Peter or Paul. If the delinquent while intending to strike the cleric Paul, by mistake strikes cleric Peter, he is liable nevertheless. This is an ancient

[33] Cf. Heiner, *Katholisches Kirchenrecht*, II, 85; Hollweck, *Die kirchlichen Strafgesetze*, note 1 *ad* par. 16, p. 78; Crnica, *Modificationes in Tractatu de Censuris* (S. Mauritii Agaunensis: Typis op. S. Augustini, 1919), p. 31.

rule of the Roman Law,[34] as well as the Common Law[35] and is in accord with traditional Canon Law doctrine.[36]

The reason for this rule is that the penal law does not punish a crime in so far as it is an injury to this or that individual, but in so far as it is a disturbance of good order, an injury to the public good. The public good is equally much disturbed in either case, consequently the error in identity of person is immaterial.[37]

If the error, however, results in a specifically different and unintended crime there is no penal imputability. The classical example is the case of A, who, while intending to shoot an animal belonging to B, by mistake kills B himself. This is not homicide (unless grave negligence can be shown), but merely an attempt to injure B's property. The homicide is the result of mere accident, as defined by canon 2203, § 2. Or again, the fact that a cleric or religious is engaged in business prohibited by canon 2380 does not make the crime

[34] Cf. *supra,* p. 8.

[35] Cf. Keedy, "Ignorance and Mistake in the Criminal Law"—*Harvard Law Review,* XXII (1908-1909), 83; Regina *v.* Lynch, 1 Cox C. C. 361; McGehee *v.* State, 62 Miss. 722. It is interesting to note the theory upon which criminal liability is based in these cases. "The rule there declared [Dunaway *v.* People, 110 Ill. 333] has not been departed from, and it established the law of this state that, where a person deliberately shoots at A. and in the direction of B., and the ball miss A. and strikes B., inflicting a wound, these facts will show the intention of the person shooting to kill and murder B., although he has no actual malice or ill-feeling toward B., and he may be convicted of an assault upon B. with intent to kill and murder him, and, proof being made that the act was committed deliberately and likely to be attended with dangerous consequences, the malice requisite to murder would be presumed."—People *v.* Cohen (1922), 305 Ill. 506, 137 N. E. 511, 513.

[36] Cf. Kuttner, *Schuldlehre,* pp. 180-181; Peckius, *Opera Omnia* (Antverpiae, 1666), *De Regulis Iuris,* reg. XIII, nn. 4-5; Vermeersch-Creusen, *Epitome,* III, 248; Coronata, *Institutiones Iuris Canonici,* IV, 426.

[37] Somewhat different is the question of restitution in case of injury to another. In this instance the injury is righted in so far as it was done to this particular individual. Moral Theologians are not in harmony regarding the obligation to restore in case an injury intended for A is erroneously done to B. Cf. Noldin-Schmitt, *Summa Theologiae Moralis,* II, *De Praeceptis* (25 ed., Oeniponte: Rauch, 1938), 434-435.

of editing or retaining a prohibited book imputable if these acts are placed through ignorance of fact.[38]

4. Ignorance, Error and Inadvertence

Quae de ignorantia statuuntur, valent quoque de inadvertentia et errore.[39]

Paragraph three of canon 2202 lays down the general rule that everything which the law ordains in regard to ignorance should also be applied to error and inadvertence. Since this paragraph is universal in its terminology, its application must also be general, so far as it does not involve contradiction with admitted legal principles. Hence, it applies alike to error and inadvertence (1) of fact; (2) of law; (3) of the penalty alone.

In regard to error the rule involves no difficulty. Error is but the logical consequence of ignorance. The mere fact that a person has formed a mistaken judgment in consequence of ignorance does not change the moral imputability of the resulting act. Hence, it makes no difference whether a man be ignorant of the law prohibiting the reading of a certain book or whether he positively believes that this particular book is not forbidden.

Of course, if a man erroneously thinks that there is a penal law forbidding a certain act, whereas in fact no such law exists, his subjectively immoral act is not a crime because the act lacks the essential objective element of a delict. Moreover, the error must concern a substantial or material element of the crime. Sometimes an error may not diminish imputability at all. For example, a man who violates a penal law with the belief that the transgression carries with it the penalty of excommunication, whereas in fact the penalty is much smaller, is not excused at all by the error. Conversely the delinquent may believe that the penalty imposed by the law is much smaller than in reality it is. In this case the judge may find the error to be a mitigating circumstance in accord with the second paragraph of canon 2202.

[38] According to the doctrine of *versari in re illicita,* one *operam dans rei illicitae* was held for all the effects resulting from the act. For the historical development of this doctrine, cf. *supra,* pp. 59-62.

[39] Canon 2202, § 3.

Hence, ignorance and error to all practical purposes have the same result upon delictual imputability. In fact, as has already been noted, the two concepts are frequently not distinguished at all in practice. What is called ignorance is in fact error in the strict sense of the term. Mere ignorance, being a negative mental state, influences imputability rather by producing a false conscience or an erroneous practical judgment. The error is not always explicitly formulated in the mind of the delinquent, but a mistake of some kind will generally accompany ignorance.

The present canon is equally explicit in regard to inadvertence. Hence, a person who knows the law and facts perfectly well can nevertheless be excused through inattention, distraction or forgetfulness, and be in the same position before the law as one who violated the law through complete ignorance. The rule, however, must be understood correctly, for in some respects inadvertence differs materially from error and ignorance with the result that not all the legal rules in regard to the latter are equally applicable to inadvertence. Some of these differences merit attention.

The most obvious exception to the general rule is the case of "culpable" inadvertence. Strictly considered "culpable" inadvertence involves a contradiction, for all moral guilt presupposes some advertence both to the physical act and to the morality of the act.

In a broader sense, that is, through a less strict use of the term which includes the case of a person who is not perfectly but merely partially aware of the facts or of the law, there may be culpable inadvertence. For instance, while engaged in a certain action a man may suddenly realize that there is something morally wrong with his conduct. Should he choose to banish the troublesome thought by centering his attention on something else the while he continue his act, then his inadvertence to this act would be culpable. In fact this case can be considered as affected inadvertence, with the result that the delinquent is liable for the results which he foresaw at the previous momentary advertence.[40]

The influence of inadvertence upon the diminution of imputa-

[40] Cf. Passerinus, *Commentaria in Sextum Librum,* lib. I, tit. II, cap. II, q. I, art. 4, n. 94.

bility is not always clear. The question is not free from all difficulties because authors are not entirely in agreement as to the degree of advertence necessary for a moral act.[41] This is rather a moral than a legal problem and hence falls outside of the scope of this study. It is now commonly admitted that the advertence necessary for grave moral responsibility must be actual, and not merely virtual or interpretative. On the other hand, it is sufficient if it is imperfect and confused in regard to the specific morality of the act.[42] Moreover, it certainly is not necessary that a man be aware of the morality of his action during the entire course of his criminal conduct. Some crimes involve a series of acts, for example, the reading of a prohibited book. In these cases it is sufficient that the delinquent advert to the illicitness of his act at some time before or during the action in such a way that the advertence will have sufficient moral connection with the act to bring it under the control or moral dominion of the delinquent.

There are especially two forms of inadvertence which in view of the accompanying negligence can easily become culpable. The one is the result of habit, and the other the consequence of passion.[43]

A person may be inclined to dismiss all doubts and disquietudes in regard to the morality of his conduct. When he becomes aware of this habit it becomes a duty to overcome it or else make himself liable for the natural, probable and foreseeable consequences thereof. Thus, an indifferent person may easily develop a lax conscience which becomes more hardened with the course of time and amid continued carelessness. If the individual realizes this and, moreover, foresees at least in a confused way that it is likely that he will violate a penal law in consequence, the subsequent violation will also be imputable to him.

Inadvertence may also come about as a consequence of passion. *Excessive* occupation with external affairs to the exclusion of any thought about the moral consequences of one's conduct may be

[41] In regard to this question see especially Passerinus, *ibidem*, nn. 85-113

[42] Noldin-Schmitt, *Summa Theologiae Moralis*, I, 287; Prümmer, *Manuale Theologiae Moralis*, I, 32-34.

[43] Cf. St. Thomas, *Summa*, I-II, q. 6, art. 8; Passerinus, *ibidem*, n. 87.

classed in this category. These cases can hardly be considered solely according to the norms applicable to ignorance. The inadvertence which results from passion, such as anger, hate or fear, should not be considered alone, but rather in relation to its sources. The culpability of the act will depend largely upon the voluntariness of the passion itself.[44]

Finally, inadvertence can scarcely be considered on an equal basis with error and ignorance in the external forum. Here a man will be considered to have acted as a normal human being, in the possession of his faculties and aware of his own conduct. If it is admitted or proved that he knew the law and the facts before the criminal act, the judge must assume as a matter of fact that the delinquent was aware of them also during the act. The delinquent would thus have the presumptions of the law and of fact against him. Furthermore, there are some laws so deeply engraven upon conscience that inadvertence can hardly be possible. Thus, the judge could not accept the plea that the delinquent forgot the natural law forbidding homicide, theft or abuse of sacred things.

From these considerations it follows that inadvertence will be very difficult to prove in the external forum and cannot be accepted by the prudent judge as equal with error and ignorance as an excusing factor.[45]

ARTICLE II. A COMPARATIVE STUDY OF THE INFLUENCE OF IGNORANCE UPON *Dolus*, PERFECT *Dolus* AND CONTUMACY

> Dolus heic est deliberata voluntas violandi legem, eique opponitur ex parte intellectus defectus cognitionis . . .[46]
> Si lex habeat verba: *praesumpserit,* . . . aliave similia quae plenam cognitionem ac deliberationem exigunt, quaelibet imputabilitatis imminutio . . . ex parte intellectus . . . eximit a poenis latae sententiae.[47]

[44] The norms for these cases are to be found in canons 2201, § 3; 2205; 2206; 2229, § 3, nn. 2-3.

[45] Cf. Coronata, *Institutiones Iuris Canonici,* IV, 33; Wernz, *Ius Decretalium,* VI, 30; Suarez, *De Censuris,* disp. IV, sect. VIII, n. 11; Lehmkuhl, *Theologia Moralis,* I, 24.

[46] Canon 2200, § 1.

[47] Canon 2229, § 2.

> Si agatur de censuris ferendae sententiae, contumax est qui, non obstantibus monitionibus . . ., a delicto non desistit vel patrati delicti poenitentiam cum debita damnorum et scandali reparatione agere detrectat; ad incurrendam vero censuram latae sententiae sufficit transgressio legis vel praecepti cui sit adnexa latae sententiae poena, nisi reus legitima causa ab hac excusetur.[48]

The first article of the present chapter considered the effect of ignorance upon imputability in general. Since not all crimes require the same degree of imputability, it follows that the general norms for imputability must be varied according to the nature of the crime and the penalty imposed when making the practical application of the law to concrete cases. There are some crimes which by their nature or by legislative definition demand a special subjective element. In these cases the lawgiver intends to penalize only those who violate the law with *dolus* or even with perfect *dolus*. On the other hand, there are crimes which demand a peculiar subjective element, not because of the nature of the crime but because of the medicinal character of the penalty to be inflicted. Ecclesiastical law has two distinct categories of penalties: those which are inflicted primarily in order to secure the amendment of the delinquent and those which directly tend to the expiation of the injury inflicted upon the moral and social order. The former are known as medicinal penalties or censures; the latter are called vindicative penalties.[49]

The nature of *dolus* and of perfect *dolus* has already been considered in the chapter on delictual imputability. A few reflections about the nature of contumacy will be necessary before one can efficaciously undertake the comparative study of the influence of ignorance upon these three types of delictual imputability.

Because of the medicinal character of censures these penalties can be employed only when the amendment of the delinquent is at least objectively possible. In order that the penalty may serve to deter the criminal it must be known. Hence it can be employed only in the cases resulting from a more open violation of the law. The

[48] Canon 2242, § 2.

[49] Cf. canons 2216; 2241, § 1; 2286.

technical term which Canon Law doctrine has long employed to express the necessary subjective element for the inflicting or incurring of a censure is *contumacy*. The introduction of "contumacy" from Roman procedural law into the Canon Law of penalties has been considered in the historical section.[50] It remains but to examine the meaning of contumacy as it is used in Canon Law at the present time.

In the pre-Code law of procedure disobedience of any kind against the judge of a tribunal was considered contumacy.[51] The Code has restored the more narrow meaning which the term *contumacia* had in the procedural law of the Romans.[52] In the words of the Rota, he alone can be declared contumacious "qui non comparet in ius sive in decursu iudicii seu qui omittit respondere post citationem seu vocationem in ius legitime factam, quae omissio in civilibus consideratur potius sub aspectu renuntiationis tuitioni iudiciali iuris." [53]

The procedural meaning of contumacy has been taken over into substantive penal law and modified to some extent. Contumacy in penal law is also disobedience but of a very specific nature, since it is a form of disobedience which implies contempt of law and authority.[54]

[50] Cf. *supra*, pp. 64-65.

[51] Cf. S. R. R., *Incidentis super contumacia*, 28 iulii 1923—*S. R. R. Dec.*, XV (1923), dec. XXI, n. 8, p. 185; Wernz, *Ius Decretalium*, V, n. 534; d'Ambrosio, "De contumacia iudiciali in antiqua et nova iuris canonici disciplina" —*Jus Pont.*, IV (1924), 11-14.

[52] Cf. *supra*, p. 65, note 46; *S. R. R. Dec.*, *ibidem*, nn. 8-10, pp. 186-187.

[53] *S. R. R. Dec.*, *loc. cit.*; cf. canons 1842; 1843, § 1; 1848; 1849.

[54] Cf. Reiffenstuel, *Ius Canonicum*, lib. V, tit. XXXIX, n. 14; Benedict XIV, *De Synodo Dioecesana*, lib. X, cap. I, n. 5; Ojetti, *Synopsis*, *v.* "censura"; Sole, *De Delictis et Poenis*, p. 82. Frequently the legal texts employ the word *contemnere* in the meaning of contumacy. This is the older and, perhaps, more frequently used term. Cf., v. gr., *contempserit evitare*—Comp. III, c. 1, *de hereticis*, V, 4; *satisfacere contempserit*—c. 13, X, *de haereticis*, V, 7; *contempta excommunicationis sententia*—c. 21, X, *de homicidio voluntario vel casuali*, V, 12; *in contemptum ecclesiasticae disciplinae*—c. 10, X, *de clerico excommunicato, deposito vel interdicto ministrante*, V, 27; "Delictum . . . debet coniungi cum contumacia, idest cum contemptu censurae."—*S. R.*

It is not necessary that the contempt of authority be express or formal, but it must at least be virtual. That is why the law demands the canonical admonition before a *ferendae sententiae* censure can be inflicted.[55]

In the case of *latae sententiae* penalties the law itself takes the place of the canonical admonition. In this case, in order that the delinquent be considered contumacious, it is necessary that he know that something is commanded or forbidden by legitimate authority under censure and nevertheless presumes to violate that law.[56]

Before one enters upon a comparison of *dolus,* perfect *dolus* and contumacy, it is useful to note that the Code defines only *dolus* when treating of criminal imputability in general. Perfect *dolus* is not expressly defined, but it is presupposed when the Code deals with the factors which excuse from *latae sententiae* penalties. A reading of the canons cited at the beginning of this article will reveal that the effect of ignorance upon *dolus* and upon perfect *dolus* is expressed in very different terminology. The mental state opposed to *dolus* is described by canon 2200, § 1, as a "defect of knowledge"; while the condition of mind which obviates perfect *dolus* is described by canon 2229, § 2, as "any diminution whatsoever of imputability on the part of the intellect." Contumacy is not defined by the Code. The canon cited above (canon 2242, § 2) is found under the title of the Code dealing with censures in general. It offers a description rather than a definition of contumacy.

From what has been said about the nature of *dolus* the difference between it and contumacy, so far as their peculiar intellectual elements are concerned, becomes evident at once. *Dolus* presup-

R., *Medellen. Excommunicationis,* 7 iulii 1924—*S. R. R. Dec.,* XVI (1924), dec. XXXII, n. 2, p. 286.

[55] Canon 2242, § 2.

[56] This is the commonly accepted definition of contumacy given by Reiffenstuel (*Ius Canonicum,* lib. V, tit. XXXIX, n. 14), who writes: ". . . sufficit enim contumacia virtualis et contemptus Ecclesiae interpretativus in hoc consistens, quod quis sciat, aliquod per Legem, aut legitimum superiorem Ecclesiasticum sub censura esse prohibitum, et tamen illud facere praesumat . . ." Cf. Ojetti, *Synopsis, v.* "censura"; Vermeersch, "De contumacia quae committendae censurae est requisita condicio"—*Periodica,* XXII (1933), 39*-42*.

poses a general knowledge of some law prohibiting or commanding a particular act; while contumacy demands a knowledge precisely of the *ecclesiastical* law together with the censure imposed upon the violation of that law. Without this knowledge the delinquent cannot be said to contemn ecclesiastical authority or to be contumacious.[57] Hence, inculpable ignorance of the censure alone, while not destroying *dolus*, negatives contumacy and excuses from all censures.

In regard to *ferendae sententiae* censures there can be no question of ignorance of the penalty during the trial proceedings, because the law expressly prescribes a special warning before the penalty can be inflicted. Contumacy, moreover, may result after the commission of a crime in ignorance of the penalty, because of a failure to heed the canonical warning and repair the injury or scandal resulting from a crime. Canon 2233, § 2, seems to presuppose contumacy in the actual commission of the crime itself, because it expressly states that the purpose of the warning is to cause the delinquent to "recede from contumacy." However, this canon explicitly refers to canon 2242, which clearly distinguishes two ways of becoming contumacious, namely, by refusing to discontinue the criminal action or by refusing to repair the criminal damage. In the latter case criminal imputability is evidently presupposed in the delictual act, otherwise no strict penalty could be imposed at all.

The next point to be considered is whether the results of ignorance are the same in cases of crimes which require only *dolus* and in those which by legislative definition presuppose perfect *dolus*. In regard to *latae sententiae* penalties canon 2229 in the second and third paragraphs leaves no doubt concerning the different effects of ignorance upon the two classes of crimes. According to one opinion, the fact that the law demands perfect *dolus* is of importance only in regard to *latae sententiae* penalties and hence no distinction is to be made between *dolus* and perfect *dolus* in regard to *ferendae sententiae* penalties.[58] The seeming justification for this view is the fact

[57] Vermeersch, *ibidem*, p. 41*; Rossi, "L'ignoranza in ordine alle censure"—*Perfice Munus*, III (1928), 31-32; Cipollini, *De Censuris Latae Sententiae*, p. 4.

[58] Moersdorf, *Die Rechtssprache des Codex Iuris Canonici*, pp. 374-375; Roberti, *De Delictis et Poenis*, I, 276.

that the Code expressly refers to this distinction only in reference to *latae sententiae* penalties.[59]

However, the conclusion drawn from the silence of the Code on this matter seems unjustified for the reason that the Code itself contains about twenty instances in which *ferendae sententiae* penalties are imposed upon crimes which according to canon 2229, § 2, would demand perfect *dolus.* The same expressions which in reference to *latae sententiae* penalties demand full knowledge and deliberation (v. gr., *praesumpserit, scienter et sponte, scienter*) are also used when the law imposes *ferendae sententiae* penalties.[60] The frequent use of terms, which are given an express and specific meaning in one class of penal laws, can hardly be supposed to be mere idle verbiage when used without further qualifications in connection with other penal laws. This is especially true of a Code in which uniformity of terminology is to be expected, at least in those laws which deal with the same subject, unless another meaning is specifically determined. The conclusion, therefore, must be that there is a distinction between laws which demand perfect *dolus* and those which do not, even in regard to *ferendae sententiae* penalties. Consequently the effect of ignorance upon these two classes of crimes must also be different.

Logically the next pertinent question is: if the effect of ignorance is different in the two cases, in what does the difference consist?

In the first place, it does not seem correct to identify perfect *dolus* with contumacy in regard to the effects of ignorance, because the law has numerous instances in which perfect *dolus* is presupposed in crimes punishable with censures. Since censures always require contumacy, the law evidently requires something more when it requires perfect *dolus* as a necessary element in these cases. It must be admitted that before the Code some authors seemed to iden-

[59] Canon 2229.

[60] Canons 2316; 2317; 2321; 2331, § 1; 2337, § 1; 2341; 2347; 2360, § 2; 2362; 2364; 2365; 2369, §§ 1, 2; 2371; 2391, § 2; 2399; 2406; 2412, n. 1. Sometimes both *ferendae* and *latae sententiae* penalties are inflicted on crimes demanding perfect *dolus,* v. gr., canons 2346; 2360; 2395.

tify contumacy and perfect *dolus*,[61] and consequently required knowledge of the penalty before the punishment could be inflicted. Thus, also after the Code, Cocchi holds that ignorance of the penalty determined by law excuses in all cases when the law requires perfect knowledge.[62] This does not seem to be the case, because the rather odd consequence flowing from this opinion would be that a *ferendae sententiae* vindicative penalty could be avoided by simple ignorance of the penalty alone. This seems out of harmony with the general canonical principles regarding vindicative penalties. Just as it is possible to have *dolus* without knowledge of the penalty inflicted by the law, so also, it seems that perfect *dolus* is possible without knowledge of the penalty imposed by the law.

The effect of ignorance upon crimes punishable by a *ferendae sententiae* penalty and requiring perfect *dolus* seems to consist in this, namely, that the judge can and must accept ignorance of law or of fact more readily in these cases. Crimes requiring *dolus* and those demanding perfect *dolus* are identical in this, that in neither case is mere negligence punishable by the penalty of the law. The reason for this inheres in the fact that the crime as defined by law was not perfectly consummated according to the strict wording of the law.[63] When the law demands full deliberation and knowledge then any diminution of knowledge in reference to the law or the facts serves to exclude criminal responsibility for the penalty of the law.

The chief difference between simple *dolus* and perfect *dolus* seems to be in the matter of evidence, *i. e.*, in the manner of proving in the external forum that *dolus* or perfect *dolus* was not present in the criminal act. Simple *dolus* is presumed by law, given the proof of the objective violation of the law.[64] But perfect *dolus* does not seem to come within this presumption of the law. In these cases criminal intent, that is, knowledge and the will to place the prohibited act, become objective characteristics of the crime and along

61 Schmalzgrueber, *Ius Ecclesiasticum*, lib. I, tit. II, n. 40; Smith, *Elements of Ecclesiastical Law*, III, 32-33.

62 *Commentarium in Codicem*, lib. V, n. 4.

63 Canon 2228.

64 Canon 2200, § 2.

with the facts of the case they must be established by convincing evidence. In a word, proof that a man actually violated a penal law does not yet prove that he did so knowingly and willingly or with presumption.

Hence, in these cases it must be proved not only that there was an objective violation of the law perpetrated by a particular individual, but also that this individual knowingly violated the law, otherwise it would not be established that the crime committed was that which was determined in the law, that is, "perfect according to the proper wording of the law," as canon 2228 indicates. For example, the evidence that a certain priest actually preached in public a doctrine condemned by the Holy See (but not as heretical) does not as yet furnish proof that the preaching was done pertinaciously, as canon 2317 demands for the incurring of the penalties. To establish the pertinacious character of his act it must be shown that the delinquent knew not only the law which he objectively violated, but also the fact that the doctrine he preached was condemned and that this condemnation was known. Evidently, proof that a canonical warning was previously given would suffice to establish the pertinacious character of the delinquent's preaching.[65]

By way of illustration (not as an argument, as is evident) one can point to a striking similarity in American criminal law. In the words of the New York Court of Appeals: "But criminal intent is always essential to the commission of crime. There are cases in which the intent may be inferred from the nature of the act. There are others where willful intent or guilty knowledge must be proved before a conviction can be had. Familiar illustrations of the latter rule are to be found in cases of passing counterfeit money, forgery, receiving stolen property, and obtaining money under false pretenses." [66]

[65] This principle was advanced already before the Code, thus Hollweck (*Die kirchlichen Strafgesetze*, note 5 *ad* § 17, p. 79) writes: "Für ein gesetzlich ausdrücklich gefordertes Merkmal steht nie die Praesumption; diese steht vielmehr für den Thäter, solange er nich aller Merkmale des Thatbestandes unterwiesen ist. Praesumendum pro reo." Cf. Heiner, *Katholisches Kirchenrecht*, II, 87.

[66] People *v.* Molineux (1901), 61 N. E. 286, 296. Cf. Perkins, "Ignorance

The results of the two preceding articles can be summed up in the following propositions:

1. Ignorance of law or of fact, which is not gravely sinful, excuses from all penal imputability. In this case the judge cannot impose a strict canonical penalty.

2. Gravely culpable ignorance of law or of fact obviates *dolus* but not *culpa*. In this case it is left to the prudence of the judge to determine whether a penalty is to be imposed at all, or whether a mitigated sentence is to be pronounced according to the degree of culpability in the ignorance. The distinctions between grave, crass or supine and affected ignorance need not be precisely differentiated by the judge. The reason for this statement is that the law does not make these distinctions in reference to *ferendae sententiae* penalties, but leaves the evaluation of the guilt to the prudence of the criminal judge. The latter can, however, use the rules and distinctions of canon 2229 as guiding norms by analogy of law to aid in arriving at a just and equitable sentence.

3. In cases wherein the law demands *dolus* as a prerequisite for the perpetration of a particular crime culpable ignorance, provided that it is not an affected ignorance of law, excuses from the penalty of the law. But the ignorance must be proved in this case because the law presumes *dolus*. In the event that the proof results in establishing culpable ignorance, it seems that the judge can impose a mitigated sentence.[67]

4. In cases wherein the law demands perfect *dolus* as a prerequisite for the perpetration of a crime, the delinquent is relieved of the burden of proof when he pleads ignorance; and in cases wherein knowledge of law and fact cannot be established the penalty of the law cannot be imposed.[68]

and Mistake in Criminal Law"—*U. of Pa. Law Review*, LXXXVIII (1939-1940), 45-51. Where specific intent is essential to a crime and ignorance of law negatives the existence of such intent, then, by way of exception, ignorance of law is sometimes admitted as a good defense.—United States *v.* One Buick Coach Automobile (Indiana, 1929), 34 F. (2d) 318, 320.

67 Using canon 2229, § 4, as a parallel. This is in accord with the powers of the judge described in canon 2223, § 2, and § 3, n. 3.

68 This point will receive more consideration in the following article.

5. In cases wherein the law requires contumacy, *i. e.*, when it imposes a censure, there must be evidence to show that the delinquent was aware of the censure at the time when he committed the crime. Proof of the canonical warning suffices.

Article III. The Admission of Ignorance in the External Forum

> Ignorantia vel error circa legem aut poenam aut circa factum proprium aut circa factum alienum notorium generatim non praesumitur; circa factum alienum non notorium praesumitur, donec contrarium probetur.[69]
>
> Posita externa legis violatione, dolus in foro externo praesumitur, donec contrarium probetur.[70]

In the present article the means of proving ignorance in the external forum are considered. As is evident, these rules are applicable to the external forum alone, because in the forum of conscience the delinquent is not judged according to presumptions and evidence, but according to his own assertions.

The Code gives expression to two traditional presumptions of law. The first concerns ignorance itself and the other has to do with criminal *dolus*. It is clear that the presumptions of canon 16, § 2, are applicable also to penal law, since the canon expressly mentions ignorance of law and ignorance of the penalty.

A comparison of the two texts of the Code cited at the beginning of this article brings out a noteworthy discrepancy between the presumptions which these two canons individually set up. According to canon 2200, § 2, the presumption of *dolus* is absolute and universal; nevertheless, according to canon 16, § 2, ignorance both of law and of fact is sometimes to be presumed. Since *dolus* presupposes knowledge both of the law and of the pertinent facts, canon 2200, § 2, apparently contains an universal presumption of knowledge in contradiction to canon 16, § 2.

One explanation for this apparent contradiction is to be found in the fact that canon 16 is applicable to both penal and civil law, while canon 2200 applies only to penal law. This consideration does

[69] Canon 16, § 2.

[70] Canon 2200, § 2.

not completely solve the difficulty, because there are instances in which ignorance is presumed in penal matters contrary to the universal presumption of *dolus.* One such instance is found in canon 16, § 2, which presumes ignorance of a *factum alienum non notorium.*[71] In this case the more potent presumption prevails according to the ancient rule of law, *generi per speciem derogatur.*[72] The presumption of ignorance in the case above is more specific and defeats the general presumption of *dolus.* Hence, there is no contradiction between the two canons. The general rule remains that, given the delictual facts, *dolus* is presumed in the external forum. If this presumption is not defeated, the delinquent will be judged guilty and the penalty imposed upon him.

This consideration suggests the division of this article, which considers first the nature and extent of the universal presumption of *dolus;* and, secondly, the means whereby this presumption can be defeated, namely, contrary presumptions and external evidence. By way of conclusion and confirmation of the principles set forth in this article a number of apparent exceptions will be discussed.

1. The General Presumption of *Dolus*

The force of canon 2200, § 2, is to presume that the delinquent knowingly and deliberately violated the law when two facts are established beyond doubt:[73]

1. That the law was actually violated (the delictual facts);
2. That this particular individual was the cause of the delictual violation of the law.

It does not imply that the law presumes a man guilty when he enters the court before he has been proved guilty. The contrary is

[71] For another example of contrary presumptions, compare canon 2200, § 2, and canon 2201, § 2 (habitually insane are presumed incapable of committing a delict).

[72] Reg. 34, *R. J.*, in VI°.

[73] These facts are never presumed but must be demonstrated as canon 2233, § 1, demands. Cf. S. R. R., *Diffamationis,* 30 iulii 1924—*S. R. R. Dec.,* XVI (1924), dec. XXXIV, n. 9, p. 301. In this case the Rota reversed a sentence because there was not *plena probatio* but only a *gravis praesumptio.* Cf. c. 14, X, *de praesumptionibus,* I, 23.

true: "Bonus quilibet praesumitur donec probetur malus." [74] The presumption that a man is good ceases when it is established that he actually committed a crime and the burden of proving that *dolus* does not exist rests with the accused.[75] The reason for the presumption is to be found in the nature of *dolus* itself. *Dolus* is something internal, consisting in knowledge of the law and facts together with the will or intent to violate the law. Since subjective or internal facts cannot be proved by merely external arguments, they can be established only by presumptions and conjectures.[76] The presumption is, moreover, in accord with common experience. Ordinarily it is assumed that when a man performs an action he is in possession of his faculties, that is, that he knows what he is doing and realizes the ordinary implications, both physical and moral, of his own conduct.

In accord with the universal presumption of *dolus* canon 16, § 2, lays down two further presumptions of law. The first presumption is that the delinquent knows the law and the penalty of the law. Since every law imposes some moral obligation, it follows that the law must be known by those upon whom it is binding. In presuming knowledge of law the legislator merely supposes that the individual has not failed in this obligation.[77]

It is to be noted that the law presumes knowledge not only of the law but also of the penalty. Consequently, not only is *dolus* presumed, but also contumacy, in the case of a crime to which a *latae sententiae* censure has been attached.[78]

[74] *S. R. R., Diffamationis et rejectionis damnorum,* 5 ian. 1920—*S. R. R. Dec.*, XII (1920), dec. I, n. 4, p. 2.

[75] Cf. *S. R. R. Dec., loc. cit.; Restitutionis in integrum,* 20 martii 1927—*S. R. R. Dec.* XIX (1927), dec. XII, n. 4, p. 94; Menochius, *De Praesumptionibus* (Coloniae Allobrogum, 1686), lib. V, praesumpt. III, nn. 45-48; Reiffenstuel, *Ius Canonicum,* lib. V, tit. XXXVI, n. 5.

[76] A *fact* that can be proved is never the subject of a presumption, which is simply a "rei *incertae* probabilis coniectura"—canon 1825.

[77] Menochius, *De Praesumptionibus,* lib. VI, praesumpt. XXIII, nn. 10-12; lib. II, praesumpt. III, n. I; Reiffenstuel, *Tractatus de Regulis Iuris,* Reg. XIII, nn. 14, 17.

[78] In case of *ferendae sententiae* censures contumacy is proved by showing that the necessary warning was given and not obeyed. Cf. canon 2233, § 2.

Secondly, the law presumes that a man is aware of the factual circumstances in which he is acting. Consequently, it presumes that a man knows his own actions and personal condition together with those things which are generally known to those about him. In the words of canon 16, § 2, a man is presumed to know *facta propria* and *facta aliena notoria*. The expression *factum proprium* needs no explanation. It can be defined as that which is done through one's own personal agency and that which one has personally sustained at the hands of others.[79]

Everything that is not a *factum proprium* must be considered a *factum alienum*. The latter are divided into facts which are notorious and those which are not notorious. Some commentators of the Code explain notorious facts by applying the definition of a notorious delict, given in canon 2197.[80]

The *notorium* of canon 16, § 2, cannot be understood in the sense of canon 2197. This involves no contradiction in the Code or even any exception to the definition of the term given in canon 2197. The latter canon defines a notorious delict, while canon 16, § 2, adopting the common terminology before the Code, speaks of a notorious fact. That a notorious fact is not to be understood according to the definition of canon 2197 is evident from the consideration that there are many facts which enter into the objective

In case of *latae sententiae* censures *lex interpellat pro homine*—S. R. R., *Medellen. excommunicationis*, 7 iulii 1924—*S. R. R. Dec.*, XVI (1924), dec. XXXII, n. 2, p. 286.

79 Cocchi (*Commentarium in Codicem*, I, n. 116) defines *factum proprium* thus: ". . . est factum quod quis posuit vel positive per actum a me elicitum, vel passive per actum a me passum; . . ." The English expression "personal affairs" renders the meaning fairly well.

80 Michiels (*Normae Generales*, I, 348-349) and Toso (*Commentaria Minora*, I, 39) apply canon 2197 without further comment. Cicognani (*Ius Canonicum*, II, 114) appeals to canon 2197 as a *locus parallelus*. Ojetti (*Commentarium*, I, 132) accepts the definition of canon 2197, but limits the application to *notorium notorietate facti* and consequently concludes that the law very rarely presumes ignorance of a *factum notorium*. Vermeersch-Creusen (*Epitome*, I, 109) give *publice notum* as the equivalent of *notorium* but, nevertheless, refer to canon 2197.

element of crimes which cannot become notorious in the sense of a notorious delict.[81]

For example, the fact that the person whom the delinquent struck is a clergyman, that this building is a religious house with papal enclosure, are facts which do not become notorious in the sense of a crime. Yet, these are the facts to be considered, when a delinquent is accused of violating the *privilegium canonis* or the law of enclosure. To apply canon 2197 in this case would limit the idea of "notorious" to only those facts of a criminal case which are in themselves already criminal. For example, the fact that another person struck the cleric could be notorious in the sense of canon 2197. But such an interpretation of canon 16, § 2, is entirely too narrow and completely out of harmony with the purpose and spirit of the presumption. Moreover, the definition of public is also inapplicable, because the possibility and likelihood that a fact will become public is of no import in considering the question whether or not this individual actually knew that fact. Only actual publicity will serve to induce the presumption that the delinquent actually knew the fact.

Hence canon 2197 is not a *locus parallelus* in the sense of canon 18. The meaning of a notorious fact must, on the contrary, not be sought in the Code but in the commonly accepted doctrine of approved authors before the Code. Canon 6, n. 2, is to be applied, because the entire canon is merely a summarized expression of commonly accepted doctrine before the Code. As is well known, the nature of a notorious, public and occult delict was not clearly defined before the Code.[82] This question was settled by canon 2197, but the meaning of a notorious fact was not touched upon.

According to the commonly accepted doctrine before the Code, the general rule was that ignorance of a *factum alienum* was pre-

[81] "Delictum est: 2°. *Notorium notorietate iuris,* post sententiam iudicis competentis quae in rem iudicatam transierit aut post confessionem delinquentis in iudicio factam ad normam can. 1750; 3°. *Notorium notorietate facti,* si publice notum sit et in talibus adiunctis commisum, ut nulla tergiversatione celari nulloque iuris suffragio excusari possit."—canon 2197. In canon 1747, n. 1, the term *factum notorium* is used in the sense of a *delictum notorium.* The meaning in this case is clear because canon 2197, nn. 2, 3, is expressly cited.

[82] Cf. Wernz, *Ius Decretalium,* VI, 21-22, note 35.

sumed.[83] The principle of canon 16, § 2, was stated as an exception to this general presumption and it comprised facts which are notorious or public, as well as those facts which are of such importance that they should be known to practically all the people. The general presumption of knowledge in regard to these facts is in harmony with common experience, because men generally know facts which are public, notorious or of general importance in the place in which they live. For example, the fact that Father X is pastor of the local parish is certainly a notorious fact within the meaning of canon 16, § 2, and knowledge of this fact by one living in the community will certainly be presumed.[84]

Hence, notorious facts which are presumed by the law to be known are those which are public or known to the people generally in the community. Such facts can be known so easily and are *de facto* generally known, and hence the law presumes that they are also known in a given instance.

2. The Means of Overcoming the Presumption of *Dolus* and Proving Ignorance

The presumption of *dolus* is a presumption of law which can be overcome by both direct and indirect proof.[85] On the other

[83] Menochius, *De Praesumptionibus*, lib. VI, praesumpt. XXXIII, n. 51; Farinaccius, *Variarum Quaestionum et Communium Opinionum Criminalium Liber Sextus. Fragmentorum Pars Secunda* (Romae, 1621), n. 91 (hereafter to be cited as *Quaestiones Criminales*); Reiffenstuel, *Tractatus de Regulis Iuris*, Reg. XIII, n. 10. In fact, the general rule, in accord with the frequently cited *Regula Iuris* (Reg. XIII, *R. J.*, in VI°): "Ignorantia facti non iuris excusat," was that ignorance of fact is ordinarily presumed. All other rules were in the nature of exceptions to this universal rule. Cf. D. (22, 6) 9, *pr.;* D. (22, 6) 2 and 3.

[84] Farinaccius, *Quaestiones Criminales*, lib. VI, P. II, nn. 102-104; Menochius, *De Praesumptionibus*, lib. VI, praesumpt. XXXIII, nn. 66, 70; Barbosa, *Collectanea Doctorum, ad* c. 1, X, *de postulatione praelatorum*, I, 5, nn. 4-6. The words of Reiffenstuel (*Tractatus de Regulis Iuris*, Reg. XIII, n. 19) can be considered a good commentary on the *notorium* of canon 16, § 2. He writes that ignorance in regard to *facta aliena* is not presumed "in casibus, et factis publicis ac notoriis, aut valde notabilibus et ponderosis, quae fere cunctis patent, et a quovis modica dumtaxat adhibita diligentia sciri possunt."

[85] Canon 1826. This is true also in regard to the presumption of knowledge

hand, the presumption is universal and consequently the delinquent must always plead and prove ignorance. The presumption of *dolus* and of knowledge of law and fact can be overcome not only by external evidence but also by contrary presumptions and conjectures.[86] In fact, direct evidence to prove ignorance is scarcely possible, because ignorance is something internal. It is a fact which can be established only by presumptions or conjectures based upon the circumstances preceding and accompanying the commission of crime and by the affirmation of the party himself, confirmed by oath. These two methods of proof, presumption and the oath, are mutually complementary, as will be seen presently.

A. Presumptions of Ignorance in Regard to Facts

The Code itself contains one presumption of ignorance in regard to *facta aliena* which are not notorious. Obviously, this is a presumption of law and can be defeated by contrary indications. For example, the presumption is overcome if it is shown that the delinquent actually discussed these facts with another, or that he was actually present when the fact took place, or, finally, if the fact concerns a person with whose condition the accused must be familiar.[87]

Even the general presumptions of knowledge stated in canon 16, § 2, admit of exceptions, as the canon itself indicates by the word *generatim*. The presumptions are not to be considered hard and inflexible rules, which must be applied with formal rigorism, but rather as guiding norms to aid the judge in arriving at a just sentence. According to the common doctrine of canonists before the Code, ignorance of notorious facts is presumed in regard to persons who do not belong to the community where the fact is pub-

of the law. Cf. Montes, "La ignorancia en el derecho penal"—*Ciudad de Dios*, CXLIX (1927), 55-60.

[86] Speaking of the presumption of *dolus* the Rota declared: "At praesumptio, nedum veritati, sed et alteri fortiori praesumptioni cedere debet."—S. R. R., *Annicien. finium parochialium*, 5 feb. 1918—*S. R. R. Dec.*, X (1918), dec. III, n. 6, p. 24. Cf. *Vladislavien. nullitatis matrimonii*, 16 martii 1920—*S. R. R. Dec.*, XII (1920), dec. VIII, n. 6, p. 58.

[87] Cf. Farinaccius, *ibidem*, nn. 105, 108, 109, 168.

lic and who were absent when a public act took place or through some impediment, such as grave illness, age, mental incapacity and the like, were prevented from getting the information.[88]

Finally, even ignorance of personal affairs is sometimes presumed. Thus, when the fact occurred a very long time ago, a lapse of memory and consequent ignorance is presumed unless the fact is of serious importance to the individual. If the delinquent is implicated in many and distracting affairs, it can be presumed that he did not actually advert to the fact. Finally, if the fact itself is extremely complicated, involved or intricate, it is presumed that the ordinary person does not understand.[89]

B. Presumption of Ignorance in Regard to the Law

Not only ignorance of facts but also ignorance of law is sometimes presumed. One case in which it seems that the law presumes ignorance and thus defeats the general presumption of *dolus* has already been considered,[90] namely, when the law expressly demands full knowledge as a prerequisite in the commission of crime. The crimes themselves in these cases are often violations of merely ecclesiastical laws, which may more easily remain unknown, or they are such serious crimes that the lawgiver rarely supposes these crimes to have been committed with full deliberation.[91] Hence, ignorance is presumed until some special reason can be shown for admitting the contrary. For example, ignorance would not be presumed on the part of one who is versed in the law, or on the part of one who holds an office, in regard to the things pertaining to his

[88] Farinaccius, *ibidem*, nn. 101, 102; Peckius, *De Regulis Iuris*, Reg. XIII, n. 3.

[89] Menochius, *De Praesumptionibus*, lib. VI, praesumpt. XXIII, nn. 32, 38, 41, 47; Reiffenstuel, *Tractatus de Regulis Iuris*, Reg. XIII, n. 11; Barbosa, *Collectanea Doctorum*, *ad* c. 41, X, *de rescriptis*, I, 3, nn. 2-3. Also at Common Law the presumption of personal facts can be rebutted. Thus, when a man relied upon the knowledge of parents and relatives concerning his age, he was held excused from the crime of illegal voting.—Gordon *v.* State (1875), 52 Ala. 308.

[90] *Supra*, pp. 175-176.

[91] Cf. Vermeersch-Creusen, *Epitome*, III, 249.

office. It is for this reason also that even though ignorance is proved, it will be judged crass and non-excusing in these cases.

The Roman Law presumed ignorance of law in certain classes of people.[92] These presumptions, founded upon natural equity, were recognized and acknowledged by the common doctrine of canonists before the Code. According to them, ignorance of law was to be presumed in women, in rustics, among ignorant and illiterate people, soldiers and minors.[93] The question can be asked whether the presumption of ignorance in regard to these classes of people is still valid today or whether it has been abrogated by the Code. It seems that these exceptions to the general presumption of knowledge of the law are still valid in the present law. In support of this view the following considerations are submitted:

1. Canon 16, § 2, gives expression to only the most general presumptions of the law in regard to ignorance. It merely repeats the general principles of the traditional doctrine, but in so doing it can scarcely be admitted that the Code abrogated the interpretation or the common acceptation of these principles. The entire canon, and hence, also the presumption of knowledge in regard to the law must be interpreted in the light of approved authors before the Code.

2. Exceptions to the presumption of knowledge of law are not contrary to the actual text of the canon which states that ignorance is not *generally* presumed. The law, therefore, implicitly admits that there are exceptions to the rule.

3. The exceptions in regard to minors, the illiterate, soldiers and women are definitely within the spirit of the present penal law. Canon 2218, § 1, expressly warns the judge that in inflicting penalties he is to have regard for the age (minors), knowledge and education (the illiterate), the sex (women) and the condition (soldiers) of the delinquent. Finally, canon 2204 expressly mentions minority as an extenuating circumstance and states that lesser imputability is presumed in minors until the contrary is proved, while canon

[92] *Supra*, pp. 12-13.

[93] Menochius, *De Praesumptionibus*, lib. VI, praesumpt. XXIII, nn. 15-24; Farinaccius, *Quaestiones Criminales*, lib. VI, P. II, nn. 275-285; Reiffenstuel, *Tractatus de Regulis Iuris*, reg. XIII, nn. 20-21; Tuschus, *Practicae Conclusiones* (3. ed., Lugduni, 1634), *v.* "ignorantia," concl. XI, nn. 11-12 and concl. XIII.

2230 declares those under the age of puberty completely exempt from *latae sententiae* penalties.

4. The doctrine is in harmony with admitted judicial practice and jurisprudence. The Rota still admitted ignorance of law in regard to women in a matrimonial case.[94] In a case of *restitutio in intetrum* for adults the Rota expressly admitted error of law among the just causes required by canon 1687, § 2, for the granting of this extraordinary remedy, but only in regard to those "to whom the law is generally unknown." As an example of the latter the Rota expressly mentions the illiterate (*rustici*) and women.[95]

5. Finally, there is substantial authority after the Code for the admission of these exceptions. Among canonists who still admit these exceptions, Van Hove,[96] Ojetti,[97] Maroto[98] and Michiels[99] may be mentioned.

The exception in regard to these four classes of people must not be taken too broadly and beyond what was admitted by the common doctrine before the Code. Hence, the presumption must be restricted to purely positive law, because knowledge of the natural law is presumed in all who have sufficient use of reason.[100] This limits the application of the presumption quite considerably in Canon Law, because by far the great majority of crimes punished by the penal laws of the Church are prohibitions and commands of the natural law. However, even in these cases ignorance of the ecclesiastical law and consequently ignorance of the penalty is presumed.

[94] *Southwarcen. nullitatis matrimonii,* 29 iulii 1926—*S. R. R. Dec.,* XVIII (1926), dec. XXXV, n. 8, p. 286. The presumption in regard to women was admitted by canonists before the Code as the weakest of the four cases. Cf. Reiffenstuel, *Tractatus de Regulis Iuris,* reg. XIII, n. 21.

[95] *Restitutionis in integrum et diffamationis,* 18 ian. 1923—*S. R. R. Dec.,* XV (1923), dec. II, n. 3, p. 12.

[96] *De Legibus Ecclesiasticis,* p. 245.

[97] *Commentarium,* I, 132.

[98] *Institutiones Iuris Canonici,* I, 469.

[99] *Normae Generales,* I, 353-354.

[100] Cf. Durandus, *Speculum Iuris,* lib. IV, partitio I, *de summa Trinitate,* n. 5; Menochius, *De Praesumptionibus,* lib. VI, praesumpt. XXIII, n. 23; Farinaccius, *Quaestiones Criminales,* lib. VI, P. II, n. 287.

Besides the presumption of ignorance regarding the law in reference to certain classes of people, canonists commonly admitted that ignorance of law was to be presumed when the law itself was obscure and difficult or extremely complicated.[101] This exception to the universal presumption of knowledge concerning the law can be admitted today. However, its application must be considered extremely limited because since the Code a great number of legal difficulties and obscurities in the law have been obviated. Moreover, if the law is in itself objectively obscure not only is ignorance of it presumed but, more than that, the law simply does not bind.[102]

C. *Proof of Ignorance by the Oath of the Accused*

Since ignorance is a mental state known by experience only to the accused himself, his assertion, confirmed by oath, has particular importance as a means of proof.[103] The oath by itself, without any

[101] Reiffenstuel, *Tractatus de Regulis Iuris,* reg. XIII, n. 22; Tuschus, *Practicae Conclusiones, v.* "ignorantia," concl. XI, n. 13.

[102] Cf. canons 15 and 19.

[103] One can seriously question whether the judge in a criminal trial can permit the use of the oath of the accused even as a supplementary means of proof to establish ignorance. The Code in Canons 1744 and 1830, § 2, apparently prohibits the use of the suppletory oath by the accused in criminal trials. Authors generally interpret canon 1830, § 2, to mean that the use of the suppletory oath is entirely forbidden in a criminal trial. Cf. Vermeersch-Creusen, *Epitome,* III, 96; Coronata, *Institutiones Iuris Canonici,* III, 266; Noval, *Commentarium Codicis Iuris Canonici,* lib. IV, *De Processibus* (Romae: Marietti, 1920-1932), I, 380. Yet, a closer inspection of canon 1830, § 2, throws some doubt upon this interpretation of the canon. The canon reads: "Sed eodem [iureiurando suppletorio] abstineat iudex tum in causis criminalibus, tum in contentiosis, si de iure vel re magni pretii agatur aut de facto nimii momenti, aut si ius, res, factum non sit proprium personae cui iusiurandum esset deferendum." The grammatical construction of this canon does not demand the interpretation given by many commentators, viz., that the oath is excluded universally in all criminal cases and in only those civil cases which are expressly mentioned in the clause beginning with *si.* Grammatically this clause refers both to *causis criminalibus* and to *causis contentiosis,* because the *tum—tum* construction places both on an equal basis. Hence, the suppletory oath is forbidden only in those criminal cases specifically mentioned in the latter part of the canon.

It is interesting to note that the source of canon 1830 does not contain any

favorable conjectures and presumptions either of law or of fact, is of no value in a criminal case. In fact, the oath could not be admitted by the judge in that event, and much less so if the presumptions were against the accused, because the supplementary oath of a party in a trial can be used only when the accused has at least some evidence of ignorance in his favor.[104]

The oath is, therefore, a proof which does not stand alone, but which together with favorable presumptions may establish reasonable certainty in the mind of the prudent judge concerning the fact of ignorance. A refusal of the delinquent to take the oath would seem to be a sufficient basis for the judge to presume that the delinquent had the knowledge.[105] But this is a conjecture which must be evaluated by the judge himself, accordingly as he thinks either

mention of either criminal or civil suits. Cf. *Regulae servandae in iudiciis apud S. R. Rotae Tribunal,* 4 aug. 1910, § 156—*Fontes,* n. 6461.

The obvious motive for prohibiting the oath in these cases is the danger of perjury. This danger can be made remote if the judge permits its use only under the following conditions:

1. If the accused has some conjectures and presumptions already in his favor;
2. If his character, as revealed in the trial, is such as to convince the judge that the accused would not resort to perjury in order to establish lack of imputability;
3. If the accused willingly offers to take the oath in order to supply what might be lacking in the evidence.

Under these conditions it would seem that the judge would be allowed to permit the suppletory oath as proof of ignorance in accord with the traditional doctrine before the Code.

[104] Canon 1829. Before the Code there was some doubt whether the oath could not be used always, even when the presumptions were against the accused. Appeal was frequently made to the *Glossa Ordinaria* which favored this view. Cf. *supra,* p. 43, note 68. The better opinion was that the oath could be used as proof only when there were presumptions in favor of the delinquent. Cf. Felinus, *Commentaria, ad* c. 2, X, *de constitutionibus,* I, 2, nn. 11-17; Menochius, *De Praesumptionibus,* lib. I, quaest. 77, n. 3; Farinaccius, *Conclusiones Criminales,* lib. VI, P. II, n. 243; Sanchez, *De Matrimonio,* lib. IX, disp. XXXII, n. 5.

[105] Cf. c. 4, X, *de sententia excommunicationis,* V, 39.

that the refusal is justified or that it is equivalent to a confession of knowledge.[106]

Since the proof of ignorance rests largely upon conjecture and presumption, it can happen that the accused, who in reality committed a crime in inculpable ignorance, fails to prove this to the satisfaction of the court. If it is hard to prove ignorance, it will be all the more difficult to prove the inculpability of the same. Proof of ignorance may suffice to rebut the presumption of *dolus*, but may simultaneously reflect that there was sufficient *culpa* for criminal liability. This is especially true in all cases of ignorance in which it can be shown that the delinquent should have known the facts and the law on account of his state in life or in view of the office that he holds. In the external forum, therefore, such ignorance must generally be considered crass or supine, or in the language of traditional doctrine, *ex lata culpa*. The latter is sufficient for penal imputability in Canon Law and the judge can justly inflict a penalty according to his prudent estimation of the subjective guilt as shown by the evidence.[107]

As was seen in the treatment of the *delictum ex culpa*, grave moral guilt always suffices for penal imputability. Hence, in the external forum it is sufficient to prove that the ignorance was the result of grave sin, without making the fine distinctions between crass and grave ignorance.[108] It seems, however, that an exception is to be made in regard to those crimes which by legislative definition require perfect *dolus*. Since perfect *dolus* is not to be presumed, but must be proved, the proof of mere negligence is not enough. It must be admitted that, if even grave negligence is shown to be present, the terminology of the law is not perfectly fulfilled and consequently the judge cannot inflict the penalty of the law according to the express prescription of canon 2228.

The same holds good for crimes which are perfectly consummated only with *dolus*, with the exception that *dolus* is presumed

[106] Canon 1831, § 2.

[107] Cf. canons 2218, § 2; 2199; 2223, §§ 2, 3; 2203, § 1.

[108] Cf. Sole, *De Delictis et Poenis*, pp. 16-17; Michiels, *Normae Generales*, I, 359.

in these cases and the burden of proving its absence is upon the accused.

When, however, the law requires neither *dolus* nor perfect *dolus* then complete penal responsibility is established by proving that the delinquent had crass or supine ignorance. In this case the judge can apply the full penalty of the law, for the delinquent's act will be regarded as the equivalent of a *delictum dolosum.* Hence, in this case the oft repeated formula for the external forum holds good: "crass and supine ignorance are equivalent to *dolus.*" [109]

In cases where *dolus* or perfect *dolus* are required by the legislative definition of the crime and *dolus* is demonstrated to have been absent in the commission of the crime, but *culpa lata* shown to be present, there seems to be no reason why the judge could not impose a milder penalty according to canon 2223. In this case penal imputability still remains, though perfect penal responsibility for the penalty of the law is not present. Moreover, in cases of grave scandal or of grave injury of a special character, canon 2222, § 1, could be applied even when it must be admitted that the crime as described by the law was not perfectly consummated.

More detailed rules for a judge would hardly be practical and the law leaves much latitude to the superior who must attempt to evaluate imputability which is influenced by almost innumerable circumstances in practical life.[110]

[109] Fagnanus, *Commentaria,* lib. V, tit. XXIX, c. 1, n. 19; Sole, *De Delictis et Poenis,* p. 17.

[110] Cf. canon 2223.

CHAPTER VIII

EFFECTS OF IGNORANCE UPON RESPONSIBILITY FOR LATAE SENTENTIAE PENALTIES

Canon 2229 in three propositions describes the limits of responsibility for *latae sententiae* penalties:

> § 1. A nullis latae sententiae poenis ignorantia affectata sive legis sive solius poenae excusat, licet lex verba de quibus in § 2 contineat.
> § 2. Si lex habeat verba . . . quae plenam cognitionem ac deliberationem exigunt, quaelibet imputabilitatis imminutio . . . ex parte intellectus . . . eximit a poenis latae sententiae.
> § 3. Si lex verba illa non habeat . . . ignorantia legis aut etiam solius poenae, si fuerit crassa vel supina, a nulla poena latae sententiae eximit; si non fuerit crassa vel supina, excusat a medicinalibus, non autem a vindicativis latae sententiae poenis.

Article I. General Observations on Canon 2229

1. Purpose of Canon 2229

The entire canon deals with the causes which excuse from *latae sententiae* penalties on account of the diminution of subjective imputability. So far as ignorance is concerned this canon provides a more detailed determination of the general principles contained in canons 2202 and 2203. The very nature of *latae sententiae* penalties makes detailed norms a necessity, because these punishments are incurred and bind the delinquent *ipso facto* upon the commission of the crime without judicial intervention. In general the application of penalties is entrusted to the prudence of an ecclesiastical court or superior, but in *latae sententiae* penalties the individual conscience must decide whether or not the penalty is incurred. Hence, the necessity not only of more detailed rules, but also of practical, simple and clear rules; for, they must serve as a guide not only for trained experts in the law but also for every confessor.

More than that, these norms should be understandable to the faithful themselves, in order that they may be capable of knowing their own condition.

The purpose of the canon is to avoid, as far as the common good will allow it, the dangerous possibility of having anyone fall under severe canonical penalties without knowledge of that fact. It was this consideration which prompted the growth of the doctrine concerning the factor of ignorance and which brought forth opinions in an almost glaring contradiction to the written law. As the often quoted decree of Boniface VIII states, the motive of this legislation is the prevention of spiritual harm to souls.[1] The same motive prompts the interpreter to go to the limits of the mild interpretation required for all penal laws. From a purely legalistic point of view the mildness of this canon almost makes the penal laws seem futile and useless. This is not true, however, for there are other measures that can be used besides resorting to the severity of *latae sententiae* penalties.

2. Some Notable Features of Canon 2229

If the provisions of canon 2229 for ignorance are brought together it will be noted that there are four parts. First there is an introductory paragraph in regard to affected ignorance and at the end there is a special provision which empowers the judge to inflict other penalties in determined cases of excuse from *latae sententiae* penalties. The principal provisions for ignorance are divided into two parts. Perhaps the most striking feature of the canon is this division, which is made on the basis of crimes requiring perfect *dolus* and such as do not require perfect *dolus*. In the light of pre-Code doctrine one would have expected a division based upon the nature of the penalties to be incurred, rather than upon the nature of the crime committed. For, if one recalls that the radical changes in doctrine occurred in regard to censures, then one would rather expect a division based upon the differences between censures and vindicative penalties. The latter distinction is made only in the third paragraph of the canon. This naturally invites the conclusion

[1] C. 2, *de constitutionibus*, I, 2, in VI°.

that the same distinction is not to be made in the first paragraph. The arrangement, moreover, obscures to an appreciable extent the importance of the difference between censures and vindicative penalties so far as ignorance is concerned. As will be seen presently, the first conclusion can perhaps be admitted without further qualification; but the second becomes tenable only after important modifications have been invoked.

Another characteristic of the canon is that whenever it mentions ignorance it expressly names ignorance of law and ignorance of the penalty alone. Hence, as far as *latae sententiae* penalties are concerned, it seemingly identifies the effects of ignorance of the penalty alone with those of ignorance of the law. But, a rigid application of this conclusion would lead to results which are not only in opposition to the general principles as defined in canon 2202, but also in contradiction to the common doctrine both before and after the Code. It is to be remembered that the canon does not mention ignorance of fact at all.

These features of the canon can be explained by supposing that the codifiers of the law desired to settle all doubts concerning excuse for ignorance of law and especially for ignorance of the penalty. While ignorance of fact was admitted from very early times and is also now admitted as an excuse by legal systems in general, this was not the case in regard to ignorance of law. But the silence in regard to ignorance of fact does nothing to contribute to clarity.

In the discussion of canons 2202 and 2203 together with 2199 it was noted that ignorance of fact was included in the general expression, *omissio debitae diligentiae.* On the basis of logic alone it may be urged that the term has the same meaning in canon 2229, § 3, n. 2. But to admit that interpretation is against all authority and general principles. For, according to the second number of the third paragraph the omission of due diligence excuses only when it is not gravely sinful, while gravely culpable ignorance, whether of law or of the penalty alone, does excuse from censures. Sound doctrine and the historical development of the legal rules concerning ignorance teach that ignorance of fact, all other things being equal, should excuse more readily than ignorance of law and far more readily than ignorance of the penalty alone.[2] Hence, the *omissio debitae diligentiae* of canon 2229 comprises only that form of negligence which results from the absence of due care when the facts are clearly known and the results of one's conduct foreseen.[3]

The next logical question is: Whence are the norms concerning ignorance of fact to be derived? The commentators of canon 2229 generally seem to admit that the rules concerning ignorance of law and ignorance of the penalty alone, are to be applied also relative to ignorance of fact.[4] In general this can be admitted, with the reservation, however, that the general principles governing penal imputability and especially the commonly accepted doctrine of canonists before the Code should not be overlooked entirely.

As will be seen presently, canon 2229 does not provide a complete set of norms regarding the effect of ignorance upon the responsibility for *latae sententiae* penalties. One of the primary purposes of the canon seems to have been to settle points which were unclear and disputed before the Code. Hence, those norms of canon 2229 which are contrary to what were probable opinions before the Code must be understood according to their own proper significance. In cases where no express rule is provided the opinions of approved authors before the Code are still valid in so far as the latter do not conflict with other provisions of the Code. Finally, those rules of canon 2229 which evidently are taken from the writings of canonists must also be interpreted in the light of pre-Code doctrine.[5]

[2] Cf. Crnica, *Modificationes in Tractatu de Censuris,* p. 31; Michiels, *De Delictis et Poenis,* I, 192-193.

[3] Canon 2203, § 1, the second part, beginning: *quod si rem praeviderit* . . .

[4] Some writers expressly state this, v. gr., Coronata, *Institutiones Iuris Canonici,* IV, 116; Michiels, *De Delictis et Poenis,* I, 193; Moersdorf (*Die Rechtssprache des Codex Iuris Canonici,* pp. 376-377, note 28) affirms this in reference to canon 2202, § 1; Ayrinhac-Lydon (*Penal Legislation,* pp. 41-42) by the examples they give show that they understand the canon to be applicable also to ignorance of fact; Chelodi (*Ius Poenale,* p. 32) thinks that this is not altogether clear. A great number of authors do not explicitly mention the question.

[5] Canon 6, nn. 2-3.

3. The Relation of Canon 2229 to pre-Code Law and the Rules Which Are Certain by Its Express Provisions

Canon 2229 can scarcely be considered a complete statement of all the legal rules concerning ignorance in relation to the responsibility for *latae sententiae* penalties. There are a number of possibilities clearly presupposed by the canon, but not expressly considered by it. This will become evident in the discussion of special problems. Indeed, a large number of possible combinations can result from the fact that in relation to two classes of penalties (vindicative and medicinal), which themselves are inflicted upon three kinds of delicts (those which require perfect *dolus* or *dolus* in general and those which are complete with imputability *ex culpa*), not only ignorance of law and ignorance of fact, but also ignorance of penalty alone, must be considered under a fourfold aspect accordingly as the ignorance itself be venially culpable, grave, crass or affected. The accompanying diagram serves at least to illustrate the complexity which arises when every possible combination of these factors is taken into consideration. The diagram also indicates the source of the legal principle which is to be applied in any given instance.

It will be noted at once that this diagram omits one form of delictual imputability completely, namely, that which is required by crimes which presuppose simple *dolus* but not perfect *dolus*. This case is not expressly provided for in canon 2229. Neither is there any justification for assuming that it is to be included among those laws which expressly demand perfect *dolus* by such terms as *praesumpserit, scienter,* and the like. This classification of delicts was omitted because it would unnecessarily complicate the diagram. It seems that this case differs from those which require general penal imputability only in regard to crass ignorance of fact.

It is submitted that crass ignorance of fact can be considered as an excuse from the incurring of a *latae sententiae* penalty imposed upon a crime which presupposes simple *dolus*. This contention is based upon the following considerations.

In the chapter on penal imputability it was shown that crimes which are fully consummated only when committed with *dolus* can-

DIAGRAM OF POSSIBLE CASES ENVISIONED BY CANON 2229

	VINDICATIVE PENALTIES		MEDICINAL PENALTIES	
IGNORANCE	*Perf. dolus*	*Dol. et cul.*	*Perf. dolus*	*Dol. et cul.*
1. *of fact:*				
a. affected.....	† c. d.	† c. d.	* p. op.	† c. d.
b. crass.......	* § 2	† c. d.	* § 2	† c. d.
c. grave.......	* § 2	† c. d.	* § 2	* c. d.
d. venial......	* 2218, § 2	* 2218, § 2	* 2242, § 1	* 2242, § 1
2. *of law:*				
a. affected.....	† § 1	† § 1	† § 1	† § 1
b. crass.......	* § 2	† § 3, n. 1	* § 2	† § 3, n. 1
c. grave.......	* § 2	† § 3, n. 1	* § 2	* § 3, n. 1
d. venial......	* 2218, § 2	* 2218, § 2	* 2242, § 1	* 2242, § 1
3. *of penalty:*				
a. affected.....	† § 1	† § 1	† § 1	† § 1
b. crass.......	* ? § 2	† § 3, n. 1	* § 2	† § 3, n. 1
c. grave.......	* ? § 2	† § 3, n. 1	* § 2	* § 3, n. 1
d. venial......	* § 2	† c. d.	* § 2	* § 3, n. 1

In this diagram "†" indicates that the respective form of ignorance does not excuse in the given case; "*" indicates that it does excuse. The paragraphs indicated refer to canon 2229. The other numbers indicate corresponding canons of the Code. All cases not clearly solved by canon 2229 or any other canon of the Code are indicated by "c. d." (common doctrine) and "p. op." (probable opinion). "?" indicates that the cases are doubtfully solved by the Code. For example, affected ignorance of fact does not excuse from a vindicative penalty imposed upon a crime which presupposes perfect *dolus* according to common doctrine. Grave ignorance of law excuses from censures not requiring perfect *dolus* according to the express provision of canon 2229, § 3, n. 1. *"Perf. dolus"* at the head of the diagram indicates a crime which presupposes perfect *dolus*. *"Dol. et cul."* stands for crimes which can be consummated with general imputability, *i. e.*, either *ex dolo* or *ex culpa*.

not be placed on the same basis with those crimes which according to canon 2229, § 2, require perfect *dolus*. Hence, the former should be judged according to the rules of the third paragraph of canon 2229, which deals with crimes that do not require perfect *dolus*. The law does not distinguish.

However, in regard to crass ignorance of fact there is a fundamental reason for supposing a difference between crimes which presuppose simple *dolus* and those which are complete even in the *culposum* form. For, it seems to be in accord with the general principles regarding *dolus* to hold that mere negligence is not the equivalent of *dolus* (at least in the internal forum), because he who acts even with crass ignorance of fact cannot be said to have a "deliberate will to violate the law." [6] An example will make this clear. The crime of abortion is committed only by those who directly procure the removal of a nonviable fetus. But one who effects an abortion through crass ignorance of fact does not directly procure the same, since it is impossible directly to intend that which is not known. Suppose, for example, that a woman is employing a certain medicine during the time of pregnancy. For some reason or other, she suspects that this medicine may result in an abortion. The particular remedy employed is not indispensable and it could readily be replaced by another which is equally good. Through gross negligence she fails to investigate the truth even though she could very easily do so by consulting her physician. If the abortion does result in this case it can scarcely be considered to have been *procured* despite the crass ignorance.[7]

The above example must not be confounded with an attempt to commit abortion. A person, who directly intends to procure abortion but through crass ignorance selects inadequate means to effect the same, is to be judged, not according to the legal rules for ignorance, but according to the principles governing criminal attempt.[8]

[6] Canon 2200, § 1.

[7] It is presumed in the above case that there is real ignorance of fact on the part of the woman. If her suspicions were so strong that they amount to practical certainty that the criminal results will follow, there is no ignorance at all.

[8] Cf. canons 2212, § 1, and 2213, § 1.

What has been said above is applicable to all crimes which presuppose at least simple *dolus* in the commission of the criminal act. In all other points, however, it seems that this classification of delicts does not differ from those which are complete when committed with either *dolus* or *culpa* so far as responsibility for *latae sententiae* penalties is concerned. Therefore, it was considered advisable not to include any mention of the former class of delicts in the above diagram.

In this connection it may be useful to recall a decision of the Holy Office in regard to the absolution of an accomplice. The Holy Office has expressly declared that crass ignorance is not an excuse from the excommunication imposed upon this crime.[9] It is necessary to remember that crass ignorance in this case (as in all others) must not be judged merely by the absence of any effort on the part of the confessor to find out whether or not the present penitent is his accomplice. Another factor, essential to all culpable ignorance, must not be overlooked, namely, the gravity of the obligation to discover the truth in the concrete circumstances of a given case. Due to the peculiar nature of this crime, there may be occasions when a confessor cannot make this inquiry because of the danger of scandal or infamy. Hence, the lack of effort on the part of the confessor to discover the truth must be balanced with the seriousness of this danger in determining whether or not the ignorance is crass.

At first sight the great number of possible cases, as revealed in the diagram above, might seem to demand a highly complex system of rules to provide for each specific case. However, the résumé placed at the end of the present chapter shows that a few simple rules can be made to cover the entire situation.

Canon 2229 is the first express and universal legislation on the subject. It is evidently designed by the codifiers of the law to settle those points of law which were doubtful and disputed at the time, thus leaving the remaining rules to be determined according to gen-

[9] The precise question was: "Utrum absolventes complicem in re turpi cum ignorantia crassa seu supina hanc excommunicationem incurrant an non." The response was: "In casu incurrere."—S. C. S. Off., 13 ian. 1892, ad 3—*Fontes*, n. 1147.

eral principles of penal imputability and the common doctrine of canonists, viewed in the light of the present legislation.

The canon, by express provisions, authoritatively settled the following points:

1. That affected ignorance either of the law or of the penalty alone never excuses from any penalty, even though the law requires perfect *dolus;*

2. That crass ignorance is distinct from grave ignorance, and that grave ignorance always excuses from censures;

3. That not only ignorance of law but also ignorance of the penalty alone excuses; thus solving any doubt concerning the old dispute regarding ignorance of the penalty alone. In regard to censures the canon is clear in determining that ignorance of the penalty alone excuses under the same conditions in which ignorance of the law excuses.

These points of law are now clear beyond all doubt and need not be considered any further. The remainder of the chapter will be devoted to the specific problems which canon 2229 offers the interpreter. Commentators of the canon have done very little to clarify questions which may be raised in regard to it; most of the writers after the Code content themselves simply with repeating the provisions or the text of the canon itself. Since the problems regarding the nature of grave, of crass and of affected ignorance, and also the question of perfect *dolus* have already been considered, it remains but to explore and delineate the specific rules which are not at once clear from the canon itself.

Article II. Ignorance in Relation to Vindicative *Latae Sententiae* Penalties

The rules concerning ignorance in relation to vindicative *latae sententiae* penalties can be summed up in two propositions:

1. When the law expressly demands perfect *dolus* as an essential condition for the incurring of these penalties, then all ignorance (*i. e.*, of fact, of the law or of the penalty), except affected ignorance, excuses.

2. When the law does not demand perfect *dolus* as an essential element of the crime, only that ignorance which does not suffice for grave penal imputability exempts from vindicative penalties. Consequently ignorance of the penalty alone does not excuse.

The first rule is a deduction from the second paragraph of canon 2229, which simply states that "any diminution of imputability on the part of the intellect" suffices to excuse from *latae sententiae* penalties when the law presupposes perfect *dolus*. The Code does not determine what is meant by *quelibet imminutio*. In general it can be said that all the causes enumerated in canons 2199-2206 are included.[10] The context of canon 2229, § 2, moreover, fixes the meaning of the phrase more precisely. In the immediately preceding paragraph of canon 2229 it is decreed that affected ignorance, whether of the law or of the penalty, does not excuse in this case. In the immediately following paragraph of the same canon it is expressly stated that crass ignorance does not excuse if the law does not presuppose perfect *dolus* in the perpetration of the crime. The logical conclusion is that crass and grave ignorance either of the law or also of the penalty alone suffices to excuse anyone from incurring those vindicative penalties which are imposed upon crimes whose perpetration presupposes perfect *dolus*. Though ignorance of fact is not mentioned in either of these paragraphs (*i. e.*, one or three), there can be no doubt that it also excuses under the same circumstances. This is evident from the general principles of the law and from the fact that the Code includes ignorance of fact among the causes which can diminish or obviate penal imputability.

In regard to ignorance of the penalty alone the Code seems to be more liberal than the common doctrine before the Code. Aside from the doctrine of individual canonists, the general opinion was expressed in the rule that ignorance of the penalty alone did not excuse unless the penalty was a censure.[11] It was in regard to cen-

[10] Cf. Berutti, *De Delictis et Poenis*, p. 91.

[11] Cf. Wernz, *Ius Decretalium*, VI, 32, note 81; Reiffenstuel, *Ius Canonicum*, lib. III, tit. XXXIX, nn. 30-31; Alterius, *De Censuris Ecclesiasticis*, lib. III, tit. II, cap. III; Suarez, *De Censuris*, disp. IV, sect. IX, nn. 19-20; Pichler, *Candidatus Iurisprudentiae*, lib. I, tit. II, n. 42; Lega, *De Delictis et Poenis*, p. 61; Montes, "La ignorancia en el derecho penal"—*Ciudad de Dios*, CL

sures, especially excommunication, that the opinion was first defended and afterwards commonly admitted. The Code evidently places vindicative penalties and censures on the same plane, so far as ignorance is concerned, when the law requires perfect *dolus* as a condition for the perpetration of the crime. The law does not distinguish. Hence no distinction is to be made unless a compelling reason can be found.

Some reason for holding that ignorance of the penalty does not excuse from vindicative penalties even in this case can be found in the nature of the penalty itself. It is inflicted primarily to expiate the crime and does not necessarily presuppose contumacy as does a censure. Yet, the law seems to overrule this objection. Moreover, the connotation of contumacy is present to some extent in the concept of perfect *dolus* and, hence, the rule of the Code in regard to these vindicative penalties is not illogical.[12]

What does, perhaps, seem strange is that even crass ignorance merely of the penalty excuses. Yet, because the canon expressly attributes the same excusing force to ignorance of law and to ignorance of the penalty alone in reference to penal sanctions which presuppose perfect *dolus*, crass ignorance of the penalty alone seems to be admitted by the Code as an excuse from the incurring of vindicative penalties. According to canon 2202, § 2, ignorance merely of the penalty diminishes imputability to some extent (*aliquantum*). It does not say what kind of ignorance is meant, but it is apparent from the first paragraph of the same canon that the degree of dimi-

(1927), 329-334. Shortly before the Code a number of authors adopted the view of Navarrus (cf. *supra*, pp. 68-69) and extended the excuse accorded for ignorance of penalty alone to crimes which were punished by "extraordinary" penalties. V. gr., D'Annibale, *Summula Theologiae Moralis*, I, 315; Noldin, *De Poenis Ecclesiasticis* (5. ed., Oeniponte, 1905), p. 23. The Code seems to have adopted the less common opinion that ignorance merely of the penalty excuses from vindicative penalties when the law demands perfect *dolus* as a prerequisite for the crime. Cf. Schmalzgrueber, *Ius Ecclesiasticum*, lib. I, tit. II, n. 40.

[12] Canon 2377, in imposing a general sanction, requires that the delinquent be contumacious: "Sacerdotes contra praescriptum can. 131, § 1, contumaces, Ordinarius pro suo prudenti arbitrio puniat . . . " The penalty in this case can be vindicative, but the delinquent must first be "contumacious."

nution is to be measured according to the degree of culpability of the ignorance. Surely, crass ignorance of the penalty diminishes responsibility for a vindicative penalty very little.

Accordingly Kinane, in reasoning from the nature of the penalty and also from the fact that ignorance of the penalty alone does not preclude imputability, holds that canon 2229, § 2, is an express exception to the general rule that ignorance of the penalty alone does not excuse from the incurring of vindicative *latae sententiae* penalties. He limits this exception to invincible ignorance of the penalty when the law presupposes perfect *dolus* for the consummation of the delict.[13]

The arguments of Kinane are in themselves correct, but the text of canon 2229 is clear and unmistakable. It puts censures and vindicative penalties on the same plane in those cases wherein perfect *dolus* is necessary for the criminal act. Hence, if crass ignorance of the penalty alone must be admitted in one case, it must be admitted also in the other. Since penal laws must be interpreted strictly[14] and in favor of the delinquent,[15] it would be contrary to the rules of interpretation to limit the scope of an excuse granted by law against the clear text of the law itself.

Commentators of the Code do not expressly bring up this question, but it seems to be in accord with the general consensus of opinion, according to which it is usually implied that ignorance, whether of the law or of the penalty alone, excuses from all penalties when the sanction of the law presupposes perfect *dolus*. The only exception to this rule is made in reference to affected ignorance.[16]

Before the discussion of this subject is brought to its conclusion,

[13] "The Effect of Invincible Ignorance of the Law or of the Punishment Alone on Vindicative Punishments 'Latae Sententiae' "—*IER*, XXXI (1928), 81-82; so also Prümmer, *Manuale Theologiae Moralis*, III, 353, note 83.

[14] Canon 19.

[15] Canon 2219, § 1.

[16] Cf., v. gr., Berutti, *De Delictis et Poenis*, p. 91; Roberti, *De Delictis et Poenis*, I, 277-278; Coronata, *Institutiones Iuris Canonici*, IV, 114, esp. note 5; Wernz-Vidal, *Ius Canonicum*, VII, 214; Vermeersch-Creusen, *Epitome*, III, 250; Woywod, "Requisites for Incurring the Penalty of the Law"—*HPR*, XXXVI (1936), 840; Michiels, *Normae Generales*, I, 359-360.

it is necessary to stress the point that the ignorance of the penalty alone, which excuses from the incurring of vindicative penalties, denotes a lack of knowledge that the law imposes any penalty at all. Anything short of that would be merely an accidental ignorance in regard to vindicative penalties. Hence, if a delinquent knows that the delict is punished by law, but does not know in what precisely the penalty consists or is in positive error regarding it, there can be no excuse. If a different view is defended in regard to censures, it is for reasons peculiar to these penalties alone.[17]

The second rule—which establishes the principle that only venially culpable ignorance exempts from the incurring of vindicative penalties when the sanction of the law does not presuppose perfect *dolus*—is evident, so far as ignorance of law and ignorance of fact are concerned. It is a necessary deduction, not so much from canon 2229, but rather from canon 2218, § 2. Ignorance of fact and ignorance of law excuse from the incurring of vindicative penalties if the ignorance is not gravely sinful, because delictual imputability is thus precluded.

The difficulty arises in regard to ignorance of the mere penalty. Sometimes the statement is made that invincible ignorance solely of the penalty excuses from the incurring of any and all penalties, hence also from *latae sententiae* vindicative penalties. For example, Cerato writes: ". . . ignorantia invincibilis . . . cum non sit voluntaria seu imputabilis, sive fuerit legis sive solius poenae, ab omni censura (itemque ab omni poena) semper excusat: c. 2218 . . ."[18] Evidently the author relies upon canon 2218, § 2, for this opinion. The reasoning is faulty, because the canon merely states the general rule that everything which precludes grave moral guilt, also excuses from all penalties. That grave penal imputability is compatible with ignorance of the penalty alone is evident from canon 2202, § 2.

Pellé, in his recent work on penal law, supports the same untenable doctrine and for practically the same reason. He writes: ". . . il est de même [*i. e.*, invincible ignorance excuses from the penalty] s'il y a ignorance invincible de la *peine;* il ne suffit pas de

[17] Cf. Haring, "Praktisches über das kirchliche Strafrecht"—*LQS*, LXXVII (1924), 536, note 1.

[18] *Censurae Vigentes*, p. 51.

savoir qu'on a fait le mal, il faut savoir, en outre, que telle faute entraîne telle sanction canonique, parce qu' elle revêt une gravité *extraordinaire*." [19] The reason here assigned is without foundation, because knowledge of the penal sanction is not necessary for penal responsibility, as canon 2202, § 2, clearly states.[20]

A cursory reading of canon 2229, § 3, n. 1, may lead to the unjustified conclusion, that both ignorance of the law and ignorance of the penalty alone (since both are mentioned together) excuse from the incurring of vindicative penalties if the ignorance is not gravely culpable. The plain fact is that canon 2229 nowhere states that either ignorance of the law or ignorance of the penalty offers such an excuse. The excuse which is offered by ignorance when the sanction of a penal law presupposes perfect *dolus*—regardless of whether the ignorance be of the law, of the fact or of the penalty, provided only that it is not an affected ignorance—is deducible from the second paragraph of canon 2229, as has already been shown.

The construction of canon 2229, § 3, n. 1, which deals with the case of crimes in whose perpetration the sanction of the law does not presuppose the existence of perfect *dolus*, is indeed somewhat strange. In the initial clause it states that crass ignorance, whether it be of the law or also of the mere penalty, never excuses from the incurring of any *latae sententiae* penalty. In the following clause it decrees that a less culpably grave ignorance than that which is crass, similarly offers no excuse in the case of vindicative *latae sententiae* penalties, though it furnishes an excuse in the case of censures. If one had to rely upon canon 2229 alone, the logical conclusion would have to be that neither ignorance of the law nor ignorance of the mere penalty excuses from the incurring of vindicative penalties.

19 *Le Droit Pénal*, p. 60. Cf. also, De Meester, *Juris Canonici Compendium*, III, P. II, 152.

20 Cocchi (*Commentarium in Codicem*, lib. V, n. 43) makes this statement: "Ignorantia invincibilis sive legis, sive tantum poenae, a poenis latae sententiae omnino excusat; deest enim in casu dolus et contumacia." The reason here assigned evidently holds only for penalties presupposing perfect *dolus* and for censures. Cocchi seems to have inadvertently erred when he wrote that sentence, because in two other places in the same work (lib. V, n. 4; lib. I, n. 116) he expressly affirms the contrary. For a refutation of the reasons assigned by Cocchi, see Kinane, *ibidem*, pp. 82-84.

The only reason for the emergence of an excuse in connection with ignorance of the law is that penal imputability is cancelled by the presence of such an ignorance according to canon 2218, § 2. But, as has already been pointed out, ignorance alone of the specific penalty that attaches to the law does not excuse from penal imputability according to the express statement of canon 2202, § 2.

Article III. Affected Ignorance of Fact in Reference to Censures

The legal rules concerning ignorance in regard to *latae sententiae* censures are for the most part clear from the text of the Code itself and need no further comment. Thus, it is certain from canon 2229, § 1, that affected ignorance, of the law and of the penalty alone, does not excuse from any censure, even if the censure be imposed for a crime whose commission presupposes the presence of perfect *dolus*. Affected ignorance of law diminishes imputability so slightly that the law justly ascribes to it the same effects that it ascribes to *dolus*. Furthermore, it would seem very strange, if the law tolerated its own deliberate circumvention and the consequent escape from the effects of its penal sanctions on the part of a delinquent, who suspects the existence of a legal prescription but designedly does all in his power to remain in ignorance in order that he may not be deterred from his course of action.

It is equally clear from the second paragraph of canon 2229 that even crass ignorance of law, of fact and of penalty alone, excuse from all censures inflicted upon crimes which by legislative definition presuppose perfect *dolus*. This proposition is evident not only from pre-Code law,[21] which is not revoked, but is implied also by the text of the canon itself, which states that any diminution of imputability whatsoever (with the exception of affected ignorance relative to the law or its penalty) excuses in these cases.

Finally, the Code clearly, though not expressly, settles the old dispute regarding grave ignorance. It is now certain that grave ignorance in relation not only to the law but also to the penalty alone excuses from the incurring of all censures. For, in the first section

[21] Cf. Lehmkuhl, *Theologia Moralis*, II, 621.

of the third paragraph of canon 2229 it is stated that all ignorance which is not crass excuses in this regard. On the other hand, it is already clear from canon 2242, § 1,[22] that anything less than grave ignorance similarly excuses from the incurring of all censures. Hence, the only form of ignorance that can be referred to in the third paragraph of canon 2229 is grave ignorance. Moreover, the Code in authoritatively adopting this opinion can certainly be understood to have accepted it also in regard to ignorance of fact, even though in the canon there is express mention solely of ignorance of law and ignorance of the penalty. It would appear illogical and altogether arbitrary to maintain that grave ignorance merely of the penalty excuses and that grave ignorance of fact does not excuse. For the latter certainly diminishes imputability more than ignorance of the penal sanction.

These principles are well established and commonly admitted. Hence, there is no need for further comment. The remaining three articles in the present chapter will be devoted to three particular difficulties which arise in regard to ignorance of censures.

The problem to be considered in the present article concerns the effect of affected ignorance of fact upon responsibility for *latae sententiae* censures imposed upon crimes which are perfectly consummated only when special *dolus* is present. Strictly considered, on the basis of the text of canon 2229 alone, the same question could be raised in reference to vindicative penalties. However, to admit affected ignorance of fact as an excuse from any vindicative penalty would be something entirely new in the law and contrary to the nature of the penalty itself. There is no basis for that view either in pre-Code doctrine or in the Code itself. Why the situation is somewhat different in regard to censures will be seen presently.

The problem arises from the fact that canon 2229, § 1, expressly mentions affected ignorance in relation only to the law or the attached penalty, when it decrees that affected ignorance never excuses from any *latae sententiae* penalties. Commentators, in speaking of canon 2229, do not expressly bring up this problem; but the general impression gained from a study of their writings is, that they

[22] Cf. also canon 2218, § 2.

do not admit affected ignorance of fact as an excuse from any *latae sententiae* penalty. Cipollini, for example, expressly states that affected ignorance of fact does not excuse from a penalty imposed upon a crime which presupposes perfect *dolus*.[23] Vermeersch-Creusen make the general statement: "Ignorantia affectata a *nullis* poenis latae sententiae excusat." [24] So also Cappello when speaking specifically of censures writes: "Ignorantia affectata numquam excusat a censura." [25] Not less clear is the general statement of Ayrinhac-Lydon that "affected or pretended [sic!] ignorance never excuses from any automatic (*latae sententiae*) penalties." [26]

But, one may ask, is this conclusion warranted by the Code? In the first place, it is evident that ignorance of fact can be affected or procured. Thus, if a person were deliberately to turn away from a friend who, he surmises, is on the point of telling him that the book he is reading is prohibited under censure, then such a person has affected ignorance of fact. A confessor who purposely requests a penitent to be silent about the circumstance of a delict, which would determine whether an excommunication reserved to the Holy See in a special manner was in reality incurred, has affected ignorance of fact in regard to the existence of that particular censure.

Does such affected ignorance excuse? The question has a twofold aspect. First, does paragraph one of canon 2229, in decreeing that affected ignorance either of the law or of the attached penalty does not excuse, include also ignorance of fact? And, secondly, does affected ignorance of fact result in a diminution of imputability within the meaning of the *quaelibet imputabilitatis imminutio* according to paragraph two of the same canon?

The first question must be answered in the negative upon the unmistakable wording of the text itself. If ignorance of fact is to be

[23] *De Censuris Latae Sententiae,* p. 21.

[24] *Epitome,* III, 249.

[25] *De Censuris,* p. 53.

[26] *Penal Legislation,* p. 41. Cf., for similar expressions, Woywod, *A Practical Commentary,* II, 421; Claeys Bouuaert-Simenon, *Manuale Iuris Canonici* (4. ed., Gandae et Leodii, 1934), III, 326; Berutti, *De Delictis et Poenis,* p. 91; Chelodi, *Ius Poenale,* p. 32; Beste, *Introductio ad Codicem,* p. 894; Michiels, *Normae Generales,* I, 359-360.

understood in the first paragraph, then why does it expressly name only ignorance of law and ignorance of the penalty? If two members of a tripartite division are expressly mentioned and the third is passed over in silence, the obvious inference is that the third member is not to be understood as included in the proposition.

On the other hand, it is equally clear that the Code adopts the distinction between ignorance of fact and ignorance of law. Ignorance of fact is expressly mentioned in canon 16, § 2, and is spoken of (though not named) in canon 2203. More specifically, canon 2229 undoubtedly presupposes the distinction, otherwise the constant mention of ignorance of law would have no meaning. Yet, when the law does make a distinction, it must be for some practical purpose. Legal distinctions are useful only if practical consequences can be predicated upon them. In a text written for instruction this is not necessarily so; for, the author may introduce distinctions merely for the sake of illustration. This, however, is not true of a Code of laws.

The more fundamental query in regard to these cases is whether affected ignorance of fact constitutes a diminution of imputability, as is required by the second paragraph of canon 2229. It seems that this question can be answered in the affirmative. This view is based upon the following considerations:

1. The silence of canon 2229 in regard to affected ignorance of fact, when it expressly states that affected ignorance of law does not excuse, may in itself be considered as an implied admission that affected ignorance of fact excuses in cases that presuppose the presence of perfect *dolus*. This conclusion is certainly in accord with the mild interpretation which must be placed upon penal law.[27] Furthermore, the first paragraph must be considered as an exception to the general principle set up in the second paragraph of canon 2229, to the effect, that every diminution whatsoever of imputability excuses in the cases that assume the necessary presence of perfect *dolus*. The exceptionary norm of the first paragraph of canon 2229 must correspondingly be subjected to a strict interpretation. Since it is not clear that ignorance of fact is comprised in the enumeration

[27] "In poenis benignior est interpretatio facienda."—canon 2219, § 1; Reg. 49, *R. J.*, in VI°.

established by the exceptional norm, this kind of ignorance must rather be regarded as being not included.[28]

2. The argument in favor of admitting affected ignorance of fact as an excuse from the incurring of *latae sententiae* penalties is, however, something more than a mere argument from silence. Canon 2229 must be viewed in its relation to pre-Code law. Prior to the Code the effect of affected ignorance upon penal imputability was the subject of a serious dispute among the authors.[29] The opinion that affected ignorance excused from the incurring of censures which were imposed upon crimes that connoted perfect *dolus*, was certainly a probable opinion before the Code. The Code settled the dispute in regard to ignorance of law and ignorance of penalty, adopting the stricter view in these cases. With regard to ignorance of fact, it must at least be admitted that the Code left the question open. According to canon 6, numbers 3 and 4, the old law is retained when the new is not clearly contrary to it. In doubt the old law remains in force and, hence, the doctrine of pre-Code authorities still must be considered the source for a norm concerning affected ignorance of fact. Therefore, the former opinion regarding affected ignorance of fact is still valid.

3. The ultimate and definitive decision in this question (barring authoritative definition) depends upon the solution of the moral problem whether or not affected ignorance diminishes imputability. It is not the purpose of this study to attempt to solve that problem. The Code does not decide it, though some seem to find an implicit solution of the question in the first paragraph of canon 2229. But the Code does not touch this question at all; it states merely that affected ignorance of law and of penalty are not a sufficient diminution of imputability for the general rule of the second paragraph to take effect.

The reasons why affected ignorance should rather be considered as diminishing imputability have already been considered. These reasons are all the more valid for ignorance of fact. There is, first of all, the general principle that ignorance of fact can be more leniently considered than ignorance of law. Moreover, in affected igno-

[28] "In obscuris minimum est sequendum."—Reg. 30, *R. J.*, in VI°.

[29] Cf. *supra*, pp. 65-69.

rance of fact there is no contempt of law or authority, but rather respect for law. In this case the agent desires to remain ignorant merely of an objective circumstance in order that he may not become guilty of a violation of the law. His purpose in deliberately seeking ignorance of fact is *not* that he may be able to *sin* more freely, but that he may *act* more freely. He seeks ignorance directly because he feels that the unwelcome knowledge would deter him from doing something that he greatly desires to do.[30] As long, therefore, as the moral question concerning affected ignorance of fact remains unsettled, it seems legitimate to adopt the milder view in penal matters.

The most serious objection to the view defended in these pages is, that it goes contrary to what is apparently the unanimous doctrine of canonists after the Code. The only answer to this objection is, that canonists generally do not expressly consider this problem at all, or, if they do, they seem to draw their conclusion from an unjustifiable interpretation of the first paragraph of canon 2229. Beyond the reasons and arguments used before the Code, at a time when the opinion favoring the excusing character of affected ignorance was simultaneously a probable opinion, nothing but this *a pari* application of canon 2229 has been advanced against the opinion that affected ignorance of fact excuses from the incurring of censures inflicted by law upon crimes that connote the accompaniment of perfect *dolus*.

From the above considerations it seems that the following principle can be set up and defended as probable and, therefore, safely followed in conscience: Affected ignorance of fact excuses from the incurring of censures imposed upon crimes that presuppose perfect *dolus*. This is especially true in regard to the enactments of such

[30] For an excellent discussion of this question see Hollweck, *Die kirchlichen Strafgesetze,* note 2 *ad* par. 16, p. 78. Hollweck seems to exclude concomitant affected ignorance of fact, *i. e.,* when a person seeks to remain ignorant, but is nevertheless minded to perform the act even if he did know the facts. This seems a very rare, if not also an oddly naïve and by the same token a highly problematical, psychological state of mind in any act that can still remain characterized as a human act. Why should anyone make positive efforts to remain in ignorance if his mind is predetermined and his will already resolved to commit the deed or to omit the duty even if he knew the act of commission or omission to be wrong?

acts as delicts which the Code has taken over unchanged from the former law and in regard to which authors before the Code expressly admitted affected ignorance of fact as an excuse; because in these cases, at least, it seems highly improbable that the silence of the Code can be considered as a departure from the earlier law.

An outstanding example of this is the penal law concerning the delict of heresy. Long before the Code it had been a probable opinion that affected ignorance of fact excused from the incurring of the penalties decreed against the pertinacious denial of a truth to be believed by divine and catholic faith. Because the denial had to be pertinacious, it was held that only a deliberate denial of a plainly proposed truth sufficed, to the exclusion of even an affected and procured ignorance, for the constitution of the delict of heresy.[31] This opinion is still taught by canonists since the publication of the Code; among whom are such authorities as Chelodi,[32] Pistocchi,[33] and Coronata.[34]

Despite the opinion of the many who reject this view[35] it can still be defended as probable, because the Code does not directly touch the question.

[31] Cf. especially De Lugo, *De Virtute Fidei Divinae,* disp. XX, sect. VI. De Lugo sums up the views of his time in five opinions. Of the fifth he writes: "Quinta et verior, ac communior sententia dicit, quamlibet ignorantiam, etiam crassam et affectatam, excusare ab haeresi et haereticorum poenis." This was the view of the commentators of the *Bullae Coenae Domini,* v. gr., Duardus, *Commentaria in Bullam Coenae Domini,* lib. II, can. I, q. 25, n. 6; and of the interpreters of the *Constitutio "Apostolicae Sedis,"* v. gr., Ballerini-Palmieri, *Opus Morale,* II, 59; Konings, *Theologia Moralis,* I, 117; Bucceroni, *Commentarii de Constitutionibus Pii IX "Apostolicae Sedis" et Benedicti XIV "Sacramentum Poenitentiae"* (3. ed., Romae, 1890), p. 5.

[32] *Ius Poenale,* p. 75.

[33] *I Canoni Penali* (Torino-Roma: Marietti, 1925), p. 8.

[34] ". . . immo idem probabilius affirmandum videtur [sc. non considerari haereticum] etiam de eo qui in fide ex ignorantia affectata errat; ratio est quia Ecclesiae non contradicit, qui nescit se Ecclesiae contradicere, ob quamvis ignorantiam hoc faciat, et ideo non potest dici pertinax contra Ecclesiae doctrinam."—*Institutiones Iuris Canonici,* IV, 281-282.

[35] V. gr., Salucci (*Il Diritto Penale,* II, 8, note 2), who appeals expressly to canon 2229 in attempting to refute Pistocchi; so also, MacKenzie, *The Delict of Heresy* (Canon Law Studies, n. 77: Washington, D. C., 1932), p. 48; Vermeersch-Creusen, *Epitome,* III, 311.

It seems that Coronata is of the opinion that affected ignorance excuses in this case on account of the unique nature of the delict of heresy, namely, because only formal heresy is a crime and to constitute it as such knowledge is necessary.[36] However, this characteristic is not exclusively proper to the crime of heresy; it obtains in every crime which requires formal and perfect *dolus* in its substantial constitution. In every case the question is the same; namely, whether affected ignorance of fact suffices to constitute the formal and perfect *dolus* required by legislative definition. Hence, to be logical one ought to admit this opinion in other cases also, because the reasoning is perfectly identical in each case.

Hence, affected ignorance of fact should be admitted as an excuse in regard to those who knowingly read or retain prohibited books. The opinion that affected ignorance of the fact that the book was forbidden under censure, or that it contained heresy, excused from the *latae sententiae* excommunication was already held by the commentators of the *Bullae in Coena Domini.*[37] It was likewise defended by the interpreters of the *Constitutio "Apostolicae Sedis."* [38]

It must be noted that the Code changed the dispositions of the old law in regard to this crime. According to the *Bullae in Coena Domini* [39] and the Constitution *"Apostolicae Sedis"* [40] the *scienter*

[36] In refuting the opinion of Salucci, who appeals to canon 2229, § 1, Coronata writes: "At ille canon ad rem non facit; non enim hic agitur de poenis incurrendis ab eo qui revera haeresim professus est, sed potius de quaestione utrum qui errat in fide ex ignorantia affectata haereticus formalis dici possit et debeat."—*Institutiones Iuris Canonici,* IV, 282, note 1.

[37] Cf. Duardus, *Commentaria in Bullam Coenae Domini,* lib. II, can. I, q. 37, n. 5.

[38] Hollweck, *Die kirchlichen Strafgesetze,* note 2 *ad* par. 106, p. 172; Ballerini-Palmieri, *Opus Morale,* VII, 77, 222; Lehmkuhl, *Theologia Moralis,* II, 658; Bucceroni, *Commentarii,* p. 7.

[39] V. gr., Gregorius XIII, const. *"Consueverunt Romani Pontifices,"* 4 apr. 1583, § 1—*Bull. Rom. Taur.,* VIII, 413; Paulus V, const. *"Pastoralis,"* 8 apr. 1610, § 1—*Bull. Rom. Taur.,* XI, 618. *Scienter* is not found in the earlier decrees; v. gr., Paulus III, const. *"Consueverunt Romani Pontifices,"* 13 apr. 1536, § 1—*Bull. Rom. Taur.,* VI, 219; Paulus IV, const. *"Dominici Gregis,"* 24 martii 1564, § 3—*Bull. Rom. Taur.,* VI, 281-282.

[40] Pius IX, const. *"Apostolicae Sedis,"* 12 oct. 1869, § 1, n. 2—*Fontes,* n. 552.

referred to the *legentes, retinentes, imprimentes,* and *defendentes,* whereas according to canon 2318 it refers only to the *legentes* and *retinentes.* This is, consequently, a change from the old law,[41] as modern authors expressly point out.[42] However, in regard to the crime of reading and retaining prohibited books the old law still remains in force as interpreted by approved authors and, hence, following the principles discussed above, affected ignorance of fact can still be admitted as probably excusing from the penalty of the law.

Article IV. The Nature of Substantial Ignorance of Penalty Alone in Reference to Censures

The second problem in reference to ignorance is one which has received scant attention by the commentators of the Code. It concerns the meaning of the phrase *ignorantia solius poenae.* Certain it is that knowledge of the penalty is not necessary for the existence of *dolus* [43] nor, in itself, for the incurring of vindicative penalties. Upon the obvious authority of the Code ignorance of the mere penalty excuses from vindicative *latae sententiae* penalties when the law presupposes perfect *dolus* by legislative definition.[44] Moreover, in regard to vindicative penalties it seems that the only ignorance of penalty that will excuse is a complete ignorance of the fact that any penalty is attached to the violation of the law. This follows from the vindicative character of the penalty, that is, from its primary purpose to expiate crime and restore the social order. If the delinquent knows that his action is *punishable* by law and nevertheless he acts, then he assumes the risk of his conduct and makes himself responsible for the penalty.

In regard to censures the situation is quite different. These penalties, it cannot be overemphasized, are medicinal. Their primary purpose is to prevent the delinquent from violating the law and also to secure his amendment after the crime has taken place. That

[41] Cf. Ballerini-Palmieri, *op. cit.*, VII, 222.

[42] Vermeersch-Creusen, *Epitome,* III, 315; Coronata, *op. cit.*, p. 309.

[43] Canons 2200, § 1, and 2202, § 2.

[44] Canon 2229, § 2.

is why censures require contumacy before they can be incurred[45] and why absolution is due in justice once amendment has been secured.[46]

The more important function of censures is to prevent crime; for, prevention is a far more effective remedy than the cure which is applied after the damage has been done. But a moral cure can be effective only if it is known and appreciated. This explains to a great extent the reason why the legislator in canon 2229 places ignorance of the penalty on practically the same plane as ignorance of the law itself. For, on the one hand, it is obvious that ignorance of the penalty does not diminish imputability to any great extent,[47] while ignorance of law may preclude imputability altogether.[48] In the moral order, upon which penal imputability is based, ignorance of the fact that a certain deed is punishable in law really changes matters very little. A violation of law with the knowledge that a penalty is attached thereto may be evidence of a more confirmed will, or of a more determined desire to commit the immoral act, but, of itself, such knowledge does not increase guilt. Hence, the only reason why the legislator ascribes to ignorance of the penalty practically the same effects as to ignorance of the law itself is, not that he judges the crime to be so much more serious when done with full knowledge of the penalty, but that his primary purpose in imposing the medicinal penalty is defeated when the penalty is not known.

More than that, not only is the medicinal purpose of censures defeated when the subject is ignorant of the penalty, but the penalty itself may become positively harmful to him if it should be incurred without knowledge of the fact. This is particularly true of the most severe of all canonical penalties, excommunication; for, if a man should fall into excommunication without his knowledge, he would unwittingly be deprived of the official prayers, suffrages and

[45] Canon 2242.

[46] Cf. canon 2241, § 1, and especially canon 2248, § 2, which decrees: "Absolutio denegari nequit cum primum delinquens a contumacia recesserit. . . ." Cf. Vermeersch-Creusen, *Epitome,* III, 253.

[47] Canon 2202, § 2.

[48] Canon 2202, § 1.

indulgences of the Church.[49] He would be deprived of that which he needs most of all not only at a time when he needs it most seriously, but also in a way that makes it extremely difficult for him again to become a partaker of these benefits.

With these observations in mind, the question can be asked: What does the law imply by its use of the phrase "ignorance of the penalty alone?" Does it mean only a complete ignorance of the fact that the action is penalized at all (*ignorantia poenalitatis*), or does it signify ignorance of the nature or species of the penalty imposed?

The text of the law itself is not very revealing. True, it does say *ignorantia solius poenae* and not *solius poenalitatis*. By insisting upon a literal interpretation of the term *solius poenae*, one might conclude that an ignorance of the specific penalty, or an ignorance of the nature of the penalty imposed, is understood by the canon. However, *ignorantia solius poenae* is a technical term and must be given its technical signification. To determine that, usage and common doctrine is the norm to be followed and a mere literal or etymological argument is of very little value. While this is true, it cannot be denied that the expression *ignorantia solius poenae*, as opposed to the phrase *solius punitionis* or *solius penalitatis*, does tend toward the interpretation that an ignorance of the specific penalty rather than a complete ignorance of penalization in general is meant.

Some commentators of the Code consider knowledge of the existence of some enacted penalty, or the knowledge that some penal sanction is imposed by law upon the crime, as a sufficient warrant for contumacy. Hence, according to these authors knowledge that the law is penal in its character suffices for the incurring of *latae sententiae* penalties.[50]

[49] Canon 2262.

[50] Thus, Vermeersch (*Theologiae Moralis Principia*, III, 767) writes: "Non censetur igitur ignorare censuram qui conluso modo novit peccato adiunctam esse quandam poenalem sanctionem ecclesiasticam. Is a contumacia minime excusatur." The same view is defended by Creusen in the *Epitome* (III, 249). Michiels (*Normae Generales*, I, 360, note 3) cites the *Epitome* with approval. The opinion is upheld by Haring, "Praktisches ueber das kirchliche Strafrecht"—*LQS*, LXXVII (1924), 536, note 1. In his article on *contumacia* (*Periodica*, XXII, 41*) Vermeersch seems to adopt the view that a knowledge of the

This view seems to be an unwarranted departure from pre-Code doctrine. By the same token it seems to be out of perfect agreement with the Code itself. It must be conceded that it is difficult to fix the exact nature of the knowledge prerequired for contumacy. Consequently, it is not easy to determine exactly what is to be understood by the *ignorantia solius poenae* which precludes contumacy and, therefore, excuses from the incurring of the censure. Perhaps the nearest approach to a definition of *ignorantia solius poenae* can be attained by using an old legal distinction between substantial and accidental ignorance. The rule could be stated thus: Ignorance of the penalty alone excuses from the incurring of *latae sententiae* censures when it is substantial, but does not excuse when it is merely accidental.[51] Yet the rule in this broad formulation is too general for practical purposes. Hence it remains to be determined what substantial ignorance in this connection really is. This must be deduced from general principles regarding censures themselves and from the common doctrine of the authors before the Code.

In the first place, the ignorance is certainly substantial if the enacted penalty is entirely unknown. For example, if a person knew that abortion was severely prohibited by the Church, but did not know that it was punishable, he would not incur the *latae sententiae* excommunication. That is admitted by all canonists.

Let it be supposed, however, that the individual has knowledge of the prohibition of the Church, and knows also that some *latae sententiae* punishment is annexed by law to this prohibition. In

fact that a *censure* is imposed by law is required for contumacy. He writes: "Ut contumacia habeatur, estne opus ut peccans noverit quanam censura suum delictum puniatur, an satis est ut cuiuspiam censurae contrahendae sit conscius?" After citing and expressly agreeing with Creusen, he continues: "Namque qui peccat, non obstante cognitione *cuiuspiam censurae* (italics added), necessario auctoritatem Superioris punientis virtualiter contemnit, ac proin contumax dicendus est." However, this text does not necessarily imply that contumacy is had only when the delinquent knows that a censure is imposed. If the observations of Vermeersch in the *Periodica* are viewed in the light of his express statement in the *Theologia Moralis,* it would seem that the learned author considers the simple knowledge that some penalty is imposed sufficient for contumacy.

[51] Cf. Prümmer, *Manuale Theologiae Moralis,* III, 353.

regard to an individual who possesses this knowledge the following hypotheses can be considered:

1. The delinquent knows that some *latae sententiae* penalty is by law imposed upon the crime, but erroneously thinks that it is a vindicative penalty; or, at least he does not know that it is a censure;

2. The delinquent knows that a censure is attached to the delict, but does not know whether it is a suspension, an interdict or an excommunication;

3. The delinquent knows precisely which censure is attached, but does not know that it is by law reserved for its absolution.

1. It seems that the delinquent in the first hypothesis is excused because there is substantial ignorance or error in regard to the penalty. In a word, his ignorance of the fact that a *latae sententiae* censure is by law attached to the crime, despite his knowledge that some penalty in general is imposed, excuses him from incurring *latae sententiae* censures. The nature of the canonical warning and of contumacy, as well as the doctrine before the Code support this view.

The canonical warning which must precede the infliction of a censure cannot be a mere general threat of punishment, but must specify that a censure will be inflicted in the event that the warning is disregarded. More than that, it is even necessary to specify exactly which censure will be inflicted in case the command or prohibition is violated.[52]

The same is true, *a pari*, when the law itself takes the place of the canonical warning. If a delinquent is unaware of the fact that a *latae sententiae* censure is imposed by law upon a certain crime, he is in reality not warned by the law and, therefore, cannot be considered contumacious. Just as in the above case the superior could

[52] Cf. canon 2242, § 2; Coronata, *Institutiones Iuris Canonici,* IV, 150; Eichmann, *Strafrecht,* p. 77. The warning was, therefore, called *comminatio censurae*—Santi, *Praelectiones Iuris Canonici,* lib. V, tit. XXXIX, n. 14. "Quisquis igitur factum aliquod, vel omissum, censuris punire vult, necesse habet eas comminari, . . . idest illud prius vetare, hoc praecipere sub censura, eaque specifica."—D'Annibale *Summula Theologiae Moralis,* I, 322. Cf. Rossi, "L'ignoranza in ordine alle censure"—*Perfice Munus,* III (1928), 31-32.

not inflict a censure in the event of a substantial defect in the warning, so in this instance the law cannot operate because the delinquent is not *de facto* warned.[53]

Moreover, the genuine notion of contumacy demands knowledge of the censure. Contumacy is not mere disobedience to authority, but a disobedience coupled with a contempt of the imposed censure. Contempt of the censure is impossible without knowledge of the same, and, consequently, ignorance of the enacted censure excuses.[54]

Finally, it seems to have been the common doctrine of authors before the Code that *ignorance of the censure* excused from the incurring of *latae sententiae* penalties, and no valid reason can be discovered in the Code for supposing a change in the law on this point. The very fact that it prescribes a canonical warning and requires contumacy before a censure can be inflicted and, furthermore, expressly states that an ignorance of the mere penalty excuses from the incurring of censures shows that this common doctrine was adopted.[55] Consequently the opinion that an ignorance concerning the censure alone, despite the general knowledge that some kind of penalty is imposed in the law, nevertheless offers an excuse relative

[53] Suarez, *De Censuris*, disp. IV, sect. IX, n. 2.

[54] ". . . la contumacia è inconceptible con l'ignoranza della censura"—Rossi, *loc. cit.* Cf. Jorio, *Theologia Moralis*, II, 250; Coronata, *ibidem*, pp. 150-151. For this reason *contumacia* is often called *contemptus censurae*. Cf. Cappello, *De Censuris*, p. 29; Lega, *De Delictis et Poenis*, pp. 144-145.

[55] Pre-Code authors generally do not discuss this precise question. Yet, their mode of expression clearly reveals their mind on this point. Frequently such statements as these are made: ". . . non incurratur censura ab ignorante, suo delicto esse annexam censuram, . . ."—Pichler, *Candidatus Iurisprudentiae*, lib. I, tit. II, n. 42; ". . . licet quis sciat actum prohibitum ab Ecclesia, ignoret autem prohibitioni adjectam esse censuram, ignorantia haec excusat a censura . . ."—Santi, *op. cit.*, lib. V, tit. XXXIX, n. 5; cf. Wernz, *Ius Decretalium*, VI, 32; Reiffenstuel, *Ius Canonicum*, lib. V, tit. XXXIX, n. 30; Suarez, *De Censuris*, disp. IV, sect. IX. That this opinion was common before the Code is evident from the words of Ferraris (*Bibliotheca Canonica Iuridica Moralis Theologica*, *v.* "ignorantia," n. 21): ". . . ex communi omnium sententia, ignorantia censurarum excusat ab eis . . . quamvis caeteroquin contra legem agendo gravissime quis peccet . . ."

to the incurring of the enacted censure seems by far the better view to adopt under the discipline of the present Code.[56]

2. One can now proceed to investigate the second of the three hypotheses mentioned above. The precise question to be considered is, whether it is necessary that the delinquent know which *specific* censure (suspension, interdict or excommunication) is imposed by law, in order that a *latae sententiae* censure can be incurred. For example, if a priest thought that a suspension was imposed upon the crime of absolving an accomplice (canon 2367), would he incur the excommunication? Or, if a layman knew that by joining a forbidden society he would be deprived of the reception of the Sacraments and that absolution from the sin would entail difficulties, but was ignorant of the excommunication,[57] would he incur that penalty?

It seems fairly clear that an ignorance through which the penalty of censure remains unidentified as an excommunication, even though knowledge be had that the law imposes some kind of penalty by way of censure, must be considered as a substantial ignorance [or error]. On the other hand, a mistake or error in regard to suspension or interdict can scarcely be considered more than accidental. Hence, the fact that a delinquent erroneously supposed an interdict to be imposed upon his crime, when in fact a suspension is inflicted, would not excuse the delinquent from incurring the suspension.

The gravity of the mistake must be judged according to the nature of the object concerning which it is had. The object in this case is the censure, the gravity of which must be measured according to the nature and extent of the goods of which it deprives the delinquent.[58] A comparison of the effects of suspension and interdict scarcely justifies the conclusion that the benefits of which these penalties deprive the delinquent are of so different a nature as to make an error in regard to these two censures substantial in character. A delinquent who falsely supposed that a personal interdict is imposed upon the simoniacal administration of the sacraments can-

[56] Cf. Sole, *De Delictis et Poenis*, p. 82; Rossi, "L'ignoranza in ordine alle censure"—*loc. cit.;* Cappello, *De Censuris*, p. 53.

[57] Canon 2335.

[58] Essentially every penalty is the privation of some good, as the definition of canon 2215 reveals.

not be said to be substantially ignorant of the penalty (suspension) actually imposed.[59]

Finally, it must not be overlooked that ignorance merely of the penalty excuses *only* because it diminishes contumacy. There is no principle in law which makes it necessary that the exact penalty of the law must be known before it can be incurred. The contumacy of a delinquent, who errs merely in regard to some of the specific effects of a censure imposed by law, is diminished very slightly if it is diminished at all. It may even happen that his erroneous belief in reality increases his imputability, because the delinquent falsely supposes that a more serious censure is imposed than actually is the case. He would thus give evidence, not of a diminished imputability, but of a more determined will to commit the crime.

However, in the case of a suspension it seems that a delinquent would be excused if he erroneously supposed that the penalty was merely a suspension *a beneficio;* whereas, in reality the law imposed a partial or total suspension from office or from the exercise of orders or jurisdiction. In this case the delinquent can be considered to have erred substantially relative to the severe canonical disabilities involved in the penalty actually annexed to the crime by the law. In other cases the mistake would imply no more than that the delinquent was unaware of the *exact extent* of the incurred privations. The nature of a penalty, in so far as it affects the individual delinquent, must be judged from the privations that it involves. If the effects of personal interdict (the only real medicinal interdict) and the effects of the various forms of suspension (excluding suspension *a beneficio*) are compared, it will be noted that the actual difference involved consists in the extent to which the exercise of orders and jurisdiction or the reception and administration of the sacraments are prohibited. A mistake in regard to these effects can scarcely be considered material and serious enough to appreciably diminish contumacy and to warrant an excuse from incurring these penalties.

With regard to ignorance or mistake in the proper identification of the censure as an excommunication there is a vast difference. True, excommunication is classed with suspension and interdict as a cen-

[59] Canon 2371.

sure, but its effects are essentially different. As a penalty it stands apart. To consider excommunication on a par with other penalties is to misunderstand completely its nature. Other penalties may involve greater difficulties in the matter of absolution or dispensation. They may even impose more serious handicaps than excommunication. Thus a degraded priest will beyond all doubt experience more difficulties in attempting to obtain a pardon than a priest who incurred a non-reserved excommunication. Yet, if the nature of excommunication be carefully examined it will appear that this penalty is the severest of all canonical sanctions. It may be that the present spirit of indifference in spiritual matters inclines men to regard excommunication lightly. But, if the language of the Church—from the time that the first sentence of excommunication was passed to the present—be examined, then no doubt will remain as to its severity.

St. Paul in excommunicating the incestuous Corinthian commanded the faithful in the name of Christ to carry out the sentence which he expressed in these words: *tradere hujusmodi Satanae in interitu carnis.*[60] There exists a striking commentary on these words, attributed to St. Augustine and incorporated in several collections of canons.[61] These words bear repetition. "Omnis Christianus . . . qui a sacerdotibus excommunicatur, sathanae traditur: . . . quia extra ecclesiam est diabolus, sicut in ecclesia Christus, ac per hoc quasi diabolo traditur qui ab ecclesiastica communione removetur."

This doctrine is not just an oratorical expression, as a study of the words which the Church used in inflicting this penalty reveal. Excommunication is called separation from the Body of Christ,[62]

[60] I Cor. V, 5.

[61] V. gr., *Ivonis Decretum,* II, 94; *Collectio Trium Partium,* III, 27 (28), 19; *Collectio Caesaraugustana,* XIV, 44; c. 32, C. XI, q. 3. Gratian (*loc. cit.*) attributes the text to St. Augustine, *Sermo LXXIX;* Ivo of Chartres (*Decretum, loc. cit.*) ascribes the same to St. Augustine, *De Unico Baptismo.* Cf. Berardi, *Gratiani Canones Genuini ab Apocryphis Discreti* (Venetiis, 1777), Pars III, cap. XIX, vol. IV, 248-249.

[62] ". . . non solum excommunicatione, que a fraterna societate separat sed etiam anathemate, quod ab ipso corpore Christi (quod est ecclesia) recidit, crebro percussam."—Letter of Pope John VIII to Liutpert, Archbishop of Mainz (872-873)—Jaffé (ed. P. Ewald), n. 2969—c. 12, C. III, q. 4.

an authoritative expulsion from the Church,[63] a separation from the communion of the faithful,[64] the death penalty by which a sinful member of the Church is condemned to die spiritually outside of the Church, so as not to infect the living members of Christ.[65]

The fact that ordinarily excommunication no longer inflicts the social disabilities which accompanied it in the ancient discipline does not change its essential nature. It is a spiritual penalty and has a real interior effect upon the excommunicated person, as the Church has expressly declared.[66]

The essential element of excommunication is, therefore, the exclusion from the communion of the faithful, as the Code clearly defines.[67] The other effects of this penalty, v. gr., deprivation of the right to assist at divine offices,[68] exclusion from the reception of the sacraments,[69] and from the public prayers, suffrages and indulgences of the Church [70] are but the natural results of the expulsion. No

[63] " . . . auctoritate Dei et iudicio sancti Spiritus a gremio sanctae matris ecclesiae et a consortio totius Christianitatis eliminamus . . ."—c. 107, C. XI, q. 3. The text is of uncertain origin, but attributed by Gratian to a Council of Orange.

[64] " . . . a caritate fratrum et ecclesiae communione priventur."—Council of Agde (506), cap. 35 Bruns, *Canones*, II, 153—c. 13, D. XVIII.

[65] " . . . cuius [*i. e.*, Sedis Apostolicae] sententiam qui superbiens contempserit observare mori praecipitur et auferri malum de Israel, id est, per excommunicationis sententiam, velut mortuus, a communione fidelium separari."—Rescript of Pope Innocent III to William of Montpellier (1202)—Potthast, n. 1794—c. 13, X, *qui filii sint legitimi*, IV, 17. The Council of Meaux (845) calls excommunication the *aeterna mortis damnatio* (c. 56)—Mansi, XIV, 832.

[66] "Propositio asserens, effectum excommunicationis exteriorem dumtaxat esse, quia tantummodo natura sua excludit ab exteriore communicatione Ecclesiae; quasi excommunicatio non sit poena spiritualis, ligans in coelo, animas obligans . . . :—falsa, perniciosa, in art. 23 Lutheri damnata, ad minus erronea."—Pius VI, const. "*Auctorem Fidei*," 28 aug. 1794, prop. 14—Denzinger, *Enchiridion*, n. 1546.

[67] Canon 2257, § 1.

[68] Canon 2259.

[69] Canon 2260.

[70] Canon 2262.

other penalty has such far-reaching consequences as this last resort of penal power, the spiritual death penalty.[71]

This rather lengthy digression upon the nature of excommunication should help one to appreciate the reasons for admitting ignorance of this penalty as an excusing factor. It is submitted that anyone who does not know precisely that an excommunication is attached to the crime he is committing is substantially ignorant of the penalty. If ignorance concerning the proper identification of an ecclesiastical penalty as an excommunication does not excuse anyone from incurring the penalty of excommunication, then it follows that a person could become excommunicated, be condemned and expelled from the spiritual communion of the Church without his knowledge of that fact.

A State may inflict its death penalty upon a criminal who, when he committed the crime, did not know that it was punishable with death. Yet, no well ordered State inflicts the death penalty except by proper and solemn process of law. Neither does the Church, in her system of *latae sententiae* penalties, inflict her spiritual death penalty except upon the contumacious subject, who with full knowledge of the threatened excommunication nevertheless despises the warning and violates the law. It seems incongruous that the Church would deprive an unsuspecting, though most gravely culpable, delinquent of all those spiritual benefits over which she has administrative control, especially at a time when the sinner needs these aids in a special way.

This opinion is not something entirely new in the law. As was shown in the historical section,[72] the opinion that an ignorance of the mere penalty excused from incurring it, was advanced first in

[71] Note that canon 2268, § 1, expressly declares that an interdict does not remove anyone from the communion of the faithful. Böhm, in his interesting study on the juridical status of non-Catholics (*Acatholicus* [Hamburg: de Gruyter, 1933], pp. 12-13) distinguishes three groups: the non-baptized; heretics; schismatics and apostates; and other excommunicates. He notes, moreover, that the heretic or schismatic does not become an *acatholicus* by the simple fact of his denial of the faith or in view of his insubordination, but because of the incurred excommunication. Cf. *op. cit.*, p. 49.

[72] *Supra*, p. 65.

regard to excommunication. Despite the unmistakable letter of the law to the contrary, canonists began to teach that, on account of the unique nature of excommunication, a knowledge specifically singling out the excommunication itself as the penalty was demanded before the delinquent could be considered contumacious and thus incur the penalty.[73] As this opinion was gradually applied to other censures, it is scarcely possible that the original doctrine came to be ignored, or even less appreciated than at the very beginning. In that contingency there would rather have emerged the odd result that as the doctrine grew milder in general relative to other penalties, it would at the same time have become stricter with relation to excommunication. For, while in the beginning ignorance concerning the specifically enacted penalty of excommunication was recognized as an excuse, the later doctrine would have accepted for an excuse only that ignorance which connoted a lack of knowledge that any censure was at all enacted by law for the delictual action concerning which the discussion arose.

The original doctrine was not, however, forgotten or discarded. It was still expressly taught by more recent authors [74] and no valid reason for rejecting that view under the Code can be shown.

3. The third hypothesis points to a delinquent who knows precisely which censure is attached to a given delictual act, but does not know that the censure is by law reserved for its absolution. The question here is concerned with a twofold aspect. It considers the effects of ignorance regarding the censure's reservation both upon penal imputability and also upon the reservation itself. The matter is sufficiently comprehensive in scope to merit treatment in a separate article.

[73] Thus, for example, Sanchez sums up the opinion of the older canonists: "At alii censent, hoc esse speciale in excommunicatione. Quia cum excommunicatio sit ultima ac summa poena, exigit *specialiter ipsius notitiam* [italics added], ut sic detur delinquentis summa contumacia . . ."—*De Matrimonio*, lib. I, tit. XXXII, n. 21; cf. Alterius, *De Censuris Ecclesiasticis*, lib. III, disp. II, cap. III.

[74] Cf. Kober, *Kirchenbann*, p. 205.

ARTICLE V. THE EFFECT OF IGNORANCE OF THE RESERVATION

The discussion insinuated by the title of this article does not very directly relate to the topic of the present study which considers ignorance in its relation to penal imputability. It is certain beyond all doubt that ignorance regarding the reservation of a censure, either to the Holy See or to the Ordinary, does not excuse anyone from incurring the censure.[75] A reservation as such does not change the nature, or, for that matter, the severity of the censure in so far as this penalty implies the privation of some good. Hence, error or ignorance about the reservation which is attached to a penalty cannot be considered a substantial mistake in regard to the penalty and, therefore, does not fall under the provisions of canon 2229. Furthermore, the reservation of a censure is not something which by way of extraordinary character is attached to a penalty, but should rather be considered the natural result of any criminal sanction. The fact that the legislator permits inferiors to absolve from the specified effects resulting from a violation of the common law is rather an exceptional favor than the general rule if the entire penal law is considered.[76]

Ignorance of the specified penalty excuses because it precludes contumacy. Contumacy consists essentially in the contempt of a known precept that is binding under threat of a definite censure. Such contumacy is not diminished by the fact that the delinquent is ignorant of the way in which he can obtain pardon after the crime has been committed and the censure incurred. Finally, if it were necessary for the delinquent to know the often rather complicated

[75] With regard to the reservation of a censure cf. canons 2245-2247. Cappello (*De Censuris*, p. 29) writes: "Nec requiritur ad conceptum contumaciae, ut quis cognoscat censuram esse reservatam specialissimo aut speciali modo S. Sedi, etc.; requiritur et sufficit ut cognoscat saltem in confuso esse reservatam." It may be true, as a matter of fact, that generally persons who know that a censure is imposed upon a crime will realize, in a confused way, that there will be some difficulty in obtaining absolution. This would certainly be sufficient. But if that confused knowledge were not had, there still would be no excuse from the incurring of the reserved censure.

[76] Cf. Canons 2236-2237; De Meester, *Juris Canonici Compendium*, III, P. II, 153.

jurisdictional question concerning the absolution of an incurred censure, it would become almost impossible for anyone who is not *ex professo* trained in law to incur any censure at all.

A different, though related, question is whether ignorance of the reservation excuses from the reservation itself. To avoid possible confusion it is important to note that the Code knows three kinds of reservations. The first is the reservation of the sin alone. In this case no penalty is inflicted; only the jurisdiction of the simple confessor is limited by revoking the case to a higher authority. This is called a *reservatio peccati ratione peccati ipsius.*[77] Secondly, those who have the power of imposing censures according to canon 2220 can also reserve the absolution of the same to their own or some other authority, thereby limiting the jurisdiction of inferiors. The restriction of the faculty to absolve a censure can be called a *reservatio solius censurae.* As a result of the reservation of a censure another form of reservation of sin may result. For, if a censure impedes the reception of the sacraments, the law decrees an *ipso facto* reservation of the sin to which the censure is attached. This is called *reservatio peccati ratione censurae.*[78] If the censure does not impede the reception of the sacraments the sin is not reserved but only the censure alone.[79]

In the case of a *reservatio peccati ratione censurae* the reservation of the sin forms one legal entity with the reservation of the censure. It begins to exist the moment the censure is incurred; it remains as long as the censure is not absolved; it ceases as soon as

[77] Canon 893, §§ 1-2.

[78] Canon 2246, § 3. Two censures impede the reception of the sacraments: excommunication (canon 2260, § 1) and personal interdict (canon 2275, n. 2).

[79] Cf. Dargin, *Reserved Cases* (Catholic University of America, Canon Law Studies, n. 20: Washington, D. C., 1924), pp. 4-6. These distinctions are sufficient for the present purpose, though it may be noted that the authors do not all agree in delineating these distinctions in the same way. For example, Farrugia (*De Casuum Conscientiae Reservatione* [2. ed., Romae: Marietti, 1922], p. 14) makes mention of a "peccatum . . . reservatum *cum censura,* quando peccatum ratione sui est reservatum, cui accessorie adiungitur excommunicationis censura, sive haec sit reservata, sive non." It is difficult to see how adding a non-reserved excommunication to a sin already reserved *ratione sui,* changes the case so far as the reservation itself is concerned.

the censure is removed. Consequently, the reservation of a sin *ratione censurae* is not "incurred" if the delinquent is excused from the incurring of the censure.[80] In this case ignorance of the censure (and not merely ignorance of the reservation attached thereto) obviously excuses from the reservation of the sin for the simple reason that the censure itself is not incurred. If the censure is not incurred, quite naturally there can arise no question of its absolution being reserved. Nor can there be any question of a non-incurred censure hindering the reception of the sacraments and thereby entailing the reservation of the sin.

The next question to be considered is, whether ignorance of the reservation alone (whether of the sin or of the censure) excuses from the reservation, even though the censure in the one case were incurred. Before the Code there were some authors who held that ignorance of the reservation exempted from the reservation.[81] The principal reason alleged in favor of this view was that the reservation must be considered penal, and therefore ignorance would excuse as in the case of other penalties. Even after the Code there are authors who defend this opinion,[82] while others hesitate to call the opinion improbable in the face of extant extrinsic authority, though they admit that the ground upon which this authority rests is very weak.[83]

A reservation, however, whether of a sin or of a censure, must be considered an administrative limitation of the jurisdiction of inferior confessors. It is not something primarily penal in character. This limitation of jurisdiction remains in force no matter if the sinner or delinquent does not know that a reservation exists.[84]

[80] Canon 2246, § 3.

[81] V. gr., Gury-Ballerini, *Compendium Theologiae Moralis,* II, 472-476; Lehmkuhl, *Theologia Moralis,* II, 294-295; Sanchez, *De Matrimonio,* lib. IX, disp. XXXII, n. 18.

[82] Farrugia, *De Casuum Conscientiae Reservatione,* pp. 29-43 (the author refers specifically to episcopal reservations); Arregui, *Summarium Theologiae Moralis* (5. ed., Bilboa: Elexpuru Hnos., 1920), p. 291, note 2.

[83] Vermeersch-Creusen, *Epitome,* II, 118-119; Coronata, *Institutiones Iuris Canonici,* IV, 160, note 1.

[84] For a more complete presentation of the arguments in favor of this view, cf. Dargin, *Reserved Cases,* pp. 13-16; Ferreres, *Compendium Theologiae*

This opinion is confirmed by a response of the Pontifical Commission for the interpretation of the Code,[85] which made it clear that a *peregrinus* (who presumably has no knowledge of local statutes) is bound by the reservations existing in the place in which he is. The opposite view has no foundation and today it can scarcely be said to have even extrinsic probability.[86]

Article VI. The Conflict of Forums and Apparent Exceptions to the Rules of Law in Regard to Ignorance

Because of the difficulties connected with the proof of ignorance in the external forum, it is apparent that a conflict can easily arise between the external and internal forums. It may happen that an individual knows for certain that he has not incurred a *latae sententiae* penalty because of his ignorance which attended the commission of the act, and yet for lack of convincing evidence he may fail to establish that fact to the satisfaction of his superior. The conflict may arise even outside of formal court proceedings, for, if the delict is notorious, the observance of the penalty imposed by law can be demanded in the external forum. It can happen, that a delinquent feels that he is not bound to the observance of a penalty because the crime was committed through ignorance, and yet his superior insists upon the observance of the penalty, since there is no evidence whatever of an excusing cause.[87]

Here the question may be asked, whether an excuse from a *latae sententiae* penalty according to canon 2229 must be admitted in the

Moralis (14. ed., Barcinone: Subirana, 1928), II, 370-372; Coronata, "Assoluzione de riservati in diocesi e in religione"—*Perfice Munus,* VII (1932), 748-753; King, "The New Code and Reservation"—*ER,* LXVI (1922), 565-568; Maroto, "De vi ignorantiae quoad falsam delationem"—*Consultationes Iuris Canonici* (Romae: Libraria Instituti Utriusque Iuris, 1934-), I, 326-335. For the opinion of pre-Code authors, cf. Sanchez, *De Matrimonio,* lib. IX, disp. XXXII, n. 18; St. Alphonsus, *Theologia Moralis,* lib. VI, tract. IV, cap. II, dub. IV, n. 581.

85 Nov. 24, 1920—*AAS,* XII (1920), 575.

86 Cf. Dargin, *ibidem,* p. 16; Maroto, *ibidem,* p. 333.

87 Canons 2232, § 1; 2197, n. 3.

external forum. According to the general norms concerning ignorance in canon 2202 a superior could impose a penalty even though the delinquent had ignorance solely of the penalty, while according to canon 2229 the same ignorance sometimes excuses entirely. Could the delinquent in this example insist upon the excuse so that the superior or judge could not pass the declarative sentence? This question must be answered in the affirmative, provided, of course, that the delinquent can prove the presence of ignorance for the time when the act was committed. This follows from the nature of a declarative sentence, which does not inflict a penalty which did not exist before, but declares the fact that a penalty has been incurred. It would seem to be a contradiction to *declare* that to exist which is proved not to exist.

This is confirmed by canon 2229, § 4, which plainly grants that on account of grave ignorance of law or even of the penalty alone an excuse from the incurring of a censure must be admitted in the external forum. It is evident, in the first place, that this paragraph is dealing with the external forum, because it declares that another penalty (besides the censures from which the delinquent is excused) can be inflicted by legitimate authority. It expressly mentions not only *poenitentia* but *alia poena,* by which latter phrase a vindicative penalty is also included. Since no one besides a legitimate superior can impose a strict canonical penalty, it follows that the external forum is spoken of.

There is no valid reason why the other instances of excuse from the incurring of *latae sententiae* censures should not be admitted in the external forum. The fourth paragraph of canon 2229 in referring expressly to paragraph 3, n. 1, is not expressly stating that only this case can be admitted in the external forum, but simply prescribes what is to be done in the case wherein a censure is avoided on account of gravely culpable ignorance.

However, it can readily happen that the delinquent will fail to prove exemption according to canon 2229 for lack of evidence. If a declarative sentence is passed in this case it would seem to be valid. At first sight it may seem to be a contradiction to declare that to exist which in fact, according to the certain knowledge of the delinquent, does not exist.

The law apparently contemplates this case, for, in canon 2232, § 2, it is stated that a declarative sentence takes effect, not from the moment that it is passed, but from the moment that the crime was committed. It may be objected that the effects spoken of in this canon are only the external consequences of the penal sentence, and not the effects that would follow from the incurring of the penalty itself. Certain it is that the external juridical effects are those which are primarily intended by the canon, but, such effects can be predicated only upon a censure, which is in reality incurred.

It may happen, therefore, that a delinquent be personally convinced that he is excused from the incurring of a penalty and yet in the external forum be obliged to observe it. Authors are unanimous in declaring that in the external forum the delinquent must obey—unless the sentence is manifestly unjust—for the sake of good order and to avoid scandal. The public good demands obedience in this case, otherwise everyone under color of some hidden excuse could avoid the legitimate sentence of proper authority and become his own judge. In the internal forum the delinquent may be excused from observing the penalty, provided that he can do so without scandal.[88]

Another question remains to be considered. It concerns the limits of the judge's or superior's power to inflict a commuted sentence according to canon 2229, § 4, in the case wherein a legitimate excuse from the incurring of a *latae sententiae* penalty has been proved. It is clear that, if the delinquent can prove that he was not guilty of grave sin in placing the objectively criminal act, no penalty can be imposed. If there is neither *dolus* nor *culpa* there can be no penal imputability. If, however, penal imputability is not obviated, the judge can ordinarily determine for what penalties the delinquent shall be held responsible. Yet, canon 2229 definitely limits penal responsibility in regard to *latae sententiae* penalties. As was shown above, if the delinquent can prove an excuse from the incurring of penalty according to the norms of canon 2229, the judge cannot declare the *latae sententiae* penalty imposed by law. But can he inflict a milder sentence? Before the Code this question was dis-

[88] Cf. Suarez, *De Legibus*, lib. V, cap. XII, n. 8; Perathoner, "Forum internum und forum externum im kirchlichen Strafrechte"—*LQS*, LXX (1917), 455; De Meester, *Juris Canonici Compendium*, III, P. II, 154.

puted,[89] and the Code itself does not entirely settle the dispute. It is now clear, by virtue of canon 2229, § 4, that the judge can, as long as the ignorance was gravely culpable, impose a mitigated sentence in case the delinquent is excused from incurring a *latae sententiae* censure which is imposed upon a crime that does not demand perfect *dolus* in the commission of the criminal act. This leaves the question open in regard to the second paragraph of the same canon. By the very fact that the Code expressly decrees that the judge can impose a mitigated penalty in the one case, it would seem to exclude the other. Hence, if a delinquent can show that he did not have perfect *dolus* and consequently did not incur the *latae sententiae* penalty imposed upon a crime which is incomplete without perfect *dolus*, the superior or judge could not impose another penalty.

This conclusion follows as a natural corollary from canon 2228, because the delict is not perfect according to the proper wording of the law. In other words, the delict as described by the law does not actually take place if there is not perfect *dolus*. Furthermore, the opinion that the judge could not impose a lesser penalty in case the delinquent escaped the *latae sententiae* penalty was the common opinion before the Code.[90] With that in mind the legislator determined that a penalty could be imposed in case the penal sanction does not presuppose perfect *dolus*, thereby implicitly affirming the common opinion in regard to penal sanctions requiring perfect *dolus* for the perpetration of the crime.

Coronata [91] argues that the crime in this case can be punished as

[89] Cf. Lega, *De Delictis et Poenis*, p. 33.

[90] Lega (*loc. cit.*) writes: "Ex adverso poenae latae sententiae delictum afficiunt quum fuerit ea ratione consummatum, uti in lege expressum est. Exinde probabilius est non esse in potestate iudicis huiusmodi poenas minuere per suam sententiam declaratoriam, etsi concurrant causae minuentes. Inquam probabilius est, quia ita opinantur communiter Doctores . . . " As is evident from this text, Lega is speaking merely of mitigating a *latae sententiae* penalty on account of partially excusing circumstances. The principle, however, is the same in both cases, for as Lega himself says: ". . . quia regula est, poenas latae sententiae non esse arbitrarias sed reum ipso facto, seu crimine consummato tenere, eo modo quo lex ipsa praecipit." Hence the principle applies *a fortiori* in the event that the delinquent is excused entirely.

[91] *Institutiones Iuris Canonici*, IV, 117.

a criminal attempt in virtue of canon 2235. This does not seem to be the case, because a delict which is not perfectly consummated on account of a defect in the subjective element (imputability) is very improperly called an attempted crime. In this case it cannot be said that the delinquent either deserted his original purpose (*consilium suum deseruit*) or that the delict actually did not take place because of insufficient or inept means.[92] Aside from the fact that most probably in Canon Law a *conatus delicti* must be *dolosus*,[93] it is not true in the case under discussion that the crime did not objectively and materially take place. On the contrary, the delict is a material fact, only it is not perfectly imputable as demanded by the law.

However, the judge or superior is not left without any means of imposing a penal remedy, in case the public good demanded that something should be done. If there is a special gravity in the delictual act despite the ignorance of the delinquent, or if there is grave scandal, the judge by a condemnatory sentence or the superior by a precept can impose a penalty in virtue of canon 2222, § 1.[94]

There are several decrees and decisions of the Holy See which seemingly run contrary to the dispositions of canon 2229. These seeming contradictions can easily be explained on the principles of the conflict of forums, and hence may well be discussed in this connection.

A striking instance of this is found in the insistence of the Holy See on the absolution from censures when heretics are received into the Church. It makes no difference whether or not the heretic was in good faith. Even if he was brought up from infancy in a heretical sect the absolution from censures must be given without considering the possibility of his good faith.[95] Seemingly, then, good faith

[92] Cf. canon 2212, § 1.

[93] Cf. *supra*, p. 106.

[94] Frequently commentators apply the rule of canon 2229, § 4, to all the cases, comprehended in the same canon, in which there is an excuse from the incurring of the *latae sententiae* penalty, provided only that there is grave imputability. Thus, v. gr., De Meester, *Juris Canonici Compendium*, III, P. II, 153; Sipos, *Enchiridion*, p. 966.

[95] Cf. S. C. S. Off. (Philadelphia), 20 iulii 1859—*Fontes*, n. 953. The regulations of this decree are incorporated in the *Rituale Romanum* (5. ed.,

and inculpable ignorance are not admitted as an excuse from this excommunication.[96]

A decree which caused a considerable amount of difficulty shortly before the publication of the Code concerns the censure imposed upon Catholics contracting marriage before a Protestant minister. There is some difficulty as to the exact wording of the decree which was issued by the Holy Office on May 12, 1892. According to the best sources the decree ran as follows:

> Quid faciendum sit de iis catholicis qui secundum veterem dioecesium nostrarum (in Borussia) usum, licet coram ministro acatholico matrimonium contraxerint, a confessariis sine speciali facultate absolvendi ad SS. sacramenta admissi sunt.
>
> ℟. Qui matrimonium coram ministro haeretico ineunt, censuram contrahere; Ordinarios autem vi facultatum quinquennalium nedum posse eos absolvere, sed alios etiam subdelegare ad eosdem absolvendos. Qui vero huc usque, nulla praevia a censuris absolutione, ab huiusmodi culpa absoluti sunt, iuxta exposita non esse inquietandos.[97]

Ratisbonae: Pustet, 1925), Supplementum, *Modus Excipiendi Professionem Fidei Catholicae.* In cases where baptism is repeated conditionally the obligation to give the absolution from censures is doubtful. Cf. Böhm, "Taufe und Absolution von der Häresie bei Konversionen"—*LQS,* LXXXVI (1933), 789; "Converts and Absolution from Censure"—*ER,* LXXIV (1926), 315; "Absolution from Censure and Profession of Faith at Conversion"—*ER,* LXXXVIII (1933), 419-420.

[96] The question whether a heretic is in good faith is a question of fact. Some authors seem to be of the opinion that heretics today cannot be inculpably ignorant in matters of faith and consequently are formal heretics under excommunication. Cf. Böhm, *Acatholicus,* pp. 17-18. This may be true in some localities, but it can scarcely be maintained that good faith is impossible. However, even granted that the heretic is in bad faith, how many of them would not be excused from the incurring of this excommunication on account of their ignorance of this censure? Even the decree, cited in the preceding note, while insisting upon the absolution from censure, admits the possibility that the excommunication might not have been incurred. For, in a note it prescribes that the word *forsan* be inserted in the formula of absolution in the event that there is doubt about the existence of the censure.

[97] This reading of the text is found in *ASS,* XXV (1892-1893), 118; *AKKR,* LXVIII (1892), 185; *Coll. S. C. P. F.,* II, n. 1793; *Fontes,* n. 1154.

Without giving his source, Noldin,[98] though not directly quoting the decree, referred to the same as containing these words in the beginning of the response: . . . *Catholici, qui censurae inscii coram ministro haeretico* . . . This evidently gives a new meaning to the decree and led Noldin to advocate the opinion that an excommunication could be incurred in the external forum without being incurred in the internal forum. Considering the nature of an excommunication, *i. e.,* an exclusion from the communion of the faithful with true internal effect,[99] it is certainly difficult to understand how especially this penalty could be really incurred only in the external forum. Ojetti,[100] therefore, opposed this view and accused Noldin of adding the phrase *censurae inscii* to the authentic text.

The opinion of Noldin was, however, not abandoned. Perathoner ardently defended it and stated that Ojetti had used a mutilated text in which the important words *inscii censurae* were omitted. According to Perathoner the text of the question presented to the Holy Office for solution was as follows:

> Sint ne etiam ii catholici, qui censurae inscii coram ministro acatholico conjunctionem matrimonialem inierunt ideoque propter ipsam censurae ignorantiam pro foro interno in eam non inciderunt, pro foro externo a censuris absolvendi, quia externe haeresi faverunt, cum Bonifacius VIII. judicaverit: Ligare nolumus ignorantes, dum tamen eorum ignorantia crassa non fuerit aut supina?

The answer according to Perathoner was the same as that given above.[101]

If this must be considered an authentic decision of the Holy Office, then one would be almost forced to admit the rather unique opinion that an excommunication can be *incurred* in the external forum, and yet because of ignorance be avoided in the internal

98 *Summa Theologiae Moralis* (Oeniponte, 1902), II, 764-765; *De Poenis Ecclesiasticis* (5. ed., Oeniponte, 1905), p. 20.

99 Cf. *supra,* p. 224, note 66.

100 *Synopsis, s. v.* "Censura"—natura censurae, I, coll. 673-675.

101 "Forum internum und forum externum im kirchlichen Strafrechte"—*LQS,* LXX (1917), 453, note 2.

forum. Neither Noldin nor Perathoner indicate the sources of their version of the text, and hence can hardly be considered compelling authorities.

A decision of the Sacred Congregation of the Council brought up the same difficulty. It, too, apparently did not admit ignorance as an excuse from crime and consequent penalty. The following question was submitted to the Congregation:

> II. Utrum Codicis canon 2381 urgeat etiam in casu non residentiae, non graviter culpabilis, vel materialiter tantum, non formaliter, culpabilis ac notoriae.

The response was:

> Affirmative, dummodo ne concurrant causae excusantes iuxta can. 420, 421, vel Pontificium indultum.[102]

It is impossible and unnecessary to enter into a discussion on the complicated details of the problem presented by this decision.[103] It is sufficient to note that canon 2381 deals with the violation of the law of residence. Those who are bound by the law of residence and are illegitimately absent, are *ipso facto* deprived of all the fruits of an office, benefice or dignity corresponding to the period of the illegitimate absence. Furthermore, those who violate the law of residence are to be deprived of their office or benefice. The latter privation is a *ferendae sententiae* penalty and must be imposed according to the procedure set forth in the Fourth Book of the Code.

Of present interest is the fact that the Congregation expressly states that no formal guilt, *i. e.*, moral imputability, is necessary in order that canon 2381 may be urged. At first sight this decision seems to be diametrically opposed to the fundamental rules of imputability discussed in the present study. According to this decision not even inculpable ignorance excuses in this case. A key to the solution of this seeming contradiction is offered by the word *notoriae*. The decision deals only with a notorious violation of canon

[102] *AAS*, XII (1920), 364.

[103] Cf. *Votum Consultoris* in S. C. C., *Toletana et Aliarum*, 10 iulii 1920—*AAS*, XII (1920), 357-364; Cozza, "In Toletana et aliarum"—*Mon. Eccl.*, XLVI (1934), 229-239; 276-287; 361-370.

2381. As is pointed out in the *votum consultoris,* given a notorious violation of the law of residence, the causes of this absence will either be admitted by law or they will not be recognized. If the causes for the absence are not admitted by law, then "posita externa legis violatione, dolus in foro externo praesumitur . . ." [104] Since *dolus,* the deliberate will to violate the law, is presumed, the person guilty of a notorious violation of the law is held liable to the penalty until he *proves* that *dolus* did not, as a matter of fact, exist on account of some defect of mind or will.[105]

The solution of this case can also be applied to the preceding two cases, viz., in regard to the usage of granting absolution from material heresy and the decision of the Holy Office in regard to Catholics who marry before a Protestant minister. In all these instances there is a notorious violation of a penal law. In the external forum *dolus* is presumed and the "delinquent" is considered to have incurred the *latae sententiae* penalty imposed by law. As far as external juridical effects are concerned, this person must be considered under the penalty of the law. In the internal forum, barring scandal, the individual need not observe the penalty, because it does not in fact exist. In the forum of conscience, the external presumptions of the law give way to fact; hence, *dolus* is not presumed and no penalty incurred.

Moreover, as was already indicated, if the delinquent should prefer to submit to trial rather than submit to the penalty, or, more precisely, the observance of the penalty, he could do so. And if he could refute the presumption of *dolus* his innocence would have to

[104] Canon 2200, § 2.

[105] *Votum Consultoris, ibidem,* p. 361. Cozza seems to be of the opinion that the privation spoken of in this decision is not a strict canonical penalty, but *una legge penale mista.* In this way he explains why the privation is sustained even in case there is no formal guilt.—*Ibidem,* pp. 233-234; 278.

In regard to this *ipso facto* privation of the fruits of a benefice the view of Cozza is correct. From a recent decision of the Sacred Congregation of the Council, April 13, 1940, it is now certain that canon 2381, n. 1, does not contain a strict penalty and that culpability is not required for the *pro rata* privation of fruits in case of illegitimate absence.—*AAS,* XXII (1940), pp. 374-378. Cf. Roelker, "The Right to Revenue during Non-residence"—*The Jurist,* I (1941), pp. 74-76.

be admitted also in the external forum.[106] When, however, the crime is notorious the delinquent is bound in conscience to submit to the penalty in the external forum, unless he prefer to undertake proof of exemption from the same. If the penalty is a censure it is much easier to submit to the absolution, which must be given as a matter of justice as soon as the delinquent asks for it and is no longer contumacious. Should he refuse to submit, he would now not only be presumed to have incurred the penalty in the external forum, but would really incur the censure and be bound in both forums.[107]

Conclusion

As stated above, the rules of canon 2229 should *a priori* be expected to be simple and easy of application. Yet, the preceding chapter may lead to quite the opposite impression. It is true, indeed, that the interpretation of the canon itself does offer serious and more or less involved legal problems. But the rules which result from the study of the canon are not complicated and can be employed by anyone. As shown above,[108] the number of hypothetical cases which must be covered is quite large and the rules covering these different cases might consequently be expected to be quite intricate. A summary of the results of the last chapter will show that the matter can be comprised in a few simple rules:

1. Affected ignorance, either of the law or also of the penalty alone, never excuses from the incurring of a *latae sententiae* penalty;
2. Affected ignorance of fact probably excuses from censures which are imposed upon crimes requiring perfect *dolus* for their perpetration;
3. Crass ignorance of fact probably excuses from censures imposed upon crimes which presuppose at least simple *dolus;*
4. Even crass ignorance (of fact, of law, and of penalty) excuses from medicinal and vindicative penalties which are im-

[106] Cf. Wernz-Vidal, *Ius Canonicum,* VII, 66; Lega, *De Delictis et Poenis,* pp. 150-151.

[107] Canon 2242, § 2.

[108] *Supra,* p. 197.

posed upon crimes demanding perfect *dolus* in their motivation;

5. Grave ignorance (of fact, of law, and of penalty) excuses from the incurring of censures even if the penal sanction does not demand perfect *dolus* as a prerequisite to make the criminal act penally imputable;
6. Ignorance of the mere penalty in regard to vindicative penalties is ignorance of the fact that a law is penal at all, and it excuses only when the crimes by legislative definition presuppose perfect *dolus*.

A consideration of these rules makes the practical conclusion inevitable, namely: censures are rarely incurred, especially by those who are poorly instructed in their religion and who are indifferent to spiritual affairs.[109] Every Catholic is, of course, bound to know those laws of the Church which relate to his state in life. Yet, it can scarcely be maintained that laymen are obliged to know the penalties of the law, nor are pastors of souls bound to give instructions in these matters as a general rule.[110] Hence, even if the number of *latae sententiae* penalties in force under the present law is considered large, the frequency with which they are incurred will be small in view of the effect of ignorance as an excusing factor. It seems that the Church in the internal forum does not wish to penalize the first-time offenders of her criminal or penal law.

It is true that the law does not require a special warning to be given before a *latae sententiae* censure is incurred. The import of the law itself constitutes the canonical warning, but because of ignorance as an excusing factor that warning will very often be ineffectual. Practically viewed, a particular warning will frequently be-

[109] Cf. Haring, "Praktisches über das kirchliche Strafrecht"—*LQS*, LXXVII (1924), 536-537; De Meester, *Juris Canonici Compendium*, III, P. II, 153; O'Neill, "Ignorance of Ecclesiastical Laws and Punishments"—*IER*, XXIX (1927), 292-293; Michiels, *Normae Generales*, I, 361, note 2. This is an effective answer to those who would find the penal laws of the Church burdensome and ill suited to modern conditions; v. gr., Geiermann, "Reserved Cases"—*ER*, LXIV (1921), 291-293.

[110] Cf. O'Neill, "Ignorance of Ecclesiastical Laws and Punishments"—*loc. cit.*

come necessary and it devolves upon the pastors of souls to issue this warning. When an abuse becomes prevalent it becomes the duty of pastors [111] and especially of bishops [112] to instruct the faithful and warn them concerning the ecclesiastical penalties. This follows from the very purpose directly or indirectly inherent in all penal legislation, viz., the protection of the public good.[113]

The individual delinquent must be considered by the prudent confessor in the light of extant facts and circumstances. Ordinarily the confessor is bound in conscience to admonish the delinquent and inform him of the penalty imposed by the law upon the delict. To hold otherwise would be to render entirely useless the penal laws that impose *latae sententiae* penalties. Under extraordinary circumstances it is permitted to omit the warning, for instance, if the penitent is in good faith and it is certainly foreseen that the admonition will not bear any fruit.[114]

Some may perhaps consider the leniency of Mother Church in the application of her penalties as a manifestation which connotes a laxity that can readily become dangerous for the public good. This is not true, because the public welfare is sufficiently safeguarded by canon 2222, § 1, which gives superiors ample coercive powers in those cases in which canonical penalties may prove to be a prudent

[111] Cf. canons 467, § 1; 469.

[112] Cf. canons 336; 343.

[113] In regard to the pastoral warning the Sacred Congregation of the Holy Office has this instructive sentence: "Ad pastoralem vero admonitionem quod attinet quid theologi doceant probe nosti, qui, si deficiente probabili spe emendationis ac fructus, prudentique metu gravioris cuiuspiam mali concurrente, differri admonendi officium, quod ex proprio munere pastorem urget, posse consentiunt, nihilominus monent, si scandalum a pastoris silentio oriatur, intermitti illud non licere."—S. C. S. Off. instr. ad *Vic. Ap. Myssurien.*, 1 febr. 1871, § 2—*Fontes*, n. 1014.

[114] "Sed si de interno [foro] res est, licet theologi doceant aliquando (hoc est debitis factis exceptionibus, . . .) dissimulari cum poenitente posse cum duo haec simul concurrunt, bona fides et indubia praevisio nullum ex admonitione fructum perceptum iri; . . . ob qualitatem Constitutionis ["*Apostolicae Sedis*"] eamdem censuram inferentis, quae recentissima est ac plane notoria, difficile dari potest bona fides quae admonitionem omitti posse suadeat."—S. C. S. Off., *loc. cit.*

means of protecting good morals. In this manner the law provides effectively for the protection of good morals in the community and at the same time secures the spiritual welfare of the individual delinquent against the harsh application of severe penalties.

The long experience of the Church and the constant efforts of profound canonists and moralists have in admirable unison achieved a harmonious balance between the two supreme laws of the Church as a perfect society: *salus reipublicae suprema lex esto* and *salus animarum suprema lex esto.* To draw either of these principles to their extreme consequences results in a sacrifice either of good morals to the individual good, or of the individual to the public good. *Summum ius est summa iniuria!* The Church by her mild rules in regard to ignorance of penal matters teaches an important lesson in the proper relation of the individual spiritual good to the public good of the entire society.

CONCLUSIONS

The study of the legal rules regarding the imputability of delicts committed through ignorance leads to the following conclusions:

1. The principles concerning ignorance must be considered in their relation to four distinct forms of penal responsibility, namely, in regard to perfect *dolus, dolus, culpa* and contumacy. The effects of ignorance upon each of these has been more accurately determined.

2. Ignorance merely of the ecclesiastical penal law or of the penalty imposed by the same upon an already existing natural law, does not preclude *dolus* if the delinquent knows that the criminal act is morally wrong.

3. Ignorance of the penalty alone, because of the clear provisions of canon 2229, must be considered as constituting a sufficient diminution of imputability to provide an excuse from even vindicative *latae sententiae* penalties which are imposed upon crimes presupposing perfect *dolus.*

4. Knowledge both of the law and of the penalty is a necessary condition for contumacy in the transgression of a penal law. Hence, the rules governing the effects of ignorance upon responsibility for censures differ substantially from those applicable to the liability for vindicative penalties.

5. Several important definitions are considered to be justified by this study:

   a. That affected ignorance is the result of a positive effort to avoid the discovery of an undesirable truth, an effort, moreover, which proceeds from a direct will to remain ignorant because of a wrongful motive;

   b. That crass ignorance can result only from a total neglect to employ any diligence in the investigation of a truth when it is realized that only a slight effort would be sufficient for the acquisition of the necessary knowledge;

   c. That all other forms of culpable ignorance must be judged to be either grave or venial according to the principles of Moral Theology.

6. As the result of a more careful study of contumacy the following rules governing the responsibility for *latae sententiae* censures are defended as at least probable opinions:

a. That affected ignorance of fact excuses from the incurring of *latae sententiae* censures which are imposed upon crimes presupposing perfect *dolus;*
b. That crass ignorance of fact excuses from the incurring of a censure imposed upon a crime which is perfectly consummated only when at least simple *dolus* is present;
c. That there is sufficient ignorance of the penalty to warrant an excuse from *latae sententiae* censures, if the delinquent is ignorant merely of the fact that any censure is imposed by law upon the crime; or—in case an excommunication is imposed—if the delinquent is ignorant solely of the excommunication. In either case he is excused from the penalty even though he knows that some penalty is attached to the violation of the law, and—in case an excommunication is inflicted—even though he knows that some censure is attached to the crime.

7. The legal rules concerning the proof of ignorance in the external forum have been studied in the light of pre-Code doctrine in order to determine the principles of law, which govern the use of the presumptions and the proofs of ignorance under the present penal law of the Church.

BIBLIOGRAPHY

Sources

Acta Apostolicae Sedis, Commentarium Officiale, Romae, 1909—

Acta Sanctae Sedis, 41 vols., Romae, 1865-1908.

Bruns, C., *Fontes Juris Romani Antiqui*, 7. ed., Gradenwitz, Tubingae, 1909.

Bullarum Diplomatum et Privilegiorum Sanctorum Romanorum Pontificum Taurinensis Editio, 24 vols. et Appendix, Augustae Taurinorum-Neapoli, 1857-1872.

Canones et Decreta Sacrosancti Oecumenici Concilii Tridentini, Lipsiae, 1866.

Codex Iuris Canonici Pii X Pontificis Maximi iussu digestus Benedicti Papae XV auctoritate promulgatus, Romae: Typis Polyglottis Vaticanis, 1917.

Codicis Iuris Canonici Fontes cura Emi. Petri Card. Gasparri editi., 9 vols., Romae (postea Civitate Vaticana): Typis Polyglottis Vaticanis, 1923-1939. Vols. VII-IX ed. cura et studio Emi. Iustiniani Card. Serédi.

Collectanea S. Congregationis de Propaganda Fide, 2 vols., Romae, ex Typographia Polyglotta Vaticana, 1907.

Corpus Iuris Canonici, ed. Lipsiensis 2., Aemilius L. Richter-Aemilius Friedberg, ed. anastice repetita, 2 vols., Lipsiae: Tauchnitz, 1928.

Corpus Iuris Civilis, Vol. I, *Institutiones*—recognovit P. Krueger; Vol. II, *Codex Iustianus*—recognovit et retractavit P. Krueger; Vol. III, *Novellae Constitutiones*—R. Schoell; opus Schoelli morte interceptum absolvit G. Kroll, Berolini: apud Weidmannos, 1928-1929.

———, *Digesta Iustiniani Augusti*—recognoverunt et ediderunt P. Bonfante, C. Fadda, C. Ferrini, S. Riccobono, V. Scialoia, Mediolani: Società Editrice Libraria, 1931.

Decretum Gratiani Emendatum et Notationibus illustratum una cum glossis, Romae, 1582.

Decretales D. Gregorii Papae IX, una cum glossis restitutae, Romae, 1582.

Denzinger-Bannwart-Umberg, *Enchiridion Symbolorum, Definitionum, et Declarationum de Rebus Fidei et Morum*, 22-23. ed., Friburgi-Brisgoviae: Herder, 1937.

Girard, Paul, *Texts de Droit Romain*, 5. ed., Paris: Rousseau, 1923.

Harduin, Jean, *Acta Conciliorum et Epistolae Decretales ac Constitutiones Summorum Pontificum*, 12 vols., Parisiis, 1714-1725.

Jaffé, Philippus, *Regesta Pontificum Romanorum ab condita Ecclesia ad annum post Christum natum MCXCVIII*, 2. ed. cura Wattenbach, Loewenfeld, Kaltenbrunner, Ewald, 2 vols. in 1, Lipsiae: Veit et Comp., 1885-1888.

Liber Sextus Decretalium, una cum Clementinis et Extravagantibus Earumque Glossis Restitutis, Romae, 1582.

Mansi, Joannes, *Sacrorum Conciliorum Nova et Amplissima Collectio*, 53 vols., Parisiis, 1901-1927.

Potthast, Augustus, *Regesta Pontificum Romanorum inde ab anno Post Christum Natum MCXCVIII ad annum MCCCIV,* 2 vols., Berolini, 1874-1875.

S. Romanae Rotae Decisiones seu Sententiae (ab anno 1909), Romae, 1912—

Reference Works

Acta Congressus Iuridici Internationalis . . . Romae 1934, 5 vols., Romae: Libraria Pont. Instituti Utriusque Iuris, 1935-1937.

Alphonsus Liguori, St., *Theologia Moralis,* ed. L. Gaudé, 4 vols., Romae, 1905-1912.

Alterius, Marius, *De Censuris Ecclesiasticis,* 2 vols., Romae, 1616.

Ayrinhac, H. A., and Lydon, P. J., *Penal Legislation in the New Code of Canon Law,* revised edition, New York: Benziger, 1936.

Azpilcueta, Martinus (Navarrus), *Consiliorum sive Responsorum Libri Quinque iuxta Ordinem Decretalium Dispositi,* 2 vols., Romae, 1602.

———, *Opera Omnia,* 6 vols., Venetiis, 1618.

[Bachofen], Charles Augustine, *A Commentary on the New Code of Canon Law,* 8 vols.; Vol. VIII, *Penal Code,* 2. ed., St. Louis: Herder, 1924 .

Ballerini, Antonius et Palmieri, Dominicus, *Opus Theologicum Morale,* 7 vols., Prati, 1889-1893.

Barbosa, Augustinus, *Collectanea Doctorum tam Veterum quam Recentorum in Jus Pontificium Universum,* 5 vols., Lugduni, 1637.

Benedictus XIV, *De Synodo Dioecesana,* 2 vols., Romae, 1806.

Berutti, Christophorus, *Institutiones Iuris Canonici,* Vol. VI, *De Delictis et Poenis,* Taurini-Romae: Marietti, 1938.

Beste, Udalricus, *Introductio in Codicem,* Collegeville, Minn.: St. John's Abbey Press, 1938.

Billuart, F. C. R., *Summa Sancti Thomas Hodiernis Academiarum Moribus Accommodata,* ed. nova, cura Lequette, 9 vols. in 8, Parisiis, *s. d.*

Blat, Albertus, *Commentarium Textus Codicis Iuris Canonici,* 6 vols., Romae, 1921-1927; Liber V, *De Delictis et Poenis,* Romae: Collegio Angelico, 1924.

Bouquillon, Thomas, *Theologia Moralis Fundamentalis,* 2. ed., Brugis, 1890.

Cance, Adrien, *Le Code de Droit Canonique Commentaire succinct et pratique,* 5. ed., 3 vols., Paris: Lecoffre, 1930.

Cappello, Felix, *De Censuris iuxta Codicem Iuris Canonici,* 3. ed., Taurinorum Augustae: Marietti, 1933.

Cerato, Prosdocimus, *Censurae Vigentes Ipso Facto a Codice Iuris Canonici Excerptae,* 2. ed., Patavii: Typis Seminarii, 1921.

Chelodi, Ioannes, *Ius Poenale et Ordo Procedendi in Iudiciis Criminalibus,* 4. ed. by Vigilius Dalpiaz, Tridenti: Ardesi, 1935.

Cicognani, Hamletus, *Ius Canonicum,* Vol. II, *Commentarium ad Librum I. Codicis,* Romae: Apollinaris, 1925.

———, *Canon Law,* authorized English version, by J. O'Hara and F. Brennan, Philadelphia: Dolphin Press, 1935.

Cipollini, Albertus, *De Censuris Latae Sententiae Iuxta Codicem Iuris Canonici*, Taurini: Marietti, 1925.

Claeys Bouuaert, F., et Simenon, G., *Manuale Juris Canonici*, 3 vols.; Vols. I, III, 4. ed., 1934; Vol. II, 2. ed., 1935, Gandae et Leodii: Dessain.

Clark, William, and Marshall, William, *A Treatise on the Law of Crimes*, 4. ed. by James Kearney, Chicago: Callaghan, 1940.

Cocchi, Guidus, *Commentarium in Codicem Iuris Canonici*, 5 vols. in 8, 1922-1930. Liber V, *De Delictis et Poenis*, 4. ed., Taurinorum Augustae: Marietti, 1938.

Coronata, Matthaeus, Conte a, *Institutiones Iuris Canonici*, 5 vols.; Vols. I-II, 2. ed., 1939; Vols. III-V, 1933-1936, Taurini: Marietti.

Corpus Scriptorum Ecclesiasticorum Latinorum, Vindobonae, 1866-

Covarrubias y Leyva, Didacus, *Opera Omnia*, 2 vols., Coloniae Allobrogum, 1679.

Crnica, Antonius, *Modificationes in Tractatu de Censuris per Codicem Iuris Canonici Introductae*, S. Mauritii Agaunensis: Typis op. S. Augustini, 1919.

D'Annibale, Iosephus, *Summula Theologiae Moralis*, 5. ed., 3 vols., Romae, 1908.

———, *In Constitutionem Apostolicae Sedis Commentarii*, 5. ed., Romae, 1909.

Dargin, Edward V., *Reserved Cases According to the Code of Canon Law*, The Catholic University of America, Canon Law Studies, n. 20, Washington: The Catholic University of America, 1924.

De Lugo, J., *Disputationes Scholasticae et Morales*, ed. nova, 8 vols., Parisiis, 1868.

De Meester, Alphonsus, *Juris Canonici et Juris Canonico-Civilis Compendium*, nova ed., 3 vols. in 4, Brugis: Descleé, 1921-1928.

Duardus, Leonardus, *Commentaria in Bullam S. D. N. D. Pauli V Lectam in Die Coenae D. Anno 1618*, Mediolani, 1620.

Eichmann, Edward, *Lehrbuch des Kirchenrechts auf Grund des Codex Iuris Canonici*, 2. ed., Paderborn: Schöningh, 1926.

———, *Das Strafrecht des Codex Iuris Canonici*, Paderborn: Schöningh, 1920.

Fagnanus, Prosper, *Commentaria in Quinque Libros Decretalium*, 4 vols., Romae, 1661.

Falchi, Giuseppino F., *Diritto Penale Romano, Dottrine Generali*, Treviso: Vianello, 1930.

Farinaccius, Prosper, *Variarum Quaestionum et Communium Opinionum Criminalium Liber Sextus, Fragmentorum Pars Secunda*, Romae, 1621.

Farrugia, Nicolaus, *De Casuum Conscientiae Reservatione iuxta Codicem Iuris Canonici*, 2. ed., Augustae Taurinorum-Romae: Marietti, 1922.

Ferraris, Lucius, *Bibliotheca Canonica Iuridica Moralis Theologica nec non Ascetica Polemica Rubricistica Historica*, 9 vols., Romae, 1885-1899.

Ferreres, Ioannes, *Institutiones Canonicae*, 2. ed., 2 vols., Barcinone: Subirana, 1920.

———, *Compendium Theologiae Moralis*, 14. ed., 2 vols., Barcinone: Subirana, 1928.

Ferrini, Contardo, *Diritto Penale Romano, Teorie Generali*, Milano, 1899.

Gabriel a S. Vincentio, *De Remediis Ignorantiae*, Romae, 1671.

Gaius, *Institutiones*, 6. ed., Seckel-Kuebler, Lipsiae: Teubner, 1928.

Gonzalez Tellez, Emmanuel, *Commentaria Perpetua in Singulos Textus Quinque Librorum Decretalium Gregorii IX*, 5 vols. in 4, Lugduni, 1715.

Gury, Ioannis, et Ballerini, Antonius, *Compendium Theologiae Moralis*, 3. ed., 2 vols., Romae, 1874-1875.

Haring, Johann, *Grundzüge des katholischen Kirchenrechts*, 3. ed., 2 vols., Graz: Mosers, 1924.

Harno, Albert, *Cases and Other Materials on Criminal Law and Procedure*, Chicago: Callaghan, 1933.

Hefele, Carolus, et Leclercq, Henricus, *Histoire des Conciles*, 10 vols. in 19, Paris: Letouzey et Ané, 1907-1938.

Heiner, Franz, *Katholisches Kirchenrecht*, 5. ed., 2 vols., Paderborn, 1909.

Hennemann, Werner, *Der Versuch im kirchlichen Strafrecht*, Limburg a. d. Lahn: Limburger Vereinsdruckerei, 1930.

Henricus Boich, *In Quinque Decretalium Libros Commentaria*, Venetiis, 1576.

Hinschius, Paul, *Das Kirchenrecht der Katholiken und Protestanten in Deutschland*, 6 vols., Berlin, 1869-1897.

Hollweck, Joseph, *Die kirchlichen Strafgesetze*, Mainz, 1899.

Hostiensis, Cardinalis (Henricus de Segusio), *Commentaria in Quinque Decretalium Libros*, 5 vols. in 3, Venetiis, 1581.

Joannes Andreae, *In Sex Decretalium Libros Novella Commentaria*, 6 vols. in 5, Venetiis, 1581.

Jolowicz, H. F., *Historical Introduction to the Study of Roman Law*, Cambridge: University Press, 1932.

Jorio, Thomas, *Theologia Moralis iuxta Methodum Compendii Joannis P. Gury et Raphaelis Tummulo*, 6. ed., 3 vols., Neapoli: D'Auria, 1938-1939.

Kantorowicz, Hermann, with the collaboration of W. W. Buckland, *Studies in the Glossators of the Roman Law*, Cambridge: University Press, 1938.

Kober, F., *Der Kirchenbann nach den Grundsätzen des canonischen Rechts*, 2. ed., Tübingen, 1863.

Konings, Antonius, *Theologia Moralis*, 4. ed., 2 vols., New York, 1880.

Kuttner, Stephan, *Kanonistische Schuldlehre von Gratian bis auf die Dekretalen Gregors IX*, Studi e Testi, n. 64, Città del Vaticano: Biblioteca Apostolica Vaticana, 1935.

Latini, Joseph, *Juris Criminalis Philosophici Summa Lineamenta*, Romae: Marietti, 1924.

Lega, Michael, *Praelectiones in Textum Iuris Canonici—De Delictis et Poenis*, 2. ed., Romae, 1910.

Lehmkuhl, Augustinus, *Theologia Moralis*, 5. ed., 2 vols., Friburgi Brisgoviae, 1888.

MacKenzie, Eric F., *The Delict of Heresy in Its Commission, Penalization, Absolution*, The Catholic University of America, Canon Law Studies, n.

77, Washington: The Catholic University of America, 1932.

Maroto, Philippus, *Institutiones Iuris Canonici,* 2 vols., 1919; Vol. 1, 3. ed., 1921, Romae: Apud Commentarium pro Religiosis.

Maschat, Remigius et Giraldi, Ubaldus, *Institutiones Canonicae,* 2 vols., Romae, 1757.

Menochius, *De Praesumptionibus, Coniecturis, Signis, et Indiciis Commentaria,* 2 vols., Coloniae Allobrogum, 1686.

Miaskiewicz, Francis S., *Supplied Jurisdiction according to Canon 209,* The Catholic University of America, Canon Law Studies, n. 122, Washington: The Catholic University of America, 1940.

Michiels, Gommarus, *Normae Generales Juris Canonici,* 2 vols., Lublin: Universitas Catholica, 1929.

———, *De Delictis et Poenis,* Vol. I, *De Delictis,* Lublin: Universitas Catholica, 1934.

Migne, Jacques P., *Patrologiae Cursus Completus,* Series Graeca, 161 vols., Parisiis, 1856-1866.

———, *Patrologiae Cursus Completus,* Series Latina, 221 vols., Parisiis, 1858-1864.

Mommsen, Theodore, *Le Droit Pénal Romain,* trans. by J. Duquesne, 3 vols., Paris, 1907.

Moriarty, Francis, *The Extraordinary Absolution from Censures,* The Catholic University of America, Canon Law Studies, n. 113, Washington: The Catholic University of America, 1938.

Moersdorf, Klaus, *Die Rechtssprache des Codex Juris Canonici,* Paderborn: Schöningh, 1937.

Mothon, Joseph, *Institutions Canoniques,* 3 vols., Paris: Desclée, 1922-1924.

Müller, Michael, *Ethik und Recht in der Lehre von der Verantwortlichkeit,* Regensburg: Josef Habbel, 1932.

Noldin, H., et Schmitt, A., *Summa Theologiae Moralis,* 3 vols.; Vol. I, 26. ed., 1939; Vols. II-III, 25. ed., 1938, Oeniponte: Rauch.

Noldin, H., et Schönegger, A., *Summa Theologiae Moralis,* Complementum II, *De Censuris,* 32. ed., Oeniponte: Rauch, 1938.

Ojetti, Benedictus, *Synopsis Rerum Moralium et Iuris Pontificii,* 4 vols., Romae, 1909-1914.

———, *Commentarium in Codicem Iuris Canonici,* 4 vols., Romae: Universitas Gregoriana, 1927-1931.

Panormitanus, Abbas (Nicolaus de Tudeschis), *Commentaria in Quinque Libros Decretalium,* 5 vols. in 7, Venetiis, 1588.

Passerinus, Petrus, *Commentaria in Sextum Librum Decretalium,* Venetiis, 1698.

Paucapalea, *Summa,* ed. J. F. von Schulte, Giessen, 1890.

Peckius, Petrus, *Opera Omnia,* Antverpiae, 1666.

Pellé, M. L'Abbé P., *Le Droit Pénal de L'Église,* Paris: Lethielleux, 1939.

Pennacchi, Josephus, *Commentaria in Constitutionem Apostolicae Sedis,* 2 vols., Romae, 1883.

Perathoner, A., *Das kirchliche Gesetzbuch*, 3. ed., Brixen: Wegers' Buchhandlung, 1923.

Pichler, Vitus, *Candidatus Jurisprudentiae Sacrae*, 5 vols., 3. ed., 1723-1728; Vol. I, 4. ed., 1733, August.

Pighi, J. B., *Censurae Sententiae Latae et Irregularitates*, 7. ed., Veronae: Sorores Cinquetti Filiae Felicis, 1922.

Pirhing, Ernricus, *Jus Canonicum Nova Methodo Explicatum*, 5 vols. in 4, Dilingae, 1674-1678.

Pistocchi, Mario, *I Canoni Penali del Codice Ecclesiastico Esposti e Commentati*, Torino-Roma: Marietti, 1925.

Pollock, Frederick and Maitland, Frederic, *The History of English Law before the Time of Edward I*, 2 vols., Cambridge, 1895.

Prümmer, Dominicus, *Manuale Theologiae Moralis*, 8. ed. by Engelbertus Münch, 3 vols., Friburgi Brisgoviae: Herder, 1935-1936.

Reiffenstuel, Anacletus, *Jus Canonicum Universum*, 7 vols., Parisiis, 1864-1870.

Roberti, Franciscus, *De Delictis et Poenis*, Vol. I, Romae: Libraria Pontificii Instituti Utriusque Iuris, 1938.

Rufinus, *Summa Decretorum*, ed. Singer, Paderborn, 1902.

Salucci, Raffaele, *Il Diritto Penale secondo il Codice di Diritto Canonico*, 2 vols. in 1, Subiaco: Tipografia dei Monasteri, 1926-1930.

Salmanticenses, *Cursus Theologiae Moralis*, 6 vols. in 4, Venetiis, 1714-1728.

Sanchez, Thomas, *De Sancto Matrimonii Sacramento*, 3 vols. in 2, Antverpiae, 1607.

Sandaeus, Felinus, *Commentaria in Quinque Libros Decretalium*, 2 vols., Venetiis, 1570.

Santi, Franciscus, *Praelectiones Juris Canonici*, 5 vols. in 3, Ratisbonae, 1886.

Sayrus, Gregorius, *Casuum Conscientiae Thesaurus*, Tom. I, *De Censuris Ecclesiasticis*, 3. ed., 1609.

Schmalzgrueber, Franciscus, *Jus Ecclesiasticum Universum*, Romae, 1843-1845.

Schmitz, H. J., *Die Bussbücher und die Bussdisciplin der Kirche*, Mainz, 1883.

Schroeder, H. J., *Disciplinary Decrees of the General Councils*, St. Louis: Herder, 1937.

Schulz, Fritz, *Principles of Roman Law*, trans. by Wolff, Oxford: Clarendon Press, 1936.

Sipos, Stephanus, *Enchiridion Iuris Canonici*, 3. ed., Pécs: Haladás R. T., 1936.

Smith, S. B., *Elements of Ecclesiastical Law*, Vol. III, *Ecclesiastical Punishments*, 3. ed., New York, 1888.

Sole, Jacobus, *De Delictis et Poenis*, Romae: Pustet, 1920.

Stephanus, *Summa*, ed. Schulte, Giessen, 1891.

Suarez, Franciscus, *Opera Omnia*, 26 vols., Parisiis, 1856-1866.

Sylvester, de Prierio (Mozolinus Sabaudus), *Summa Summarum*, Venetiis, 1601.

Thesaurus, Carolus, et Giraldi, Ubaldus, *De Poenis Ecclesiasticis*, nova editio, Romae, 1831.

Thomas Aquinas, St., *Summa Theologica*, diligenter emendata Nicolai, Sylvii,

Billuart et C.-J. Drioux notis ornata, 6. ed., 8 vols., Barri-Ducis, 1870.

———, *Opera Omnia,* studio ac labore Stanislai Fretté et Pauli Maré, 34 vols., Parisiis: apud L. Vivès, 1871-1880.

Toso, Albertus, *Ad Codicem Iuris Canonici Commentaria Minora,* Vol. I, Tiferini Tiberini: Officina Typographica Vinciana, 1921.

Tuschus, Cardinalis, *Practicae Conclusiones Iuris,* 3. ed., 8 vols., Lugduni, 1634.

Van Hove, A., *Commentarium Lovaniense in Codicem Iuris Canonici,* Vol. I, Tom. II, *De Legibus Ecclesiasticis,* Mechliniae: H. Dessain, 1930.

Vermeersch, Arthurus, *Theologiae Moralis Principia, Responsa, Concilia,* 3. ed., 4 vols., Romae: Universitas Gregoriana, 1933-1937.

Vermeersch, A., Creusen, J., *Epitome Iuris Canonici,* Vol. I, 6. ed., 1937; Vols. II-III, 5 ed., 1934-1936, Mechliniae: H. Dessain.

Wernz, Franciscus, *Ius Decretalium,* 6 vols., Romae et Prati, 1906-1913.

Wernz, Franciscus, et Vidal, Petrus, *Ius Canonicum,* 7 vols., in 8, Romae: Universitas Gregoriana, 1923-1938.

PERIODICALS

Analecta Ecclesiastica, Romae, 1893-1911.

Apollinaris, Romae, 1928—

Archiv für katholisches Kirchenrecht, Innsbruck, 1857-1861; Mainz, 1862—

Ciudad de Dios, La (formerly, *Revista Agustiniana* [13 vols., 1881-1887]), Valladolid, 1881-1889; Madrid, 1890—

Collationes Brugenses, Bruges, 1895—

Diritto Ecclesiastico, Il, Romae, 1890—

Ecclesiastical Review, The [originally, *The American Ecclesiastical Review*], Philadelphia, 1889—

Harvard Law Review, Cambridge, Mass., 1887—

Homiletic and Pastoral Review, The, New York, 1900—

Irish Ecclesiastical Record, The, Dublin, 1864—

Jurist, The, Washington, D. C., 1941—

Jus Pontificium, Romae, 1921—

Monitore Ecclesiastico, Il, Romae, 1876—

Perfice Munus, Torino, 1926—

Periodica de Re Canonica et Morali utili praesertim Religiosis et Missionariis, Brugis, 1905-1927;

———, *de Re Morali, Canonica, Liturgica,* Brugis, 1928-1936; Romae, 1937—

Recherches de Théologie Ancienne et Médiévale, Louvain, 1929—

South African Law Journal, The, Capetown, 1884—

Theologisch-praktische Quartalschrift, Linz, 1832—

Zeitschrift der Savigny-Stiftung für Rechtsgeschichte, Roman. Abtlg., Weimar, 1880—

———, *Kanon, Abtlg.,* Weimar, 1911—

ARTICLES

Anon. "Absolutio haereticorum"—*Periodica,* XXIII (1934), 55*-57*.

Badii, Cesare, "Il dolo nel codice de diritto canonico"—*Il Diritto Ecclesiastico,* XL (1929), 305-326.

Binding, Karl, "Culpa, Culpa lata und culpa levis"—*Zeitschrift d. Savigny-Stiftung, Roman. Abtlg.,* XXXIX (1918), 1-35.

Bodenstein, H., "Phases in the Development of the Criminal *Mens Rea*"—*South African Law Journal,* XXXVI (1919), 323-349; XXXVII (1920), 18-34.

Brys, J., "De ignorantia ejusque influxu in actum humanum"—*Coll. Brug.,* XXX (1930), 116-121.

Bucceroni, Januarius, "De ignorantia a censura excusante"—*Analecta Ecclesiastica,* XIII (1905), 318-319.

Carraresi, N. Papafava dei, "Ad can. 2314. Quaestio quaedam circa haeresim" —*Jus Pont.,* XI (1931), 52-55.

Checchi, Petrus, "De contumacia requisita ad incurrendam censuram"—*Analecta Ecclesiastica,* XIII (1905), 227-229.

———, "De culpa requisita ad incurrendam censuram"—*ibidem,* pp. 185-187.

Coronata, Matteo da, "Assoluzione di riservati in diocesi e in religione"—*Perfice Munus,* VII (1932), 748-753.

Cozza, Luigi, "In *toletana et aliarum*"—*Mon. Eccl.,* XLVI (1934), 229-239; 276-287; 361-370.

D'Ambrosio, Fran. Xav., "De contumacia iudiciali in antiqua et nova iuris canonici disciplina"—*Jus Pont.,* IV (1924), 11-20.

Galtier, Fr., "De Ignorantia et errore in censurarum specialissimo modo reservatarum absolutione"—*Periodica,* XVII (1928), 55-58.

Haring, Joh., "Praktisches über das kirchliche Strafrecht"—*LQS,* LXXVII (1924), 536-539.

Keedy, Edwin, "Ignorance and Mistake in the Criminal Law"—*Harvard Law Review,* XXII (1908), 75-96.

King, Richard, "The New Code and Reservation"—*ER,* LXVI (1922), 558-586.

Kinane, J., "Effect of Ignorance on Censure"—*IER,* IX (1917), 233-236.

———, "The Effect of Invincible Ignorance of the Law or of the Punishment Alone on Vindicative Punishments 'Latae Sententiae' "—*IER,* XXXI (1928), 81-84.

Köck, Johann, "Die Zensuren latae sententiae des Codex Iuris Canonici"—*LQS,* LXXII (1919), 502-518.

Lenel, Otto, "Culpa lata und culpa levis"—*Zeitschrift d. Savigny-Stiftung, Roman. Abtlg.,* XXXVIII (1917), 263-290.

Lottin, D. O., "Le problème de l'*ignorantia iuris* de Gratien à St. Thomas d'Aquin"—*Recherches de Théol. ancienne et médiévale,* V (1933), 345-368.

Maroto, P., "De vi ignorantiae quoad falsam delationem, qua sacerdos innocens accusatur de crimine sollicitationis"—*Apollinaris*, V (1932), 96-105.

Montes, J., "La ignorancia en el derecho penal"—*Ciudad de Dios*, CXLVIII (1927), 354-369; CXLIX (1927), 43-60; 213-226; CL (1927), 39-53; 277-297; 321-338.

Noval, "De conatu delicti et eius punitione iuxta Codicem Iuris Canonici"—*Jus Pont.*, IX (1929), 118-127.

O'Neill, "Ignorance of Ecclesiastical Laws and Punishments"—*IER*, XXIX (1927), 292-293.

Perathoner, Anton, "Forum internum und forum externum im kirchlichen Strafrechte"—*LQS*, LXX (1917), 443-457; 726-743.

Perkins, Rollin M., "Ignorance and Mistake in Criminal Law"—*U. of Pa. Law Review*, LXXXVIII (1939-1940), 35-70.

Pernice, Alfred, "Der verbrecherische Vorsatz im grieschish-römischen Rechte" —*Zeitschrift d. Savigny-Stiftung, Roman. Abtlg.*, XVII (1896), 205-251.

Pistocchi, M., "Natura e divisione del delitto"—*Mon. Eccl.*, XLVI (1934), 17-23.

———, "Il dolo"—*ibidem*, pp. 39-46.

———, "Influsso dell'ignoranza e della inavvertenza nella imputabilità del delitto"—*ibidem*, pp. 211-216.

———, "La colpa nella imputabilità del delitto"—*Mon. Eccl.*, XLVII (1935), 26-29.

———, "De subjecto coactivae potestati obnoxio"—*Mon. Eccl.*, XLIX (1937), 171-180; 204-209.

Roelker, Edward, "The Right to Revenue during Non-residence"—*Jurist*, I (1941), 74-76.

Romani, Sylvius, "De ignorantia legis"—*Acta Congressus Iuridici Internat.*, IV, 61-119—*Jus Pont.*, XVII (1937), 218-234; XVIII (1938), 24-56.

Rossi, Giuseppe, "L'ignoranza in ordine alle censure"—*Perfice Munus*, III (1928), 31-34.

Syre, Francis, "Mens Rea"—*Harvard Law Review*, XLV (1931-1932), 974-1026.

Vermeersch, A., "De contumacia quae committendae censurae est requisita condicio"—*Periodica*, XXII (1933), 39*-42*.

Woywod, Stanislaus, "Ecclesiastical Penalties. Transgression of the Law Through Ignorance"—*HPR*, XXXV (1935), 268-276.

———, "Penal Law of the Code. Requisites for Incurring the Penalty of the Law"—*HPR*, XXXVI (1936), 838-847.

ABBREVIATIONS

AAS—*Acta Apostolicae Sedis.*
ASS—*Acta Sanctae Sedis.*
C.—*Codex* (Iustinianus).
Coll.—*Mosaicarum et Romanarum Legum Collatio.*
Coll. Brug.—*Collationes Brugenses.*
Coll. S.C.P.F.—*Collectanea S. C. de Propaganda Fide*, ed. 1907.
CSEL—*Corpus Scriptorum Ecclesiasticorum Latinorum.*
D.—*Digestum* (Iustinianum).
ER—*Ecclesiastical Review.*
Fontes—*Codicis Iuris Canonici Fontes cura . . . Gasparri editi.*
Harduin—*Acta Conciliorum*, etc.
HPR—*Homiletic and Pastoral Review.*
IER—*Irish Ecclesiastical Record.*
Jaffé—*Regesta Pontificum Romanorum.*
Jus Pont.—*Jus Pontificium.*
LQS—*Theologisch-praktische Quartalschrift* (Linz).
Mansi—*Sacrorum Conciliorum Nova et Amplissima Collectio.*
Mon. Eccl.—*Monitore Ecclesiastico.*
MPG—Migne, *Patrologia Graeca.*
MPL—Migne, *Patrologia Latina.*
Periodica—*Periodica de Re Canonica et Morali.*
Potthast—*Regesta Pontificum Romanorum.*
S. R. R. Dec.—*S. R. Rotae Decisiones seu Responsae* (from 1909).

ALPHABETICAL INDEX

BIOGRAPHICAL NOTE

Innocent Robert Swoboda was born on October 12, 1910, at Union, Missouri. He attended the parochial schools of St. Peter near Washington, Missouri, and of the Immaculate Conception at Union, Missouri. On June 8, 1930, he graduated from St. Joseph's College at Hinsdale, Illinois; entered the Novitiate of the Franciscan Order at Teutopolis, Illinois, and in the following year made his religious profession as a member of the Order of Friars Minor. After completing his philosophical studies in Our Lady of Angels Seminary at Cleveland, Ohio, and his theological studies at St. Joseph's Seminary at Teutopolis, Illinois, he was ordained to the priesthood on June 24, 1937. After he had completed his final year of theology, in 1938, he was sent to the Athenaeum Antonianum in Rome, from which he received the Baccalaureate in Canon Law in June, 1939. The following year he continued his Canon Law studies at the Catholic University of America, from which he received the Licentiate in Canon Law in June, 1940.

CANON LAW STUDIES

1. Freriks, Rev. Celestine A., C.PP.S., J.C.D., Religious Congregations in Their External Relations, 121 pp., 1916.
2. Galliher, Rev. Daniel M., O.P., J.C.D., Canonical Elections, 117 pp., 1917.
3. Borkowski, Rev. Aurelius L., O.F.M., J.C.D., De Confraternitatibus Ecclesiasticis, 136 pp., 1918.
4. Castillo, Rev. Cayo, J.C.D., Disertacion Historico-Canonica sobre la Potestad del Cabildo en Sede Vacante o Impedida del Vicario Capitular, 99 pp., 1919 (1918).
5. Kubelbeck, Rev. William J., S.T.B., J.C.D., The Sacred Penitentiaria and Its Relation to Faculties of Ordinaries and Priests, 129 pp., 1918.
6. Petrovits, Rev. Joseph, J.C., S.T.D., J.C.D., The New Church Law on Matrimony, X-461 pp., 1919.
7. Hickey, Rev. John J., S.T.B., J.C.D., Irregularities and Simple Impediments in the New Code of Canon Law, 100 pp., 1920.
8. Klekotka, Rev. Peter J., S.T.B., J.C.D., Diocesan Consultors, 179 pp., 1920.
9. Wanenmacher, Rev. Francis, J.C.D., The Evidence in Ecclesiastical Procedure Affecting the Marriage Bond, 1920 (Printed 1935).
10. Golden, Rev. Henry Francis, J.C.D., Parochial Benefices in the New Code, IV-119 pp., 1921 (Printed 1925).
11. Koudelka, Rev. Charles J., J.C.D., Pastors, Their Rights and Duties According to the New Code of Canon Law, 211 pp., 1921.
12. Melo, Rev. Antonius, O.F.M., J.C.D., De Exemptione Regularium, X-188 pp., 1921.
13. Schaaf, Rev. Valentine Theodore, O.F.M., S.T.B., J.C.D., The Cloister, X-180 pp., 1921.
14. Burke, Rev. Thomas Joseph, S.T.D., J.C.D., Competence in Ecclesiastical Tribunals, IV-117 pp., 1922.
15. Leech, Rev. George Leo, J.C.D., A Comparative Study of the Constitution "Apostolicae Sedis" and the "Codex Juris Canonici," 179 pp., 1922.
16. Motry, Rev. Hubert Louis, S.T.D., J.C.D., Diocesan Faculties According to the Code of Canon Law, II-167 pp., 1922.
17. Murphy, Rev. George Lawrence, J.C.D., Delinquencies and Penalties in the Administration and the Reception of the Sacraments, IV-121 pp., 1923.
18. O'Reilly, Rev. John Anthony, S.T.B., J.C.D., Ecclesiastical Sepulture in the New Code of Canon Law, II-129 pp., 1923.
19. Michalicka, Rev. Wenceslas Cyrill, O.S.B., J.C.D., Judicial Procedure in Dismissal of Clerical Exempt Religious, 107 pp., 1923.

20. DARGIN, REV. EDWARD VINCENT, S.T.B., J.C.D., Reserved Cases According to the Code of Canon Law, IV-103 pp., 1924.
21. GODFREY, REV. JOHN A., S.T.B., J.C.D., The Right of Patronage According to the Code of Canon Law, 153 pp., 1924.
22. HAGEDORN, REV. FRANCIS EDWARD, J.C.D., General Legislation on Indulgences, II-154 pp., 1924.
23. KING, REV. JAMES IGNATIUS, J.C.D., The Administration of the Sacraments to Dying Non-Catholics, V-141 pp., 1924.
24. WINSLOW, REV. FRANCIS JOSEPH, M.M., J.C.D., Vicars and Prefects Apostolic, IV-149 pp., 1924.
25. CORREA, REV. JOSE SERVELION, S.T.L., J.C.D., La Potestad Legislativa de la Iglesia Catolica, IV-127 pp., 1925.
26. DUGAN, REV. HENRY FRANCIS, A.M., J.C.D., The Judiciary Department of the Diocesan Curia, 87 pp., 1925.
27. KELLER, REV. CHARLES FREDERICK, S.T.B., J.C.D., Mass Stipends, 167 pp., 1925.
28. PASCHANG, REV. JOHN LINUS, J.C.D., The Sacramentals According to the Code of Canon Law, 129 pp., 1925.
29. PIONTEK, REV. CYRILLUS, O.F.M., S.T.B., J.C.D., De Indulto Exclaustrationis necnon Saecularizationis, XIII-289 pp., 1925.
30. KEARNEY, REV. RICHARD JOSEPH, S.T.B., J.C.D., Sponsors at Baptism According to the Code of Canon Law, IV-127 pp., 1925.
31. BARTLETT, REV. CHESTER JOSEPH, A.M., LL.B., J.C.D., The Tenure of Parochial Property in the United States of America, V-108 pp., 1926.
32. KILKER, REV. ADRIAN JEROME, J.C.D., Extreme Unction, V-425 pp., 1926.
33. MCCORMICK, REV. ROBERT EMMETT, J.C.D., Confessors of Religious, VIII-266 pp., 1926.
34. MILLER, REV. NEWTON THOMAS, J.C.D., Founded Masses According to the Code of Canon Law, VII-93 pp., 1926.
35. ROELKER, REV. EDWARD G., S.T.D., J.C.D., Principles of Privilege According to the Code of Canon Law, XI-166 pp., 1926.
36. BAKALARCZYK, REV. RICHARDUS, M.I.C., J.U.D., De Novitiatu, VIII-208 pp., 1927.
37. PIZZUTI, REV. LAWRENCE, O.F.M., J.U.L., De Parochis Religiosis, 1927. (Not Printed.)
38. BLILEY, REV. NICHOLAS MARTIN, O.S.B., J.C.D., Altars According to the Code of Canon Law, XIX-132 pp., 1927.
39. BROWN, MR. BRENDAN FRANCIS, A.B., LL.M., J.U.D., The Canonical Juristic Personality with Special Reference to its Status in the United States of America, V-212 pp., 1927.
40. CAVANAUGH, REV. WILLIAM THOMAS, C.P., J.U.D., The Reservation of the Blessed Sacrament, VIII-101 pp., 1927.
41. DOHENY, REV. WILLIAM J., C.S.C., A.B., J.U.D., Church Property: Modes of Acquisition, X-118 pp., 1927.

42. Feldhaus, Rev. Aloysius H., C.PP.S., J.C.D., Oratories, IX-141 pp., 1927.
43. Kelly, Rev. James Patrick, A.B., J.C.D., The Jurisdiction of the Simple Confessor, X-208 pp., 1927.
44. Neuberger, Rev. Nicholas J., J.C.D., Canon 6 or the Relation of the Codex Juris Canonici to the Preceding Legislation, V-95 pp., 1927.
45. O'Keefe, Rev. Gerald Michael, J.C.D., Matrimonial Dispensations, Powers of Bishops, Priests, and Confessors, VIII-232 pp., 1927.
46. Quigley, Rev. Joseph A. M., A.B., J.C.D., Condemned Societies, 139 pp., 1927.
47. Zaplotnik, Rev. Johannes Leo, J.C.D., De Vicariis Foraneis, X-142 pp., 1927.
48. Duskie, Rev. John Aloysius, A.B., J.C.D., The Canonical Status of the Orientals in the United States, VIII-196 pp., 1928.
49. Hyland, Rev. Francis Edward, J.C.D., Excommunciation, Its Nature, Historical Development and Effects, VIII-181 pp., 1928.
50. Reinmann, Rev. Gerald Joseph, O.M.C., J.C.D., The Third Order Secular of Saint Francis, 201 pp., 1928.
51. Schenk, Rev. Francis J., J.C.D., The Matrimonial Impediments of Mixed Religion and Disparity of Cult, XVI-318 pp., 1929.
52. Coady, Rev. John Joseph, S.T.D., J.U.D., A.M., The appointment of Pastors, VIII-150 pp., 1929.
53. Kay, Rev. Thomas Henry, J.C.D., Competence in Matrimonial Procedure, VIII-164 pp., 1929.
54. Turner, Rev. Sidney Joseph, C.P., J.U.D., The Vow of Poverty, XLIX-217 pp., 1929.
55. Kearney, Rev. Raymond A., A.B., S.T.D., J.C.D., The Principles of Delegation, VII-149 pp., 1929.
56. Conran, Rev. Edward James, A.B., J.C.D., The Interdict, V-163 pp., 1930.
57. O'Neill, Rev. William H., J.C.D., Papal Rescripts of Favor, VII-218 pp., 1930.
58. Bastnagel, Rev. Clement Vincent, J.U.D., The Appointment of Parochial Adjutants and Assistants, XV-257 pp., 1930.
59. Ferry, Rev. William A., A.B., J.C.D., Stole Fees, V-136 pp., 1930.
60. Costello, Rev. John Michael, A.B., J.C.D., Domicile and Quasi-Domicile, VII-201 pp., 1930.
61. Kremer, Rev. Michael Nicholas, A.B., S.T.B., J.C.D., Church Support in the United States, VI-136 pp., 1930.
62. Angulo, Rev. Luis, C.M., J.C.D., Legislation de la Iglesia sobre la intencion en la application de la Santa Misa, VII-104 pp., 1931.
63. Frey, Rev. Wolfgang Norbert, O.S.B., A.B., J.C.D., The Act of Religious Profession, VIII-174 pp., 1931.
64. Roberts, Rev. James Brendan, A.B., J.C.D., The Banns of Marriage, XIV-140 pp., 1931.
65. Ryder, Rev. Raymond Aloysius, A.B., J.C.D., Simony, IX-151 pp., 1931.

66. Campagna, Rev. Angelo, Ph.D., J.U.D., Il Vicario Generale del Vescovo, VII-205 pp., 1931.
67. Cox, Rev. Joseph Godfrey, A.B., J.C.D., The Administration of Seminaries, VI-124 pp., 1931.
68. Gregory, Rev. Donald J., J.U.D., The Pauline Privilege, XV-165 pp., 1931.
69. Donohue, Rev. John F., J.C.D., The Impediment of Crime, VII-110 pp., 1931.
70. Dooley, Rev. Eugene A., O.M.I., J.C.D., Church Law on Sacred Relics, IX-143 pp., 1931.
71. Orth, Rev. Clement Raymond, O.M.C., J.C.D., The Approbation of Religious Institutes, 171 pp., 1931.
72. Pernicone, Rev. Joseph M., A.B., J.C.D., The Ecclesiastical Prohibition of Books, XII-267 pp., 1932.
73. Clinton, Rev. Connell, A.B., J.C.D., The Paschal Precept, IX-108 pp., 1932.
74. Donnelly, Rev. Francis B., A.M., S.T.L., J.C.D., The Diocesan Synod, VIII-125 pp., 1932.
75. Torrente, Rev. Camilo, C.M.F., J.C.D., Las Processiones Sagradas, V-145 pp., 1932.
76. Murphy, Rev. Edwin J., C.PP.S., J.C.D., Suspension Ex Informata Conscientia, XI-122 pp., 1932.
77. MacKenzie, Rev. Eric F., A.M., S.T.L., J.C.D., The Delict of Heresy in its Commission, Penalization, Absolution, VII-124 pp., 1932.
78. Lyons, Rev. Avitus E., S.T.B., J.C.D., The Collegiate Tribunal of First Instance, XI-147 pp., 1932.
79. Connolly, Rev. Thomas A., J.C.D., Appeals, XI-195 pp., 1932.
80. Sangmeister, Rev. Joseph V., A.B., J.C.D., Force and Fear as Precluding Matrimonial Consent, V-211 pp., 1932.
81. Jaeger, Rev. Leo A., A.B., J.C.D., The Administration of Vacant and Quasi-Vacant Episcopal Sees in the United States, IX-229 pp., 1932.
82. Rimlinger, Rev. Herbert T., J.C.D., Error Invalidating Matrimonial Consent, VII-79 pp., 1932.
83. Barrett, Rev. John D. M., S.S., J.C.D., A Comparative Study of the Third Plenary Council of Baltimore and the Code, IX-221 pp., 1932.
84. Carberry, Rev. John J., Ph.D., S.T.D., J.C.D., The Juridical Form of Marriage, X-177 pp., 1934.
85. Dolan, Rev. John L., A.B., J.C.D., The Defensor Vinculi, XII-157 pp., 1934.
86. Hannan, Rev. Jerome D., A.M., S.T.D., LL.B., J.C.D., The Canon Law of Wills, IX-517 pp., 1934.
87. Lemieux, Rev. Delise A., A.M., J.C.D., The Sentence in Ecclesiastical Procedure, IX-131 pp., 1934.
88. O'Rourke, Rev. James J., A.B., J.C.D., Parish Registers, VII-109 pp., 1934.

89. TIMLIN, REV. BARTHOLOMEW, O.F.M., A.M., J.C.D., Conditional Matrimonial Consent, X-381 pp., 1934.
90. WAHL, REV. FRANCIS X., A.B., J.C.D., The Matrimonial Impediments of Consanguinity and Affinity, VI-125 pp., 1934.
91. WHITE, REV. ROBERT J., A.B., LL.B., S.T.B., J.C.D., Canonical Ante-Nuptial Promises and the Civil Law, VI-152 pp., 1934.
92. HERRERA, REV. ANTONIO PARRA, O.C.D., J.C.D., Legislacion Ecclesiastica sobra el Ayuno y la Abstinencia, XI-191 pp., 1935.
93. KENNEDY, REV. EDWIN J., J.C.D., The Special Matrimonial Process in Cases of Evident Nullity, X-165 pp., 1935.
94. MANNING, REV. JOHN J., A.B., J.C.D., Presumption of Law in Matrimonial Procedure, XI-111 pp., 1935.
95. MOEDER, REV. JOHN M., J.C.D., The Proper Bishop for Ordination and Dimissorial Letters, VII-135 pp., 1935.
96. O'MARA, REV. WILLIAM A., A.B., J.C.D., Canonical Causes for Matrimonial Dispensations, IX-155 pp., 1935.
97. REILLY, REV. PETER, J.C.D., Residence of Pastors, IX-81 pp., 1935.
98. SMITH, REV. MARINER T., O.P., S.T.Lr., J.C.D., The Penal Law for Religious, VII-169 pp., 1935.
99. WHALEN, REV. DONALD W., A.M., J.C.D., The Value of Testimonial Evidence in Matrimonial Procedure, XIII-297 pp., 1935.
100. CLEARY, REV. JOSEPH F., J.C.D., Canonical Limitations on the Alienation of Church Property, VIII-141 pp., 1936.
101. GLYNN, REV. JOHN C., J.C.D., The Promoter of Justice, XX-337 pp., 1936.
102. BRENNAN, REV. JAMES H., S.S., M.A., S.T.B., J.C.D., The Simple Convalidation of Marriage, VI-135 pp., 1937.
103 BRUNINI, REV. JOSEPH BERNARD, J.C.D., The Clerical Obligations of Canons 139 and 142, X-121 pp., 1937.
104. CONNOR, REV. MAURICE, A.B., J.C.D., The Administrative Removal of Pastors, VIII-159 pp., 1937.
105. GUILFOYLE, REV. MERLIN JOSEPH, J.C.D., Custom, XI-144 pp., 1937.
106. HUGHES, REV. JAMES AUSTIN, A.B., A.M., J.C.D., Witnesses in Criminal Trials of Clerics, IX-140 pp., 1937.
107. JANSEN, REV. RAYMOND J., A.B., S.T.L., J.C.D., Canonical Provisions for Catechetical Instruction, VII-153 pp., 1937.
108. KEALY, REV. JOHN JAMES, A.B., J.C.D., The Introductory Libellus in Church Court Procedure, XI-121 pp., 1937.
109. McMANUS, REV. JAMES EDWARD, C.SS.R., J.C.D., The Administration of Temporal Goods in Religious Institutes, XVI-196 pp., 1937.
110. MORIARTY, REV. EUGENE JAMES, J.C.D., Oaths in Ecclesiastical Courts, X-115 pp., 1937.
111. RAINER, REV. ELIGIUS GEORGE, C.SS.R., J.C.D., Suspension of Clerics, XVII-249 pp., 1937.

112. Reilly, Rev. Thomas F., C.SS.R., J.C.D., Visitation of Religious, VI-195 pp., 1938.

113. Moriarity, Rev. Francis E., C.SS.R., J.C.D., The Extraordinary Absolution from Censures, XV-334 pp., 1938.

114. Connolly, Rev. Nicholas P., J.C.D., The Canonical Erection of Parishes, X-132 pp., 1938.

115. Donovan, Rev. James Joseph, J.C.D., The Pastor's Obligation in Prenuptial Investigation, XII-322 pp., 1938.

116. Harrigan, Rev. Robert J., M.A., S.T.B., J.C.D., The Radical Sanation of Invalid Marriages, VIII-208 pp., 1938.

117. Boffa, Rev. Conrad Humbert, J.C.D., Canonical Provisions for Catholic Schools, VII-211 pp., 1939.

118. Parsons, Rev. Anscar John, O.M.Cap., J.C.D., Canonical Elections, XII-236 pp., 1939.

119. Reilly, Rev. Edward Michael, A.B., J.C.D., The General Norms of Dispensation, XII-156 pp., 1939.

120. Ryan, Rev. Gerald Aloysius, A.B., J.C.D., Principles of Episcopal Jurisdiction, XII-172 pp., 1939.

121. Burton, Rev. Francis James, C.S.C., A.B., J.C.D., A Commentary on Canon 1125, X-222 pp., 1940.

122. Miaskiewicz, Rev. Francis Sigismund, J.C.D., Supplied Jurisdiction According to Canon 209, XII-340 pp., 1940.

123. Rice, Rev. Patrick William, A.B., J.C.D., Proof of Death in Prenuptial Investigation, VIII-156 pp., 1940.

124. Anglin, Rev. Thomas Francis, M.S., J.C.L., The Eucharistic Fast.

125. Coleman, Rev. John Jerome, J.C.L., The Minister of Confirmation.

126. Downs, Rev. John Emmanuel, A.B., J.C.L., The Concept of Clerical Immunity.

127. Esswein, Rev. Anthony Albert, J.C.L., Extrajudicial Penal Powers of Ecclesiastical Superiors.

128. Farrell, Rev. Benjamin Francis, M.A., S.T.L., J.C.L., The Rights and Duties of the Local Ordinary Regarding Congregations of Women Religious of Pontifical Approval.

129. Feeney, Rev. Thomas John, A.B., S.T.L., J.C.L., Restitutio in Integrum.

130. Findlay, Rev. Stephen William, O.S.B., A.B., J.C.L., Canonical Norms Governing the Deposition and Degradation of Clerics.

131. Goodwine, Rev. John, A.B., S.T.L., J.C.L., The Right of the Church to Acquire Property.

132. Heston, Rev. Edward Louis, C.S.C., Ph.D., S.T.D., J.C.L., The Alienation of Church Property in the United States.

133. Hogan, Rev. James John, S.T.L., J.C.L., Judicial Advocates and Procurators.

134. Kealy, Rev. Thomas M., A.B., Litt.B., J.C.L., Dowry of Women Religious.

135. Keene, Rev. Michael James, O.S.B., J.C.L., Religious Ordinaries and Canon 198.
136. Kerin, Rev. Charles A., S.S., M.A., S.T.B., J.C.L., The Privation of Christian Burial.
137. Louis, Rev. William Francis, M.A., J.C.L., Diocesan Archives.
138. McDevitt, Rev. Gilbert Joseph, A.B., J.C.L., Legitimacy and Legitimation.
139. McDonough, Rev. Thomas Joseph, A.B., J.C.L., Apostolic Administrators.
140. Meier, Rev. Carl Anthony, A.B., J.C.L., Penal Administrative Procedure Against Negligent Pastors.
141. Schmidt, Rev. John Rogg, A.B., J.C.L., The Principles of Authentic Interpretation in Canon 17 of the Code of Canon Law.
142. Slafkosky, Rev. Andrew Leonard, A.B., J.C.L., The Canonical Episcopal Diocesan Visitation of the Diocese.
143. Swoboda, Rev. Innocent Robert, O.F.M., J.C.L., Ignorance in Relation to the Imputability of Delicts.
144. Dubé, Rev. Arthur Joseph, A.B., J.C.L., The General Principles for the Reckoning of Time in Canon Law.
145. McBride, Rev. James T., A.B., J.C.L., Incardination and Excardination of Seculars.

www.ingramcontent.com/pod-product-compliance
Lightning Source LLC
LaVergne TN
LVHW050254080826
844660LV00012B/639

* 9 7 8 0 8 1 3 2 2 3 3 2 2 *